STUDIES IN THE HISTORY OF AMERICAN LAW

WITH SPECIAL REFERENCE TO THE SEVENTEENTH AND EIGHTEENTH CENTURIES

BY

RICHARD B. MORRIS, Ph.D.

GOUVERNEUR MORRIS PROFESSOR OF HISTORY
COLUMBIA UNIVERSITY

SECOND EDITION

1963
OCTAGON BOOKS, INC.
NEW YORK

FOREWORD TO THE SECOND EDITION

More than a quarter of a century has elapsed since *Studies in the History of American Law* appeared. That pilot study constituted a challenge to American legal scholarship to rescue the law of the British colonies in North America from the obscurity in which it had long lain. Since that time there has been an increasing awareness of the need for closer study into the origin and development of American legal institutions. A few significant monographic studies have appeared, and a systematic program was launched for the publication of early American court records. If that program has not gathered too much momentum to date, it has nonetheless admirably served its purpose of illuminating diverse facets of our legal experience. A modest amount of attention is now paid to American legal history in the law school curricula, considerably more than was the case a generation ago. The founding of the American Legal History Society, recently resuscitated as the American Society for Legal History, and the appearance of *The American Journal of Legal History* are heartening to those who have had to fight an uphill battle against that most insidious of all foes of intellectual enterprise—incuriosity.

It seems appropriate at this time to review the contributions which have been made in this field since the publication of the *Studies* in 1930. "Sufficient reasons" then existed, I stated in the Bibliographical Essay, for publishing at least important selections from the abundant judicial records on a scale commensurate with the notable work of the Selden Society in the field of early English legal records. A first step toward realizing that long-range objective was the inauguration of the series of *American Legal Records* by the American Historical Association, acting through its Committee on the Littleton-Griswold Fund. The spadework for this program was started by examining the principal archival depositories along the Atlantic seaboard, from Wiscasset, Maine, to St. Augustine, Florida,[1] and by the systematic inventorying of federal and county archives carried on in the 1930s by the nationwide Survey of Federal Archives[2] and the Historical Records Survey. While the former project completed its important assignment, the latter dissipated its energies by undertaking a variety of heroic enterprises, and when it was terminated had published inventories for a relatively small proportion of the total number of counties in the United States. Despite the shortcomings of the Historical Records Survey, that project did prepare some useful inventories and bibliographies of court records for some of the older counties and transcribed and published several records of the early courts.[3] In addition, over the past

---

[1] R. B. Morris, "Early American Court Records: A Publication Program," *Anglo-American Legal History Series*, I, No. 4 (1941).

[2] For early court records uncovered by that program, see R. B. Morris, "The Federal Archives of New York City: Opportunities for Historical Research," *American Historical Review*, XLII (1937), 256-262. Inventories of these records are now on file in the National Archives. Older judicial records, such as the minutes of the Vice Admiralty Court of the province of New York, have in some cases been transferred from the custody of the clerks of the district courts to the National Archives. See *National Archives Guide* (Washington, D.C., 1948) and H. T. Ulasek and Marion Johnson, "Records of the U. S. District Court for the Southern District of New York," *Preliminary Inventories*, No. 116 (Washington, 1959).

[3] For evaluations of this project, see *American Historical Review*, Oct. 1939 and April, 1941. Among the court records published were those of the early court of constables and overseers of Newtown, 1656-90, and of Staten Island, 1678-1813. See also Historical Records Survey, *Abstract and Index of the Records of the Inferior Court of Pleas (Suffolk County Court) held at Boston, 1680-98* (Boston, 1940).

fifteen years substantial progress has been made in the microfilming of public records, including legislative and judicial materials of interest to the legal historian.4 Finally, legal scholars need hardly be reminded of the value to legal history of the editorial enterprises now moving forward under the sponsorship of the National Historical Publications Commission for collecting and publishing the papers of American statesmen. In the case of lawyers of the stature of Jefferson, Hamilton, John Adams, and John Jay such editorial projects are calculated to disclose significant, if hitherto discrete, legal papers.

To supplement the listing of published court records in the "Bibliographical Essay" and bring it up to date, one should mention, first of all, the seven volumes of judicial records published so far in the *American Legal Records* series. These have ranged in locale from Connecticut to South Carolina and in jurisdiction from a provincial court of appeals to some county courts,5 with an impressive backlist of volumes still to come. Attention also should be called to the judicial records published in the *Archives of Maryland,* which now provides the scholar with a complete cross-section of the judicial activity of the province for the middle of the seventeenth century.6 Indubitably the models for the publication of inferior court records are the two volumes of Suffolk County court records, 1671-80, skillfully edited by Samuel Eliot Morison, with a perceptive introduction by the late Zechariah Chafee, Jr.7 The publication of the Old Norfolk County Records of the Bay State was continued in the 1930s in the *Historical Collections of the Essex Institute,* and to date four volumes have appeared of the province and court records of Maine from 1636 down to the first decade of the eighteenth century. If one keeps in mind the previously published and extensive records of the Essex quarterly and probate courts, it is evident that the Bay Colony, at least for the seventeenth century, boasts the most representative and complete collection of inferior court records of any of the original Thirteen Colonies.8. Pennsylvania is represented by the publication of the Phila-

4 Among the items microfilmed by the National Archives, for which positive prints can be obtained, are the records of prize cases heard on appeal from state courts by committees of the Continental Congress (1776-80) and by the Court of Appeals in Cases of Capture (1780-86). See *List of File Microcopies of the National Archives* (Washington, D.C., 1950). The State Records Microfilm Project is making available in microfilm a large variety of state public records. See *A Guide to the Microfilm Collection of Early State Records,* comp. under the direction of William S. Jenkins and ed. by Lillian A. Hamrick (Washington, D.C., 1950; *Supplement,* 1951), which organizes the material into such categories as legislative records, statutory laws, constitutional records, court records, etc. *The Union List of Microfilms* (rev. ed., Ann Arbor, 1951) lists 25,000 items owned by 197 institutions.

5 *Proceedings of the Maryland Court of Appeals, 1695-1729,* ed. by C. T. Bond and R. B. Morris (1933); II: Select Cases of the Mayor's Court of New York City, ed. by R. B. Morris (1935); III: Records of the Court of Vice Admiralty of Rhode Island, ed. by Dorothy S. Towle; IV: The Superior Court Diary of William Samuel Johnson, 1772-73, ed. by J. T. Farrell (1942); V: The Burlington Court Book, ed. by H. Clay Reed and G. J. Miller (1944); VI: Records of the Court of Chancery of South Carolina, 1671-1779, ed. by Anne K. Gregorie (1950); VII: County Court Records of Accomack-Northampton, Virginia, 1632-1640, ed. by Susie Ames (1954).

6 The Provincial Court, 1637-67 (*Md. Arch.,* IV, X, XLI, XLIX, LVII, LXV-LXVII); Chancery, 1669-79 (*ibid.,* LI); and four county court records for the middle of the 17th century (*ibid.,* LIII, LIV). Abstracts of the New Hanover, North Carolina, C. P. and Q. S. minutes have recently been compiled for the years 1738-1769, 1771-1785, by Alexander M. Walker and privately printed (Bethesda, Md., 1958, 1959).

7 Colonial Society of Massachusetts, *Publications,* XXIX, XXX (1933).

8 See also William Jeffrey, Jr., "Early New England Court Records: A Bibliography of Published Material," *Boston Public Library Quarterly* (July, 1954). Herter Prager and Willa W. Price, "A Bibliography on the History of the Courts of the Thirteen Original States, Maine, Ohio, and Vermont," *American Journal of Legal History,* II (1958), *passim.*

delphia Court of Quarter Sessions and Common Pleas for the year 1695,[9] by the records of the Bucks County courts of quarter sessions and common pleas, 1684-1700, as well as those of the Court at Upland 1676-1681, followed by the court records for the years 1681 to 1697 of Chester County. Delaware is represented by the Record of the Court at New Castle, covering the years 1676-1699.[10]

The publication and study of the court records of the seventeenth and eighteenth centuries poses a continuing challenge to the legal scholar and provides the social historian with a vast corpus of intimate and authentic details of the life, loves, and labors of the average man. The evidence upon which my study of labor relations in the colonial and Revolutionary periods[11] was based came in large part from the unpublished inferior court records of the American colonies. The twenty thousand cases reviewed in the course of that investigation demonstrated that in the field of labor relations the law-in-action did not necessarily correspond to the law-on-the-books. In subsequent investigations into freedom and bondage in the slave states the inferior court records, police jury minutes, jail records, grand jury presentments, and other judicial archives are continuing to shed considerable light on shadowland areas of labor relations.[12] Jack Kenny Williams has recently given us a useful analysis of more than ten thousand South Carolina grand jury indictments during the ante-bellum period, from which he has drawn some conclusions about the state of law enforcement, while at the same time furnishing the social historian with some valuable insights,[13] and Guion Griffis Johnson has effectively utilized county court and parish records to illuminate the subject of poor relief and other aspects of the social life of ante-bellum North Carolina.[14] Many more areas in social history remain to be given the kind of microscopic examination that is so often made possible by the existence of full court papers.

The reception of the common law in America is a complex subject and the last word has not been said about it. The *Studies* demonstrated that the authority of the common law was far less influential in some colonies than in others, and far more pervasive in the eighteenth century than in the seventeenth. Thus it was appropriate that in May, 1959, a plaque commemorating the establishment of legal institutions in the New World was set in the wall of the seventeenth-century church on Jamestown Island by the Virginia State Bar. Had Boston provided the site the choice would have been less suitable, for the General Assembly Act of 1661 formally recognizing the common law in Virginia merely gave

9 *Pa. Mag. of Hist. and Biog.*, LXXVII (1953), 457-480, and in *Amer. Jl. of Leg. Hist.*, I (Jan., 1957), passim.

10 The Bucks Q. S. and C. P. records were published by the Colonial Society of Pennsylvania (Meadville, Pa., 1943); the Chester records were reprinted by Joseph M. Mitchell Co. (Philadelphia, 1959); and the 2 vols. of New Castle records were issued by the Colonial Society of Pennsylvania (1904, 1935). Daniel J. Boorstin's edition of *Delaware Cases, 1792-1830* (3 vols., St. Paul, 1943), is a notable addition to the later sources for that state. Paul M. Hamlin and Charles E. Baker have recently brought out the records of the New York Supreme Court of Judicature, 1691-1704 (2 vols., New York, 1952).

11 *Government and Labor in Early America* (New York, 1956).

12 See, for example, three of my published studies in this area: "White Bondage in Ante-Bellum South Carolina, *S. C. Hist. and Geneal. Mag.*, XLIX (1948), 191-207; "Labor Controls in Maryland in the 19th Century," *Journal of Southern History*, XIV (1948), 385-400; "The Course of Peonage in a Slave State," *Political Science Quarterly*, LXV (1950), 238-263.

13 *Vogues in Villainy: Crime and Retribution in Ante-Bellum South Carolina* (Columbia, S. C., 1959).

14 *Ante-Bellum North Carolina: A Social History* (Chapel Hill, N. C., 1937).

official sanction to what had long been the general practice. But even where, as in the tobacco provinces, the common law was well entrenched almost from the start, there were notable deviations from the procedure in force in the royal courts in England, such as the use of the informal petition in master-servant cases, and, in Maryland, the trial of criminal cases without juries. If the law of the tobacco provinces was fundamentally the law of England, it was, as one legal scholar has perceptively remarked, "the law of England with a difference."[15]

What was substantially true for Virginia and Maryland did not necessarily hold elsewhere, particularly among the Puritan and Quaker colonies which were established under the reformist impulse. Hence, it is now pretty generally recognized that Mr. Justice Story's classic dictum that the common law of England was substantially in force in the colonies from the time of their settlement, at least so much of it as "was applicable to their situation,"[16] is one of those generalizations which more accurately describe what American judges in the nineteenth century thought had happened than the actual facts of colonial legal experience.

Story's view of the reception has been challenged on the one hand by those who maintain that the American legal system was indigenous[17] and by an opposing school[18] that insists that it was not the common law of the royal courts but rather local custom and the practice of English borough and county courts which was transplanted to the colonies in the seventeenth century. Professor Aumann[19] has chosen to consider me as a proponent of the former position, but I must decline that distinction unless it is properly qualified. A careful reading of the *Studies*, as well as an examination of my subsequent writings in this field, will show that, while I have given ample recognition to the numerous and important indigenous elements in the early American legal system, I have been careful to circumscribe my generalizations both by chronological periods and by regions. I have, moreover, devoted a good deal of attention to the influence of English local customs on colonial legal development. In chapter II of the *Studies* I have shown how local custom, modified by Biblical precepts, influenced the introduction into a number of the American colonies of a system of partible descent differing from the rule of primogeniture prevailing at common law. Working in a similar area, George L. Haskins[20] has demonstrated that the recording system in Massachusetts was not indigenous. The practices of Leyden, where the Pilgrims resided for a time, and the customs of many manorial and borough courts in England, set the pattern for the system that was adopted in the Bay Colony. In my *Select Cases of the Mayor's Court* I stressed the impact in the colonies of English borough and local customs and procedures, and demonstrated how that most notable seat of the

---

15 Carroll T. Bond, *The Court of Appeals of Maryland: A History* (Maryland, 1928), pp. 17-21.

16 *Commentaries on the Constitution of the United States*, 2d ed. (Boston, 1851).

17 For example, by Paul S. Reinsch, "The English Common Law in the American Colonies," in *Select Essays in Anglo-American Legal History*, I, 367, et seq.; C. J. Hilkey, *Legal Development in Colonial Massachusetts, 1630-1686*, p. 144.

18 Julius Goebel, Jr., "King's Law and Local Custom in Seventeenth New England," *Columbia Law Review*, XXXI (1931), 416; prefatory note by Francis S. Philbrick in *County Court Records of Acomack-Northampton*, pp. xiii, xiv.

19 Francis R. Aumann, *The Changing American Legal System: Some Selected Phases* (Columbus, 1940).

20 "The Beginnings of the Recording System in Massachusetts," *Boston University Law Review* (April, 1941), pp.28 1-304.

law merchant in England, the London mayor's court, served as the prototype for the institution of the same name which was transplanted in the seventeenth century to settlements as widely separated as the English colonies in North America and the Indian municipalities of Madras, Bombay, and Calcutta. In my *Government and Labor in Early America* I pointed out how the Tudor industrial code patterned colonial legislation and administrative practice, although both the colonial entrepreneur and the free worker, owing to the widely divergent conditions obtaining in this country, enjoyed a larger measure of freedom from restriction than they would have had they chosen to stay at home. In other cases, too, where English law was seemingly adopted, significant variations were introduced. For instance, the Massachusetts Dower Act of 1647 has been shown to have been based upon the rules of common law dower prevailing in England, but to have been interpreted by the courts in a manner which was in many instances at variance with the common law rules.[21]

When we give proper recognition to the impact of English local customs on early colonial law and to the transplantation and adaptation, often in scarcely recognizable form, of the common law, we should not forget that novel, numerous, and significant departures from English law and practice were introduced in the colonies. Many examples could be cited. Recent scholars have shown how the peculiar system of appeals of the General Court of Massachusetts for the greater part of the seventeenth century worked out quite differently from English practice and constituted strong testimony to the indigenous and reformist impulses prevailing in Puritan New England.[22] Lest we forget, too, the American law of slavery was an innovation, without support in contemporary English law,[23] although centuries of villeinage had lent precedence for a system of bondage, and white servitude in the colonies, founded in the main on debt bondage, represented a significant deviation from the relations of master and servant prevailing in the mother country.[24] Finally, it must be borne in mind that in the mid-seventeenth century England herself was in the throes of political and social reform, but it is safe to say that the modifications of the criminal code in the Puritan colonies went a good deal further than the tentative experiments in England, and that in the Quaker colonies the criminal codes, until modified or supplanted, were representative of the most liberal thought of the time and widely departed from English practice.[25]

In view of the strength of the reformist program, the pull of half-remembered customs, and the streamlining of archaic procedure and practice to meet the needs of agrarian communities largely without trained lawyers, it is perhaps remarkable that the conservative reaction of

---

21 G. L. Haskins, "A Problem in the Reception of the Common Law in the Colonial Period," *University of Pennsylvania Law Review* (May, 1949), XCVII, 842-853.

22 See Mark De Wolfe Howe and Louis F. Eaton, Jr., "The Supreme Judicial Power in the Colony of Massachusetts Bay," *New England Quarterly*, XX (1947), 1-26.

23 "One may be a villein in England, but not a slave." Holt, C. J., in Smith v. Brown and Cooper, 2 Salkeld 666 (c. 1706). For Lord Stowell's ironic comment on the view "that England was too pure an air for slaves to breathe in," see Slave Grace, 2 Hagg. Adm. 1904 (1827).

24 See my *Government and Labor in Early America*, pp. 310 *passim*.

25 See Herbert K. Fitzroy, "The Punishment of Crime in Provincial Pennsylvania," *Pa. Mag. of Hist. and Biog.* (July, 1936), pp. 242-269; *The Burlington Court Book*, p. xlviii, xlix.

the eighteenth century described in the Introduction to the *Studies* was able to make such headway, even in colonies ideologically unsympathetic to large chunks of the common law. But the facts must be faced. Although the Connecticut reporter Root insisted that "we need only compare the laws of England with the laws of Connecticut to be at once convinced of the difference which pervades their whole system,"[26] and although Thomas Jefferson and John Adams both felt that the common law was little attended to in New England, a close look at a Connecticut higher court on the eve of the Revolution suggests that the contrast between the legal systems of New England and the practices prevailing elsewhere in the colonies was becoming more blurred as time went on. Indeed, as one recent editor has pointed out, "the picture of this framework of the law in an eighteenth century corporate colony is a picture of the framework of the law of England at the same time."[27] In the shaping of its legal system as well as in the functioning of its political system Connecticut had abandoned utopian idealism and embraced normalcy.

If Hartford and Westminster were getting closer together on the eve of the Revolution, we should expect that Charleston would have bridged the gap with London even more quickly, and we would be justified in such expectations. English law was sweepingly adopted by that province's act of 1712[28] and the South Carolina court act of 1721, setting as a requirement for admission to practice that the applicant have had at least five years at one "of the four Law Colleges" of England and have "kept eight terms common," guaranteed a fairly close observance of English common law and equity. As lawyers trained in the common law came to dominate the profession in every colony, the reception of the common law gained increasing momentum. After all, the English reported cases were available, the colonial judicial records were not. As one attorney pithily put it, in an argument in a Virginia case, "we are to take as our guide the rules and principles of the English law, as we have none other to follow."[29]

The impact of a frontier environment upon the shaping of the American legal system deserves close evaluation, region by region. A more recent generation is less inclined than its elders to accept without serious qualifications the thesis of Frederick Jackson Turner as applied to the law in still starker form by F. L. Paxson, that liberalizing currents originated in frontier areas. This pregnant, but highly debatable thesis remains to be tested by examining the transmission of legal institutions into the Western territories. A gratifying number of significant investigations into the law of the territories have been carried out by scholars in recent years. The first returns suggest less resistance to the common law than the Turner-Paxson school might have predicted. For example, the records of the Michigan courts offer considerable evidence of a large-scale reception of English law, a process which was stepped up as the nineteenth century advanced.[30] A bewildering conglomeration of English

---

26 Preface to 1 Root's Reports (1798).

27 John T. Farrell, ed., *The Superior Court Diary of William Samuel Johnson, 1772-73*, p. xxxviii.

28 *S. C. Stat.*, II, 401.

29 Ross v. Poythress, 1 Wash. 120, 121 (Va., 1792).

30 See *Transactions of the Supreme Court of the Territory of Michigan, 1825-1836*, ed. by W. W. Blume (6 vols., Ann Arbor, 1940).

statutes, acts of the territorial governors and judges, statutes of the Northwest territorial legislature, acts of Congress, and French law left over from early times, had to be digested until order was created out of the confusion.[31] Even in the Southwest Territory the English common law and equity were virtually from the start the accepted base of the law even though the Spanish had only just relinquished the Mississippi Territory.. Far less hostility to the common law is found in the Southwest than in the Northwest Territory, although a number of innovations and deviations from the common law are found there, too.[32] In short, whether on the seaboard or the frontier, no monolithic interpretation will suffice to explain the course and reception of the law. Many strains were woven into the fabric and the patterns vary from place to place.

Much work still remains to be done in the field of American legal history. We need more monographic studies in depth.[33] Opportunities are at hand for further searching investigations into the role of the lawyer in colonial society and politics and into the economics of the legal profession in the eighteenth century.[34] Recent researches into the careers of the Dulanys of Maryland, of William Livingston and John Tabor Kempe of New York, and of William Paterson of New Jersey help fill an enormous gap in our knowledge of the colonial and Revolutionary lawyer.[35] Perhaps before the younger scholar sets out to write a monograph he would do well to try his hand at editing a legal text. We need, and need desperately, a group of dedicated and trained minds who will be prepared to assume the task of editing our legal records, a task which summons those prepared to master the disciplines of law and history. Microfilm, Xerography, and other photocopying devices might well be utilized to supplement present programs for printing the unpublished court records of the colonial period. The great body of statutes still remains to be systematically reviewed and collated; the business of the courts still awaits study and interpretation. We must do first things first. The voyages of discovery preceded the age of colonization. Before we can write the history of the law we must discover for ourselves what the law really was.

RICHARD B. MORRIS

December 1, 1959

---

31 See Pease, ed., *Laws of the Northwest Territory* and F. S. Philbrick's edition of the *Laws of the Indiana Territory.*

32 See William B. Hamilton, *Anglo-American Law on the Frontier*: *Thomas Rodney and His Territorial Cases* (Durham, N. C., 1953), pp. 117-135.

33 Two penetrating studies are Julius Goebel, Jr. and T. Raymond Naughton, *Law Enforcement in Colonial New York*: *A Study in Criminal Procedure* (New York, 1944), and Joseph Henry Smith, *Appeals to the Privy Council from the American Plantations* (New York, 1950).

34 For a suggestive approach, see my "Legalism versus Revolutionary Doctrine in New England," *New England Quarterly*, IV (1931), 195-215. The perceptive analysis by James W. Hurst (*The Growth of American Law*: *the Law Makers* [Boston, 1950], pp. 249-375) suggests a significant area worth exploring for the colonial period.

35 Aubrey C. Land, *The Dulanys of Maryland* (Baltimore, 1955); Milton M. Klein, "The Rise of the New York Bar; The Legal Career of William Livingston," *William and Mary Quarterly*, XV (July, 1958); Catherine S. Crary, "The American Dream: John Tabor Kempe's "Rise from Poverty to Riches," *ibid.*, XIV (1957), 176; Richard C. Haskett, "William Paterson, Attorney General of New York," *ibid.*, VII (1950), 26-38; Paul M. Hamlin, *Legal Education in Colonial New York*, (New York, 1939).

TABLE OF CONTENTS

CHAPTER I

An Introduction to the Early History of American Law

A. THE PROBLEM FOR THE LEGAL HISTORIAN

IF one were gifted with the ability to give melodic expression to the juristic ideas and experiences that comprise the early American legal system with its fascinating number of counter-themes, he might turn for his medium to a classic symphony in the polyphonic style. In the first movement of this hypothetical juristic symphony, the composer might present the opposing themes of the seventeenth-century law. The strings would introduce a majestic theme expressive of the tenet that all positive law was declaratory of the law of nature and that the source of this ideal law might be found in the Scriptures. In contrast, the woodwinds would take up the counter-theme, representing secular tradition, deriving its inspiration from the common-law precedents of the English system. In the final section of the movement the original subject in the strings would be transformed in character. Freedom and self-assertion due to the radical changes in economic outlook and the environment of the frontier would now be expressed in a theme of pioneer pattern. At this point the brass would blare forth defiantly against the commentary of the strings, and herein might be discerned the Calvinist motif, inhibiting human behavior and expression, and imposing a system of paternalism in the law.

The eighteenth century in American law — the second

movement of the juristic symphony—would present a single dominant theme which might best be expressed in the homophonic style. The fundamental voice which would now be heard is the common law of England, a melody supported by harmonic chords known as natural rights. These natural rights have evolved out of the seventeenth-century principles of eternal validity, and the positive law, in this instance the common law, is expected to give effect to them. Virile survivals of seventeenth-century progress and premature instances of deference to modernity might be expressed in this movement by an occasional and intriguing dissonance.

The dominant theme of the second movement would not be completely abandoned in the third, representative of nineteenth-century legal experience. As it proceeds, a new voice would sweep upward and lead on to a vigorous climax. The eighteenth-century theme would emphatically recur throughout. The conflict between the progressive legal demands of the industrial age and those of habit and tradition might thus be disclosed.

In the finale the composer might introduce his theme, illustrative of recent juristic tendencies, by a series of questions. The experiences of the three earlier centuries would then return to perplex him and to guide him. Against the dominant and clear voice of progressive reform in the strings, the woodwinds might still be faintly audible, issuing an occasional disturbing challenge in the name of tradition.

1. *The American Common Law*

Modern historical scholarship has considered the American Revolution in broader aspects than simply the military and political. It has recognized the struggle with Great Britain as evidential of a great social movement. This movement can be projected back into the middle of the seventeenth century. Profound changes in social outlook can be traced to conditions on the frontier and to a changed intellectual and theological equipment. No more concrete evidence of these social transformations can be found than in the evolution of the law as administered in the colonial courts and as enacted by the colonial legislatures. No clearer illustration can be seen of the application of the working rule that changing *mores* bring changing law. Certain common tendencies and certain common characteristics appearing in the law of the British colonies in America are in some respects without parallel in the history of the common law in the seventeenth and eighteenth centuries. Their existence justifies the term, " American law." In fact, as early as 1704 it was recognized that the laws of the various colonial jurisdictions had some common basis and that British traders and those engaged in inter-colonial trade could not take refuge in the books of the common law but were charged with notice of the colonial systems. In that year an *Abridgment* [1] was printed in London of the laws of Virginia, Barbados, Maryland and Massachusetts, together with a few scattering items from Jamaica, New York and the Carolinas.

2. *The Theory of the Transplantation of the Common Law*

The distinctively American characteristics of the colonial law have gained little recognition in the modern courts. A convenient theory has been evolved by the courts which has in this country undoubtedly discouraged serious legal historical scholarship in the field of American law prior to the

---

[1] The full title reads: *An Abridgement | of the | Laws | In Force and Use in | Her Majesty's Plantations; | (Viz.) Of | Virginia, Jamaica, Barbadoes, Maryland, New England, New York, Carolina, &c. | Digested under proper Heads in the Me- | thod of Mr. Wingate, and Mr. Washington's | Abridgements. London | Printed for John Nicholson at the King's-Arms in | Little Britain, R. Parker, and R. Smith, under | the Royal-Exchange, and Benj. Tooke at the Middle- | Temple-Gate in Fleetstreet, 1704.*

Revolution. This theory relates to the transplantation of the common law to this country.[1] It is presented in different forms. One form is that the common law was enforced and all statutes in affirmance thereof passed in England antecedent to the settlement of the colony in the absence of specific legislation to the contrary.[2] Another view is that adoption and usage are essential to the authority of the common law,[3] that portion being adopted which was applicable to colonial conditions.[4] The success with which this latter variant has been applied bears a direct relation to the knowledge which the court possesses of colonial legal practices and of colonial social and economic conditions. Experience has shown that in many cases the *dicta* of modern decisions have been predicated on untenable historical grounds. Specific instances will be found throughout these *Studies*. No general rule can be formulated. In many respects early American law was indigenous. Therefore the court cannot rest content after an examination of the Year Books, the Abridgments, and the early English reports. The extent to which the common law was adopted in the colonies must be actually determined in each specific situation. This principle was recognized by Chief Justice Tilghman of Pennsylvania, in 1813, in *Poor v. Greene*:[5]

Every country has its Common Law. Ours is composed partly of the Common Law of England and partly of our own

[1] See R. C. Dale, " The Adoption of the Common Law by the American Colonies," *Amer. Law. Reg.*, n. s., XXI, 554.

[2] *Cf.* opinion of Attorney-General West, 1720, in Chalmers, *Opinions of Eminent Lawyers on various Points of English Jurisprudence chiefly concerning the Colonies* (Burlington, 1858), p. 206; Comm. *v.* Churchill (1840) 2 Metc. (Mass.) 123; Sackett *v.* Sackett (1829) 8 Pick. 309.

[3] Comm. *v.* Leach (1804) 1 Mass. 60, 61.

[4] Story, *J.,* in Van Ness *v.* Packard (1829) 2 Peters 144.

[5] 5 Binney 554.

usages. When our ancestors emigrated from England, they took with them such of the English principles as were convenient for the situation in which they were about to place themselves. It required time and experience to ascertain how much of the English law would be suitable to this country. By degrees, as circumstances demanded, we adopted the English usages, or substituted others better suited to our wants, till at length before the time of the Revolution we had formed a system of our own.

In frequent cases when the courts have been presented with specific instances of colonial divergence from the beaten track, they have found refuge in the maxim of *stare decisis.* Similarly, where modern legislation has found its origins in colonial practices, the courts have in many cases resorted to the traditional rule of construction that statutes in derogation of the common law are to be strictly construed.[1]

3. *The Dark Ages in American Law*

The neglect of the general field of American colonial law is not assignable alone to the conservatism of the bench. Other factors have played a part. In the first place, great difficulties have confronted the historian and the lawyer in search of the evidence. Primary obstacles have been the absence of reports and legislative records. It was not until 1843, for example, that the *Body of Liberties,* adopted by the colony of Massachusetts Bay in 1641, the first code of laws established in New England, was brought to light. Only within recent years has a copy of the printed *Book of the General Lawes and Libertyes* (Cambridge, 1648) of that colony, a collection of paramount importance, been un-

[1] Sir Frederick Pollock accounts for the rule on the ground of a traditional distrust of statutes and legislatures. *Essays in Jurisprudence and Ethics* (London, 1882), p. 85. This practice has been severely arraigned by Dean Pound. "Common Law and Legislation," *Harvard Law Review,* XXI, 383.

earthed. The second book of the seventeenth-century records
of the Particular Court of Connecticut, which had disap-
peared for many years and was finally discovered in New
York City in 1861, has only recently been printed. Certain
problems in connection with the Duke of York's code of laws
for the jurisdiction of New York and neighboring regions
are still obscure.[1] The loss and mutilation of colonial legal
manuscripts have complicated the problem. In addition,
until recent times official records of this kind in public
archives were virtually inaccessible.

A further reason for the survival of misconceptions of
early American legal history has been the undue weight
accorded to statements of legal policy authorized by the colonial officials on one occasion or another.[2] In Massachusetts
preeminently, historians, in seeking to comprehend the
rationale of early legal development, have here encountered
a decoy leading far afield. An example of this is the cred-
ulity with which they have accepted the Declaration of 1646,
drawn up by a Committee of the General Court to answer a
group of remonstrants. These critics of the Puritan régime
had included, among other grievances, the absence of " a
settled form of government according to the laws of England." [3] The committee proceeded in an ingenious manner
to show that the laws of Massachusetts were at one with the
common law. An examination of these *Parallels,* as they
have been called, reveals that such statements of important
law as are included are often incomplete, garbled and misleading. In addition, the absence from the Declaration of

---

[1] Dr. Julius Goebel's forthcoming critical edition of that code will undoubtedly clarify many moot points.

[2] This problem is discussed in detail in my "Massachusetts and the
Common Law: The Declaration of 1646," *American Historical Review,*
XXXI, 443-453.

[3] Hutchinson Papers, *Prince Society Publications,* I, 214 *et seq.*

many important legal practices of a pioneer character bears eloquent testimony to its apologetic nature. The document appears disingenuous, and is not a fair presentation of fundamental law in this constructive period.

Rhode Island was not averse to similar methods. When, after a long delay, the Lords of Trade received what the colonists sent over as a true copy of their laws, that body complained that " the blots in some places, the blanks in others, the want of sense in some expressions, the want of titles to the Acts, and the disorderly placing of them " were such that no dependence could be placed upon them. Bellomont himself reported them to be "such a parcel of fustian" as he had never seen.[1]

A third reason for the obscurity in which early American law has lain is the failure of the colonists themselves to formulate a definite theory as to the extent of the transplantation of the common law and of the application of English statutes to the colonies. This confusion resulted in legislation in several colonies, notably Maryland and North and South Carolina, specifically adopting such English statutes as were believed to be applicable to colonial conditions.[2] In " An Essay on the Government of the English Plantations," published at the beginning of the eighteenth century, " An American " voiced his complaint that

No one can tell what is law and what is not in the plantations.

[1] *Cal. State Pap., Col. Ser.*, 1699, p. 388; 1700, p. 13; *R. I. Col. Rec.*, III, 376; cited by J. T. Adams, *Revolutionary New England* (Boston, 1923), p. 55. Francis Brinley and others in a letter to the Earl of Bellomont, Newport, Dec. 23, 1699, charges the authorities with omitting embarrassing acts from their abstract and with resorting to deliberate deception. *R. I. Col. Rec.*, III, 396, 397.

[2] For the theory of the extension of English statutes to the plantations, see St. George L. Sioussat, " The English Statutes in Maryland," *Johns Hopkins Univ. Studies in History and Political Science* (Baltimore, 1913), vol. XXXI, reprinted in part in *Select Essays in Anglo-American Legal History* (hereafter *Select Essays*), II, 416-430.

Some hold that the law of England is chiefly to be respected, and, where that is deficient, the laws of the several colonies are to take place. Others are of the opinion that the laws of the Colonies are to take the first place and that the laws of England are in force only where they are silent. Others there are who contend for the laws of the colonies, in conjunction with those that were in force in England at the first settlement of the colony, and lay down that as the measure of our obedience, alleging that we are not bound to observe any late acts of parliament in England except such only where the reason of the law is the same here that it is in England.[1]

The opponents of the colonial position held that the colonies were erected as corporations within the kingdom of England with legislative power limited to the making of by-laws and ordinances only for their own good government, provided the same were not contrary to the laws of England. A second group maintained that the colonists brought with them the common law and statutes in force before the settlement of the plantations. To these were to be added later acts of Parliament which specifically mentioned the colonies. A third group denied the authority of the common law in colonial jurisdictions.[2]

It is thus seen that in the past the investigator of our early legal institutions faced the prospect of entering a realm of obfuscation. Modern scholarship, which has overthrown the

[1] Quoted in C H. Lincoln, *Revolutionary Movement in Pennsylvania* (Philadelphia, 1901), pp. 17, 18, and in Sioussat, *Select Essays*, II, 429, 430. A later illustration of the vagueness of the theory of transplantation is found in a tract written by Anthony Stokes, Chief Justice of Georgia, *View of the Constitution of the British Colonies of North America and the West Indies* (London, 1783), pp. 9, 10.

[2] This division of opinion is clearly seen in the controversy over the Connecticut intestacy law, which has been treated in detail by Professor C. M. Andrews, " The Influence of Colonial Conditions as illustrated in the Connecticut Intestacy Law," *Yale Review* (1894), III, 261-294; *Select Essays*, II, 431-463.

traditional concept of the "Dark Ages" in European history and has gradually narrowed the span of years allotted to an epoch distinguished chiefly by the obscurity of historical knowledge concerning it, will find in the "Dark Ages" of American law another field of surprising revelations. The elaborate series of publications of colonial records, the modernization of facilities at important depositories of judicial archives, notably at the Suffolk Court House in Boston, and the advance which has been made in research in the field of English legal history, constitute a challenge to American legal scholarship to reveal the continuity of American legal institutions from their colonial foundations to the present day.[1]

B. SEVENTEENTH-CENTURY INFLUENCES IN AMERICAN LAW

1. *The Frontier*

In the seventeenth century American law was born. It grew amid the surroundings of the first American frontier which nurtured self-assertion and independence. By its very isolation from established centers of culture, the frontier created of necessity a culture peculiarly its own. As conditions on the first frontier of the seaboard became stabilized, the conservative interest in static security thwarted further independent development. In the western movement of the American population new frontiers were established which fashioned the political and social institutions of the old along characteristically independent lines adapted to their conditions. From the new frontiers emanated new social currents which reacted on the older settlements. This frontier pro-

---

[1] A complete denial of the significance of early American legal history is found in J. M. Zane's *The Story of Law* (New York, 1927), p. 358, wherein the author maintains that "as soon as the Colonies reached a stage where there was need of any developed system of law, the whole of the English law was introduced in its system of common law and equity, with exceptions that are not important."

cess, which has been called the "American great first cause," brought about in the field of law the scrapping of what Professor Paxson has termed " Englishism." [1]   In the colonies most exempt from English supervision this tendency to disregard the authority of the common law was frequently given public expression.   These colonies were Massachusetts, Plymouth, New Haven, Connecticut, Rhode Island, Pennsylvania, and Maryland.   To a lesser degree in the provinces generally frontier innovation was present in the seventeenth century; outward deference was paid to English legal institutions.

The officials in the corporate colonies were in general disinclined to confess a legal policy at variance with English law lest their charters be revoked.   Governor Winthrop of Massachusetts in a memorandum under date of November, 1639, admits that the delay in acceding to the will of the people in their demand for codification was due to the belief that laws " should arise *pro re nata* upon occasions " and that specific legislation " would professedly transgress the limits of our charter, which provide we shall make no laws repugnant to the laws of England, and that we are assured we must do." [2]   And Winthrop's words contain the key to the study of the law in early Massachusetts: no definitive information can be procured from the codes and legislation of the General Court; in all cases resort must be had to the administration of justice in the colonial and county tribunals.   On occasion the authorities could be more outspoken, however. In reply to the remonstrants in 1646 the General Court courageously declared:

[1] F. L. Paxson, "Influence of Frontier Life on the Development of American Law," State Bar Association of Wisconsin, *Reports*, XIII (1919-1920-1921), p. 485.

[2] John Winthrop, *History of New England* (or *Journal*), edited by James Savage (Boston, 1853), vol. i, pp. 388, 389.

Our allegiance binds us not to the laws of England any longer than while we live in England, for the laws of the parliament of England reach no further, nor do the king's writs under the great seal go any further. . . . And whereas they seem to admit of laws not repugnant, etc., if by repugnant they mean, as the word truly imports, and as by the charter must needs be intended, they have no cause to complain, for we have no laws . . . contrary to the law of God and of right reason, which the learned in those laws have anciently and still do hold forth as the fundamental basis of their laws, and that, if anything hath been otherwise established, it was an error, and not a law, being against the intent of the law-makers, however it may bear the form of a law (in regard of the stamp of authority set upon it) until it be revoked.[1]

The pursuance of this policy evoked repeated attacks [2] and contributed to the annulment of the charter.

In 1665 the General Court of Connecticut decided that the colony should resort to the word of God in the absence of

[1] *Ibid.*, II, 352. For a similar honest renunciation of English law, see Winslow, " New England's Salamander," Mass. Hist. Soc., *Collections*, 3d ser., II, 137. Prior to the Child petition of 1646 the legislative independence of the *de facto* commonwealth had been asserted whenever its divergence from the laws of England was challenged. In 1630 the protest of Watertown drew forth a declaration in which the corporation's legislative powers were likened to those of Parliament. Winthrop, *Journal*, I, 84. In the Hingham affair of 1645, Winthrop, on trial, asserted the prerogative to govern and "judge over causes by the rule of God's laws and our own" (*ibid.*, II, 280) ; and on the eve of the Child incident, the demands of the Gorton faction that " in their public courts the laws of our native country should be named amongst them " had proved an embarrassing pretension. Samuel Gorton, "Simplicity's Defence against Seven-Headed Policy," edited by William R. Staples, R. I. Hist. Soc., *Collections*, II, 80.

[2] Edward Randolph was the most indefatigable opponent of colonial separatism. For pertinent reports to the council, see Hutchinson Papers, II, 210; Prince Society, *Publications*, II, 311. A subsequent assertion of independence from English laws was made by the General Court. *Mass. Col. Rec.*, V, 198, 200.

specific law.[1] Robert Quary commented on this statement
in the *Book of Laws* as follows:

The people are of a very turbulent, factious and uneasy
temper. I cannot give their character better than by telling
your Lordships that they have made a body of laws for their
government which are printed; the first of which is that no
law of England shall be in force in their government till made
so by act of their own. Having told your Lordships this, I
think there is no further room to admire at any extravagancy
acted in the government.[2]

The rugged independence which was born of the frontier
brought about the scrapping of important common-law practices incompatible with life in the new agrarian communities.
In these *Studies* three types of social engineering evolving
out of the frontier are developed. The first relates to land.
New economic and social conditions favored a legal technique
which would facilitate the transfer of land, give property
security in addition to liquidity, and respond the more readily
to the demands for equality of distribution. The second
study concerns laws tending toward the establishment of a
greater equality of persons. Simple agrarian conditions of
the seventeenth century revived the function of the family
as the unit of production. As a result of this development,
there was imposed greater economic responsibility upon the
married woman, and the enlargement of her legal personality
was the consequence. Social regulation of family life was

[1] *Conn. Col. Rec.*, II, 184.

[2] Quary to the Board of Trade, *B. T. Papers, Plantations, General,
Entry Book D*, fol. 201, quoted by Andrews, *op. cit.*, p. 435 n. In 1698
Gov. Nicholson wrote the Board of Trade that in Rhode Island, among
other colonies, a great many people believed "that no law of England
ought to be in force and binding to them without their own Consent for
they foolishly say they have no represent[a] sent from themselves to the
Parlia[t] in England And they look upon all laws made in England that
put any restraint upon them to be great hardships." Chalmers MSS.,
R. I., fol. 13 (transcript), NYPL.

intensified not alone through the influence of Puritanism but through the absence of real urban life. In general, the smaller the group the greater is the intensity with which group restrictions and norms are imposed upon the individual. The third study deals with the transplantation to the colonies of common-law notions of responsibility for wrongful acts, and with the modifications thereof which were the resultant of a new humanitarian concept and a revolt against the archaic restrictions of the English system.

2. *Theologico-political Concepts: the Law of Nature and the Law of God*

A second major theme in early American law was founded on an appeal from positive law to fixed standards of justice, to a " higher law " which prescribes the consequences to be attached by judicial action to particular relations. The concept of a law of nature, superior to positive law and embracing a body of moral principles recognized always and everywhere by man's reason as binding, was by no means peculiar to the colonists. The doctrine, acquired from classical antiquity, was developed by medieval jurists and schoolmen on the ground of Roman and canon law and of patristic and classical philosophy. In the Middle Ages theologians and canonists associated the concept of a law of nature with that of a law of God. Thomas Aquinas, the great schoolman, postulated a *lex aeterna* derived from the divine reason. Man's participation in the *lex aeterna* constituted the law of nature. This natural law was considered as comprising the instincts of nature, often identified with the will of God, the *jus gentium* and the moral law of the Scriptures. The fundamental principles of the law of nature endured without change owing to the unchangeableness and perfection of the Divine Reason, but the human or positive law was subject to the sovereign power of the state and therefore was mutable. By elevating this law of nature above the will of sovereigns and above positive law, the churchmen sought to gain additional sanction for the civil jurisdiction of the clergy; anti-papalists, on the other hand, employed the *jus naturale* in behalf of the Empire.[1]

While it is true that the canon law was the principal vehicle of the law of nature, and that there was considerable hostility to the canonists among the common lawyers,[2] nevertheless the concept was by no means unimportant in English law. Equity was in theory a generalization from the law of reason or the law of God.[3] Furthermore, additional authority for the concept of fundamental law might be derived from the view that medieval English statutes were declaratory of pre-existing law and that conscious legislation is difficult to find much before the fifteenth century.[4] While this opinion has

[1] Aquinas, *Summa Theologica*, Part II, i, Q. 91, art. 1, 2; Q. 97, art. 1, 3; Placentinus, *Summa Institutionum* (Mairitz, 1535), i, 2; Azo, *Summa Institutionum*, i, 2; Otto Gierke, *Political Theories of the Middle Ages*, translated with an Introduction by F. W. Maitland (Cambridge, 1922), pp. 74-77; 172-174.

In reducing the medieval concept of the law of nature into its component parts, it is impossible to make any clear-cut distinction between law founded upon reason and that found in revelation. Human reason appears to be a derivative of eternal reason; and man's rationalism is founded upon dogma. Aquinas, *Summa Theologica*, Part II, i, Q. 91, art. 2; Étienne Gilson, *Études de Philosophie médievale* (Strasbourg, 1924), p. 28.

[2] W. S. Holdsworth, *A History of English Law* (London, 1909), vol. ii, pp. 512, 513.

[3] *Cf*. e. g., *Doctor and Student*, Dial. I, c. xi, wherein it is maintained that the law of England has authority "where the law of reason, the law of God, customs, maxims, ne other grounds of the law seem not to be sufficient to punish evil men and to reward good men." *Cf*. also Sir Frederick Pollock, "Transformation of Equity," *Essays in Legal History*; Roscoe Pound, *Harvard Law Review*, XXI, 393 *et esq.*; L. O. Pike, "Common Law and Conscience in the Ancient Court of Chancery," *Select Essays*, II, 722; Sir Paul Vinogradoff, "Reason and Conscience in Sixteenth Century Jurisprudence," *Law Quarterly Review*, XXIV, 373.

[4] C. F. McIlwain in *Magna Carta Commemoration Essays*, edited by H. E. Malden (London, 1917), pp. 140, 141, 145; *The American Revolution* (New York, 1923), pp. 63, 73.

been challenged for the first half of the fourteenth century,[1] it is none the less clear that a general principle held for the seventeenth as well as for the thirteenth century: " There is a fundamental law which binds a king, and beyond which he may not go." [2] English political philosophers of diverse views found this fundamental law in the law of nature which they identified with the law of God. Wycliffe advanced the fundamental basis for anti-papal arguments: *" Non enim est jus humanum nisi de quanto fundatum fuerit in lege Dei divina."* Hobbes frequently mentioned " a Law of Nature (which is undoubtedly God's law)," and John Locke, who perpetuated the intellectual traditions of Calvinism, identified the will of God with the law of nature, accepting the " Word of God " as fundamental law and utilizing it as " a rule of righteousness to influence our lives " and as a concrete means of checking arbitrary government.[3]

In the great constitutional conflict of the seventeenth century both the prerogative and parliamentary parties drew their arguments from the law of God and the law of nature. Upon these foundations they superimposed the structure of the common law.[4] The broadest authority was bestowed

[1] T. F. T. Plucknett, *Statutes and their Interpretation in the First Half of the Fourteenth Century* (Cambridge, 1922), part i, chap. iv.

[2] C. F. McIlwain, *The High Court of Parliament* (New Haven, 1910), chap. II.

[3] J. N. Figgis, *The Divine Rights of Kings*, 2d edition (Cambridge, 1914), p. 311; Hobbes, Leviathan [reprinted from the edition of 1651 (Oxford, 1909)], pp. 220, 221; John Locke, *Two Treatises on Civil Government. Cf.* also H. D. Foster, " International Calvinism through John Locke and the Revolution of 1688," *Amer. Hist. Rev.*, XXXII, 475-499.

[4] " Laws," said the Speaker of the House of Commons in 1604, " whereby the ark of this government hath ever been steered, are of three kinds; the 1st, the Common Law, grounded or drawn from the Laws of God, the Law of Reason, and the Law of Nature, and not mutable; the 2d,

upon the law of God and the law of reason by the radical groups, particularly the Levellers, who accepted them as the fundamental law of the kingdom which no Parliamentary act could contravene.[1]   The proposition that the law must be in accord with reason is now " the major premise of the new political logic." [2]   Lilburne in *Londons Liberty In Chains* defined the law of England as

the Perfection of Reason, consisting of Lawful and Reasonable Customes, received and approved of by the people: and of the old Constitutions, and modern Acts of Parliament, made by the Estates of the Kingdome.   But such only as are agreeable to the Law Eternall and Naturall, and not contrary to the word of God: For whatsoever lawes, usages, and customes, not thus qualified: are not the law of the land; nor are to be observed and obeyed by the people, being contrary to their Birthrights and Freedoms, which by the Law of God, and the great Charter of Priviledges, they ought not to be.[3]

It is not therefore in the least surprising to find that similar sentiments should have been voiced by contemporaries in the New England colonies.   In Puritan America, not only was the supremacy of the law of nature maintained and identified with the law of God, but the source of the law was found in the scriptural word.   This thesis was good Calvinism,[4] and was upheld by the leading Protestant Reformers.   Even Richard Hooper, opponent of Puritanism in

the positive Law, founded, changed, and altered by and through the occasions and policies of times; the 3d, Customs and Usages, practised and allowed with time's approbation, without known beginnings." *Parl. Hist.,* I, 1046.   *Cf.* also Coke, *Law Tracts,* 1746 edition, p. 224.

[1] T. C. Pease, *The Leveller Movement* (Washington, D. C., 1916), p. 342.

[2] *Ibid.,* pp. 137, 138.

[3] *Londons Liberty In Chains Vindicated against Slavery* (London, 1646), p. 41.

[4] Calvin, *Institutes,* bk. I, cc. 7, 8; IV, cc. 8-10.

England, urged in his *Ecclesiastical Polity* that " laws human must be made according to the general laws of nature, and without contradiction to any positive law of Scripture, otherwise they are ill made." [1] The American Puritans gave this theory concrete application. The law of nature, which had always been something of an abstraction, was with them associated with the Deuteronomic code. "The Law of Nature is God's law," declared John Davenport in 1669.[2] It had been planted by God deep in the hearts of men, " written as with a pen of iron and the point of a diamond," before the fuller revelations of the written law, and there it was still to be found,[3] eighteenth-century divines continued to maintain.[4]

Such doctrines, generally held among the Puritan clergy in England and America, account for the assertion of Jeremy Taylor that " amongst us there are or have been a good many Old Testament Divines, whose Doctrines and manner of talk and arguments and practices have too much squinted towards Moses." [5] There was at least as much foundation for the application of this criticism to American Puritanism

[1] Richard Hooker, *Of the Laws of Ecclesiastical Polity*. See especially Bk. I, pp. 147-232. Hooker cites Gratian's definition of natural right: "*Jus naturale est, quod in Lege et Evangelio continetur.*" p. 1, d. I. (*Corp. Jur. Can.*, p. 2. Jugd. 1586).

[2] *Mass. Election Sermon*, 1669, p. 4; cited by Alice M. Baldwin, *The New England Clergy and the American Revolution* (Durham, N. C., 1928), p. 15.

[3] Jonathon Mayhew, *Sermons*, 1755, p. 258; cited by Baldwin, *op. cit.*, p. 15.

[4] [Elisha Williams] *A seasonable Plea For The Liberty of Conscience And The Right of private Judgment In Matters of Religion, Without any Control from human Authority*, Boston, 1744. See also Appleton, *Mass. Election Sermon*, 1742, pp. 11-13, 49; Cutler, *Conn. Election Sermon*, 1717, p. 17; cited by Baldwin, *op. cit.*, p. 16.

[5] Quoted by H. G. Wood, " The Influence of the Reformation on Ideas concerning Wealth and Property," *Property: Its Duties and Rights*, edited by Charles Gore, Bishop of Oxford (New York, 1922), p. 166.

as there was to English. The scriptural influence in American Puritan polity is attributable (1) to the dominating position of the clergy in New England; and (2) to the Hebraic or Old Testamentarian Renascence nurtured by the non-conforming sects in England and America.

(1) Although the Protestant Revolution has been regarded as the responsible cause for the reduction of the power of the clergy, it must be remembered that outstanding Reformers such as Cartwright and Knox maintained that the ministers " should teach the magistrates how to exercise civil jurisdiction according to the Word of God." [1]   In the New England theocracies, at least down to 1660, the secular functions of the clergy were greatly expanded.   A contemporary, writing of conditions in Massachusetts Bay in the early period, observes:

> The preachers by their power with the people made all the magistrates, and kept them so entirely under obedience that they durst not act without them.   Soe that whenever anything strange or unusual was brought before them, they would not determine the matter without consulting the preachers.[2]

Thomas Lechford pointed out in 1642 that " the ministers advise in making of laws, especially ecclesiastical, and are present in courts and advise in some special causes annual and in framing of fundamental Lawes." [3]   In the period of legal origins the prestige of the clergy in civil affairs was of first magnitude.   To list but a few instances: in Massachusetts, John Cotton, the proponent of a Mosaic code of laws, and Nathaniel Ward, the compiler of the *Body of Liberties,* were members of the clergy; and so were Roger Williams in Rhode Island, Thomas Hooker in Connecticut, and John

---

[1] Figgis, *op. cit.*, pp. 190, 191.

[2] Winthrop, *Journal*, I, 194.

[3] *Plaine Dealing or News from New England* (Boston, 1867).

Davenport, co-founder of New Haven. The Cambridge Platform and the writings of Cotton and Davenport laid the foundations for the Puritan theocracies.[1]

(2) No small share in the Hebraic and Old Testamentarian Renascence which accompanied and followed the Protestant Revolution may be assigned to the non-conforming sects in England and America. The period from 1600 to 1650 was marked in England by a revival of interest in the Hebrew language and its literature. A number of sects, notably the Levellers, favored resorting to the Old Testament as the norm of English laws. At this time Millenarian enthusiasm, spreading from the Orient and continental Europe, penetrated England; the Fifth Monarchy Men were steeped in Hebraic doctrines.[2] This literary renascence manifested itself in Puritan America in numerous ways. Old Testament nomenclature, for one thing, was fashionable, although by no means universally adopted.[3] The Independents, both in the Old World and in the New, claimed distinguished Hebraists. The reverence for Hebrew which was held by Henry Ainsworth was transplanted in this country by William Bradford. Among others, John Cotton, the Mathers, Michael Wigglesworth, Nathaniel Ward, Henry Dunster, Charles Chauncy, John Clarke, and Roger Wil-

---

[1] *Cf.* Cotton Mather, *Magnalia Christi Americana* (London, 1702), Bk. V, Platform, chap. xvii; letter of John Cotton to Lord Say and Sele, in Hutchinson, *History of the Colony of Massachusetts Bay* (2d ed., London, 1765), vol. i, appendix; John Cotton, [John Davenport] *A Discourse about Civil Government in a New Plantation whose design is* religion (Cambridge, 1663), p. 14; John Eliot, *The Christian Commonwealth.*

[2] *Cf.* Louis I. Newman, *Jewish Influence on Christian Reform Movements* (New York, 1925), pp. 631-633, and literature cited.

[3] New Testament and non-Biblical names probably comprised a clear majority among the American Puritans. *Cf.* D. K. Dodge, " Puritan Names," in *New England Quarterly*, I, 467-475.

liams, were all seriously engaged in Hebrew studies.[1] Finally, the reverence for the Old Testament led to its being
held by some of the outstanding public officials among the
American Puritans as a pattern for legislation and a guide
for judicial decisions.

The early history of the law in Massachusetts Bay in-
volves a struggle between the desire of the governing group
for discretionary powers in the administration of justice, and
the popular demand for security — a conflict analogous in
some respects to the plebeian demand for the codification of
early Roman law and the establishment of limitations upon
the arbitrary consular powers, culminating in the Twelve
Tables.   Prior to 1643 such legislation as emanated from
the General Court was of a desultory character.   In 1635,
at the behest of the deputies, who objected to the discretion
lodged in the magistrates, a drafting committee was appointed,[2] and again in the following year a new committee,
of which John Cotton was one of the members, was chosen
" to make a draught of laws agreeable to the word of God,
which may be the Fundamentals of this Commonwealth." [3]
In the interim, the law of God was to guide in the absence
of specific law.   In 1636 Cotton presented to the General
Court a copy of his proposed code, " Moses his Judicialls,"
which, as the title fairly implies, was a rearrangement and
almost a complete copy of Pentateuchal enactments.[4]   This
code was published in 1641 in London under the misleading
title, *An Abstract of the Lawes of New England, as they are
now established*.   It was reprinted in London in 1655 and
its editor, William Aspinwall, disclaims any legal authority

---

[1] Newman, *op. cit.*, pp. 635-645.

[2] *Mass. Col. Rec.*, I, 147; Winthrop, *Journal*, I, 191.

[3] *Mass. Col. Rec.*, I, 174, 175.

[4] Winthrop, *Journal*, I, 240.

for the text.[1]   The medieval notion that fundamental law
could merely be declared, but not changed, by statutory enactment is presented by the editor in his Preface, wherein he
states: " These are not properly Laws, but prudentiall Rules,
which he recommended to that Colonie," for " it would be
an intrenchment upon the Royall power of Jesus Christ "
for the freemen " or any other of the sonnes of Adam to
ordain Lawes."   Cotton's object was " to show the complete sufficiency of the word of God alone to direct his people
in judgment of all causes, both civil and criminal."   The
medieval conception of sovereignty emanating from God is
tersely stated in the conclusion of the code by a quotation
from Isaiah 32 : 22 : " The Lord is our Judge, the Lord is
our Lawgiver, the Lord is our King: he will save us."

While there is no evidence that any action was taken on
the Cotton code, significant parallels may be drawn with the
subsequent code attributed to Nathaniel Ward—a member
of the 1638 committee — which was adopted in 1641 and
bears the name, *Body of Liberties*.[2]   This collection of broad

1 *Cf.* the reprint in Hutchinson Papers, Prince Society, *Publications*
(Boston, 1865), I, 181-205; *cf.* also W. C. Ford, " Moses his Judicialis,"
Mass. Hist. Soc., *Proceedings*, 2d ser., XVI, 274-284.

2 These parallels may be enumerated as follows: Cotton (C), chap. i,
1, i with Liberty (L) 67; C chap. iv, 6 with L 81; C chap. vi, 1 with
L 94, 3; C chap. vii, 3 with L 94, 2; C chap. vii, 5, 7, 8 with L 94, 1;
C chap. vii, 16 with L 94, 4; C chap. vii, 19 with L 94, 7, 8; C chap. vii,
17 with L 94, 9; C chap. vii, 22 with L 94, 10; C chap. vii, 23 with L
94, 11; C chap. vii, 11, 14 with L 94, 12; C chap. ix, 2 with L 29;
C chap. ix, 6 with L 43.

Mr. Max Farrand in his Introduction to the recent imprint (Cambridge, 1929) of the *Lawes and Libertyes* (Cambridge, 1648) appears
doubtful " as to whether the Liberties were ever formally made law."
In fact, he asserts that " the Epistle in the present work . . . states posi-
tively that the Liberties were prepared ' with intent to make use of them
in composing our lawes, but not to have them published as the lawes of
this Jurisdiction: nor were they voted in Court.' "   This is a miscon-
struction of the sentence which actually refers to " a modell of the

generalizations was by no means comprehensive; its ninety-eight articles comprising fundamental liberties, immunities, and sanctions. Because of its content and its incomplete character, it bears analogy to the medieval charters and partial codes.[1]

The very first article of the *Body of Liberties* provides that no man shall be deprived of life, liberty, or property except by a specific law established by the General Court " or in case of the defect of a law in any particular case by the word of God. And in Capitall cases, or in cases concerning dismembering or banishment, according to that word to be judged by the General Court." [2]   The law committee of 1647 was even more positive. In the preamble to the code of 1648 we find the codifiers asserting that the rules of civil polity were framed according to the law of God, and further that

   . . . *That distinction which is put between the Lawes of God and the lawes of men, becomes a snare to many* as it is misaplyed on the ordering of their obedience to civil Authorities; for when the Authoritie is of God, and that in way of an Ordinance Rom. 13, 1, and when the administration of it is according to deductions, and rules gathered from the word of God, and the clear light of nature in civil actions, *surely there*

Judiciall lawes of Moses," meaning the Cotton Code. The Epistle further states that, while a number of the Liberties have been repealed or altered, the compilers make no pretense in their present effort to establishing an unchangeable and perfect code. Attention may be called in this connection to the authoritative statement of Winthrop, writing of the General Court of December, 1641: " This session continued three weeks, and established one hundred laws, which were called the Body of Liberties . . . they were revised, amended and presented, and so established for three years, by that experience to have them fully amended and established to be perpetual." *Journal*, II, 66.

   [1] *Cf.* Paul Viollet, *Histoire du Droit Civil Français* (Paris, 1893), p. 139.

   [2] *Mass. Col. Laws* (*1660-1672*), edited by W. H. Whitmore, pp. 33, 121; *Lawes and Libertyes* (Cambridge, 1648), p. 1.

is no human law that tendeth to common good (according to these principles) but the same is mediately a law of God, and that in way of an Ordinance which all are to submit unto and that for conscience sake. Rom. 13. 5.

It was but a logical step to assert, as was done at a later day, that, where the authority exercised by the executive and the legislature exceeds the bounds of the law of God, the acts of these bodies are *ipso facto* void.[1] The natural antipathy which a common lawyer would have for a legal system constituted along these lines was reflected in the caustic comment of Lechford:

I feare it is not a little degree of pride and dangerous improvidence to slight all former lawes of the Church or State, cases of experience and precedents, to go to hammer out new, according to the Severall exigencies, upon pretence that the Word of God is sufficient to rule us. It is true, it is sufficient, if well understood. But take heede my brethren, despise not learning, nor the worthy Lawyers of either gown, lest you repent too late.[2]

The theocracies of Connecticut and New Haven took their cue from Massachusetts, and Plymouth anticipated her neighbor. In November, 1636, before the adoption of a body of laws, the General Court of Plymouth declared that no law should be imposed upon the jurisdiction without its consent.[3] In the celebrated foreword to the 1658 revision of the laws, its authors confess their indebtedness to the Scriptures in these words:

[1] Rev. Stephen Johnson, *Fast Day Sermon*, Dec. 1765; cited by Baldwin, *op. cit.*, p. 101. *Cf.* also Thomas Aquinas, who states that, if in any point human law deflects from the law of nature, it is no longer a law but a perversion of law. *Summa Theologica*, Part II, i, Q. 95, art. 2; Gierke, *op. cit.*, p. 174.

[2] *Plaine Dealing*, p. 86.

[3] Brigham, *Compact, Charter, and Laws*, p. 36.

It was the great privilege of Israel of old, and soe was acknowledged by them, Nehemiah the 9th and 13th. That God gave them right judgements and true Lawes for God being the God of Order, and not of Confusion hath comaunded in his word, and put man into a capacitie in some measure to observe and bee guided by good and wholesome Lawes: which are soe fare good and wholsome, as by how much they are derived from and agreeable to the ancient Platforme of Gods Lawe; for although sundry particulares in the Judiciall lawe which was of old enjoyed to the Jews, did more espetially (att least in some Circumstances) befitt theire Pedagogye, yet are they for the mayne soe exemplary, being grounded on Principles of Morall Equitie, as that all men Christians espetially, ought alwaies to have an eye thereunto, in the framing of theire Politique Constitutions; And although several of the Heathen Nations whoe were ignorant of the time (true) God and of his Lawe, have bine famous in theire times, for the Enacting and Execution of such Lawes as have proved profitable for the Government of theire Comonwealthes in the times wherein they lived: Notwithstand theire excelency appeered soe fare as they were founded upon grounds of Morall Equitie, which hath its Originall from the Law of God. And accordingly wee whoe have bine Actors in the framing of this smale body of the Lawes, together with other useful instruments whoe are gone to theire rest, can safely say both for our selves and them, that wee have had, an eye primarily and principally unto the aforsaid Platforme. . . .[1]

Along similar lines was the Connecticut Code of 1650 constituted. Thomas Hooker, the guiding spirit of the colony, in a letter to Governor Winthrop of Massachusetts in 1648, justified his fundamental doctrines of government by citing " the practice of the Jewish Church directed by God, Deut. 17: 10, 11; II. Chron. 19." [2]   In general, it may be said that

[1] Brigham, *op. cit.*, p. 106.
[2] Conn. Hist. Soc., *Collections*, I, 11, 12.

Connecticut legislation in the seventeenth century closely followed the precedents of its parent colony. When, in June, 1639, the free planters of New Haven gathered to discuss " settling civil government according to God," the first question propounded by Davenport was: " Whether the Scriptures do hold forth a perfect rule for the direction and government of all men in all duties which they are to perform to God and men, as well in the government of families and the commonwealth as in matters of church." " This was assented unto by all, no man dissenting." The second question, whether the word of Scripture should guide public officials in the performance of their official duties, was answered in the same way. Therefore, it was unanimously voted " that the Word of God shall be the only rule to be attended unto in ordering the affairs of government in this plantation." [1] The Plymouth declaration was anticipated by that of New Haven, which recognized the non-local and non-ceremonial laws of God, " as they were delivered by Moses," as having binding force in the courts of law in that jurisdiction, " till they be branched out in particular(s) hereafter." [2] Such an elaboration was found in the New Haven code of laws of 1655, which quotes liberally from both the Old and New Testaments, but looks more frequently to the former dispensation. Although Rhode Island was much less affected by theocratic legalism, this characteristic veneration for the law of God was shown in the compact adopted by the settlers of Aquidneck. [3]

Contemporary American Puritan literature affords considerable insight into the rationale of the concept of the law of God. An important commentary is found in a manuscript attributed to John Cotton, which Mr. Worthington Ford has assigned to the period between 1636, when the

---

[1] *New Haven Col. Rec.*, I, 11-13.   [2] *Ibid.*, p. 191.
R. I. *Col. Rec.*, I, 52, 63, 64.

" Judicialls " were framed, and 1640, when they were rejected. The document, entitled " How Far Moses Judicialls Bind Mass[achusetts]," [1] contends that the foundation of natural equity is to "give every man his due" and the means are specially set forth in the Scriptures. The author differentiates between these Scriptural laws in the manner of the New Haven lawmakers. The " perpetual " laws in the Old Testament are separated from those of purely local or temporary application. The binding validity of these perpetual laws is clearly upheld. Cotton dogmatically states that " naturall Judicialls bind all." Laws excluded as peculiar to the local circumstances of the ancient Hebrews include ceremonial laws, laws forbidding intermarriage and the alienation of land from the family, etc. In this respect the New England divine is merely reiterating the doctrine of the European Calvinists that the law of nature was " corroborated," " contained," or " summarized " in that part of the Mosaic law which was fundamental and moral, not ceremonial.[2] These Mosaic judicials, according to the thought of this scholastic discussion, are not superseded by the New Testament. Aspinwall, the editor of the second edition of the *Abstract*, advanced the three-fold attributes of the laws of God as: " 1. They are unvariable, and bind all persons in all ages, and in all Nations.[3] 2. They are undispensable by any created powers. 3. They bind not only the outward man to obedience, but also the spirit and conscience." [4]

[1] Mass. Hist. Soc.., *Proceedings*, 2nd ser, XVI, 280-284.

[2] Foster, "International Calvinism," *Amer. Hist. Rev.*, XXXII, 488. *Cf.* also Aquinas, *Summa Theologica*, Part II, i, Q. 100, art. 1 ; Q. 103, art. 3 ; Q. 104, art. 3.

[3] In 1639 Lechford proposed to the General Court that a record be kept of all actions, and, among the benefits which would accrue thereby to the public good, he declared that "hereby shall the law of God and justice be Duly administered to the people according to certain unchangeable rules." Lechford, *Note Book*, pp. 88, 89.

[4] Foreword to the second edition of the *Abstract*, edited by William Aspinwall (London, 1655).

Just as Cotton distinguishes between the perpetual and temporary laws of the Scriptures, so Winthrop advances a distinction well known in English constitutional law, between fundamental and introductory or secondary law, arguing that

it is well proved & concluded by a late Juditious writer, in a book newly come over, intituled an Answ: to Dr. Ferne, that thoughe all Lawes, that are sup' structive may be altered by the representative bodye of the Com:w: yet they have not power to alter anythinge w'ch is fundamental.[1]

Such a distinction was to be drawn by the magistrate, who, in accord with the Calvinist concept, was the " viceregent of God," and exercised a patriarchal supervision over society. Therefore, law-making, as Cotton asserted, was fundamentally a divine function, for " the more any Law smells of man, the more unprofitable " it is. In fact, such law-making as there was, was a matter of interpretation, a function reserved chiefly for the judiciary, and legislation consisted in broad generalizations declaratory of fundamental legal concepts. In accord with this notion, Winthrop, in his treatise on " Arbitrary Government," written in 1644 while he was deputy-governor to determine the respective powers of the magistrates and the deputies, declared that "the determination of law belongs properly to God : He is the only lawgiver, but He hath given power and gifts to man to interpret His laws; and this belongs principally to the highest authority in a commonwealth, and subordinately to other magistrates and judges according to their several places." [2] Winthrop comes out flatly against specific penalties. The whole problem, he contends, resolves itself into the question of Rule *versus* Discretion. The deputy-governor advocates discretion, with

---

[1] *Journal*, II, 438.

[2] Robert C. Winthrop, *Life and Letters of John Winthrop* (Boston, 1864-1895), vol. ii, pp. 440 *et seq.*

the Scriptures as the source of judicial interpretation.   Penalties should be prescribed as the case arises, *pro re nata*. The legislator, according to Winthrop, cannot prescribe penalties as equitably as the judge who can take into consideration the specific circumstances of the case before him.   In 1646, in answer to a contention between the magistrates and deputies as to whether the magistrates " in cases where there is noe particular expresse law provided, were to be guided by the Word of God till the generall courte give particular rules in such cases," the elders, acting as arbiters, replied:

Wee do not find that by the pattent they are expressly directed to proceed according to the Word of God, but we understand that by a law or libertie of the country they may act in cases wherein as yet there is no express law, soe that in such cases they proceed according to the Word of God.[1]

This discretionary power which Winthrop and his colleagues sought to keep in the hands of the magistrates was a subject of caustic criticism by the House of Deputies.   Discretion was regarded as a potentially dangerous cryptogram to which each judge possessed the key.[2]   Thomas Hooker frankly rejected the system of magisterial omnipotence, and argued:

That in the matter which is referred to the judge, the sentence should lie in his breast, or be left to his discretion, according

[1] Hutchinson Collection, *op. cit.*, pp. 179, 180.

[2] Among the offensive charges in the letters of the " Gortonoges," which Winslow summarizes, appears this: " That the whole Word of God is a parable to them, as their conversation in all points daily declare it." *Hypocrisie Unmasked*, edited by H. M. Chapin (Providence, 1916), p. 40. In a report in 1733 in regard to a Connecticut law founded on the Massachusetts precedent giving the judges the power to resort to the word of God where the statute book was silent, Francis Fane, standing counsel to the Board of Trade and Plantations, wrote: " To which Act I apprehend there is no objection except to the last clause, which seems to leave too great a discretionary power in the Court." Francis Fane, *Reports on the Laws of Connecticut*, edited by Charles M. Andrews (New Haven, 1915), pp. 57, 58.

to which he should go, I am afraid it is a course which wants both safety and warrant. I must confess, I ever looked at it as a way which leads directly to tyranny, and so to confusion, and must plainly profess, if it was in my liberty, I should choose neither to live nor leave my posterity under such a government.[1]

The acceptance of the law of God as fundamental law is in part accountable for the identification by Calvinist jurists in America of law with morality, sin with crime. This theory of criminal administration was not unique in Puritan America. In medieval Europe morals as well as belief were subject to the authority of the church. In Anglo-Saxon England immorality was a subject of penitential discipline, and down to 1640 the Ecclesiastical Courts exercised a wide disciplinary control over the moral life of the members of the church.[2] Calvinism intensified this social discipline, for, according to Calvin,[3] discipline was the nerve of religion. The vigorous arm of the state was now raised to enforce the moral dictates of the church. In New England, because of the close affiliation of church and court and of the homogeneous character of the community, it was possible to make practically every breach of the moral code a crime punishable by law. In the *Body of Liberties,* for example, it was provided that " no custome or prescription " should prevail in any moral cause, which could be proved " morallie sinfull

[1] Quoted in J. T. Adams, *Founding of New England* (Boston, 1921), p. 194.

[2] *Cf.* Von Bar, *History of Continental Criminal Law* (Boston, 1916), pp. 81-94; H. C. Lea, *History of Auricular Confession and Indulgences* (Philadelphia, 1896), II, 106-107; J. P. Oakley, *English Penitential Discipline and Anglo-Saxon Law in their Joint Influence* (New York, 1923), pp. 45, 141; Stephen, *History of the Criminal Law of England* (London, 1883), II, 402; Hale, *Precedents in Criminal Causes*, pp. 180, 220, 247; Godolphin, *Reportorium Canonicum*, pp. 469, 474, 475, cited by Julius Goebel, Jr., *Materials for the Development of Legal Institutions* (New York, 1928), pp. 366, 367.

[3] Calvin, *Inst.*, bk. iv, chap. xii, p. 1.

by the word of God." [1]   Thus, among the capital offences, idolatry, witchcraft, blasphemy, adultery, bestiality, and sodomy were included.   By the same token, unmitigated lying, common barratry, scolding, fornication, and acts conducive of unchaste behavior, idleness, drunkenness, and swearing were all criminal offences to which a penalty was attached. [2]

Two decades after the founding of Plymouth, according to the reports of contemporaries, there was an outbreak of crime and immorality before which the authorities of the colony were impotent.   The " crime wave " was not restricted to Plymouth, but swept over the colony of Massachusetts Bay.   Early in 1643 Richard Bellingham, then Governor of Massachusetts, began a correspondence with the magistrates and ministers of Plymouth, in which their advice was sought. [3]   In the replies of Bradford, Partridge, Reynors and Chauncy of Plymouth, Old Testament precedents were quoted as foundation for laws necessary to curb these crimes of sensational character.   Finally, Bradford himself recorded that in 1642 capital punishment was inflicted " according to ye law, Levit. 20: 15." [4]

[1] Lib. 65, *Mass. Col. Laws*, pp. 47, 186; *Lawes and Libertyes* (1648), p. 45.

[2] There was European precedent for such legislation outside of Geneva. From the Middle Ages down through the seventeenth century considerable sumptuary legislation was enacted both in England and on the continent.   But in contrast with the mass of sumptuary laws found in central Europe, the English statutes were almost entirely concerned with the regulation of food and clothing.   The economic policy of mercantilism and the desire for class distinctions appear to be more determining than any deep-seated moral convictions.   It was found impossible to enforce this legislation. *Cf.* Frances E. Baldwin, *Sumptuary Legislation and Personal Regulation in England* (Baltimore, 1926). *Cf.* also act of 1651 relating to apparel, *Mass. Col. Laws*, p. 123.

[3] William Bradford, *History of Plimoth Plantation* (Boston, 1900), pp. 459 *et seq.*

[4] *Ibid.*, pp. 474, 475.

This inter-colonial correspondence illustrates the characteristic resort to the opinions of the clergy and the confident acceptance of the literal precepts of the Pentateuchal code in matters of this kind. In the seventeenth-century legislation of a majority of the colonies there is manifest to a greater or less degree this desire to make palpable violations of the moral code penal offences and to assimilate sin and crime; it appears in more highly concentrated form, however, in Massachusetts, Plymouth, New Hampshire, Connecticut, New Haven, and East Jersey.

The influence of the New England codes extended beyond the confines of their respective jurisdictions. Thus, the " Duke's Laws " of 1664 bear close resemblance in wording to the New Haven codes of 1642 and 1650. Similarly, strict regulation of sexual morality was enacted among the Quakers. The " Great Law " of 1682, which may be regarded as representing Penn's ideal of a criminal code, contained elaborate provisions regulating sexual morality.[1] Throughout the colonies, furthermore, the lawmakers frowned fiercely upon intemperance, although it is doubtful whether the laws against drunkenness were as strictly enforced in the plantation provinces as in the Puritan colonies.[2]

The intensified social discipline of the Puritan in the New World was advertised in the Old by the publication in London of a broadside of the capital laws of the *Body of Liberties* of Massachusetts and of the alleged *Abstract of the Laws of New England*. A reflex of this experience appears during the period of the Puritan Revolution in England in the attempt to regulate sexual morality by criminal prosecution. A comparative study in law enforcement, based on the *Middlesex* (England) *Sessions Rolls* and the *Records of the*

[1] *Charter and Laws*, pp. 109, 110.

[2] John Allen Krout, *The Origins of Prohibition* (New York, 1925), pp. 26 *et seq.*

Quarterly Court of Essex County, Massachusetts, for the period of the middle seventeenth century, affords concrete evidence of the legislative warfare against sin carried on under the Puritan aegis. Beginning with the year 1651 a sudden increase in the number of indictments for the offences of adultery, fornication, lewdness and incest is found in Middlesex County, reaching a surprising figure in the year 1656 when there were ten indictments for crimes against property, i. e., burglary, robbery, embezzlement and larceny, and eleven for sexual offences. After 1661 indictments for sexual offences disappear from the *Rolls.* The Commonwealth act of 1650, making adultery a non-clergyable felony with mitigating circumstances,[1] and the proposals of the law committee of 1653,[2] illustrate the Calvinist influence in the law. It must be conceded that the surface was barely scratched in this attempt during the Commonwealth to enforce a strict moral standard. In the great metropolitan area of Middlesex County there were only forty-eight indictments for sexual offences for the period 1649-1660, as against eighty-six in Essex County, Massachusetts, a homogeneous district about one one-hundredth the former's numerical size. In fact, the Essex *Records* reveal the more telling figures that for the period 1636-1662 there were ninety-two indictments for crimes against property as against 122 for sexual offences.

The Puritan has in recent times been severely criticized by some writers for sponsoring a systematic policy of suppression which could only result in frequent moral explosions.[3] Corroborative of this view are the early admission by the Massachusetts legislators of their failure to suppress illicit

---

[1] Scobell's *Acts,* pt. 2, 121; 3 Bl. *Comm.* 139.

[2] Robinson, "Anticipation under the Commonwealth of Changes in the Law," *Select Essays,* I, 483.

[3] *Cf.* L. H. Gibson, *Jared Ingersoll* (New Haven, 1920), pp. 51-53; Myers, *Ye Olden Blue Laws* (New York, 1921), p. 114.

relationships entered into by husbands who had left their wives in England,[1] and, late in the century, the admission by the Connecticut General Court, acknowledging the futility of laws for the suppression of vice.[2] Bradford, commenting on the crime wave of 1642, manifests a clearer understanding of the effects of drastic criminal codes on human behavior than do his contemporaries in New England:

It may be in this case as it is with waters when their streams are stopped or dammed up, when they gett passage they flow with more violence, and make more noys and disturbance, than when they are suffered to rune quietly in their owne chanels. So wikednes being here more stopped by strict laws, and the same more nerly looked unto, so as it cannot rune in a comone road of liberty as it would, and is inclined, it searches every wher, and at last breaks out wher it getts vente.[3]

Although the Connecticut Court in 1684 confessed to the prevalence of tippling and immorality, it stoutly held that it was not the laws which were responsible, but the " want of due prosecution of offenders that are guilty of the breach of them." This was the reason why these laws had " not answered that expectation of reformation which this Court aimed at." [4] Such an argument sounds painfully familiar to a generation which has wrestled with the problem of the relationship between paternalistic legislation and law enforcement.

3. *Limitations on the Acquisition of the Common-Law System*

The fundamental limitation on the growth of American law in the seventeenth century was the scarcity of lawyers. Yet the absence of the professional class was to a consider-

---

[1] *Lawes and Libertyes* (Cambridge, 1648), p. 37.
[2] (1690) *Conn. Pub. Rec.*, IV, 28, 29.
[3] *Op. cit.*, p. 386.
[4] *Conn. Pub. Rec.*, III, 148.

able degree accountable for the liberation of American law from many of the shackles of English medievalism. I do not intend to go into detail in regard to a subject ably treated by Mr. Charles Warren in his *History of the American Bar,* but merely to summarize the conditions briefly.

The legal profession in New England in the seventeenth century was inconsequential. Of the sixty-five men who landed at Plymouth in 1620, not one was a lawyer. Although there was some legal talent in Massachusetts Bay, there was no lawyer actually practising at the time of the settlement. The first educated attorney who practised in the colony was Thomas Lechford, whose activities, dating from 1637 or 1638, were limited. He was disbarred from pleading shortly thereafter because of an alleged attempt to influence the jury out of court, and returned to England within a few years having few illusions about the regard for the legal profession in Massachusetts. The eccentric career of the other early Massachusetts lawyer, Thomas Morton of Merrymount notoriety, is too well known to be elaborated; but Morton was in no sense active in the practice of the law. Article twenty-six of the *Body of Liberties,* providing that attorneys might plead causes other than their own, but disallowing all fees or rewards was a further blow to the profession. Within a few years, however, this policy was abandoned. Because of the scarcity of legal talent, it became customary for parties to a suit to consult the magistrate privately.

Hostility to the legal profession was by no means confined to New England. As late as 1762 a prominent New York merchant uttered the complaint that " the Subject is tore to pieces by Robbers, Lawyers & all sorts of Vermin." [1] The

[1] John Watts to Lieut. Col. Isaac Barré, New York, Feb. 28, 1762, *Letter Book of John Watts* (New York, 1928), edited by D. C. Barck, p. 27.

popular attitude toward the profession in Pennsylvania is shown in a remark of Gabriel Thomas, writing in 1690:

Of Lawyers and Physicians I shall say nothing, because this country is very peaceable and healthy: Long may it so continue and never have occasion for the tongue of one nore the pen of the other—both equally destructive of men's estates and lives.[1]

The informal methods of trying a lawsuit and the non-professional character of the bench, which twice a year does

> gravely meet,
> Some to get drink, and some to eat
> A swinging Share of County Treat,

is brought out in a well-known colonial poem attacking the unjust treatment of strangers in the courts of colonial Maryland.[2] In that province the frontier hostility to lawyers was carried over into the eighteenth century. In 1725 the legislature passed an act regulating lawyer's fees with extreme strictness and giving an option to the planter to pay in tobacco or currency at a fixed rate. Despite the protests of the profession, the act was in 1729 extended for three years. At that time the lawyers petitioned the Proprietary in London, who gave his dissent on the ground that such a law " was not agreeable to any known law here." One interesting result of the controversy was the famous pamphlet of Daniel Dulany, published in 1728 at Annapolis, entitled, *The Right of the Inhabitants of Maryland to the Benefit of the English Laws*. In Virginia the prejudice was deep-seated. An act of 1645 virtually disbarred paid attorneys. The repeal of this act in 1656 was followed by a renewal of perse-

[1] *An Historical and Geographical Account of the Province and County of Pennsylvania and of West Jersey in America* (London, 1698); quoted by Warren, *op. cit.*, pp. 106, 107.

[2] Ebenezer Cooke, *The Maryland Muse containing . . . The Sotweed Factor, or Voiage to Maryland* (3d ed., Annapolis, 1731), pp. 20, 21, 24, 25.

cution.   In the next year a heavy fine was imposed upon lawyers for appearing in court in behalf of a client.   In 1680 lawyers were again allowed to practice under rigid restrictions and after license by the Governor.   After further vicissitudes, the position of the colonial attorney was stabilized in 1748, when a general statute was passed providing for the licensing of all lawyers.[1]

The acquisition of legal information concerning the common-law system was also hindered by the lack of law reports and legal texts.   In 1647 the General Court of Massachusetts was compelled to order a number of well-known English lawbooks, including *Coke on Littleton* and on *Magna Charta, New Terms of the Law,* Dalton's *Justice of the Peace,* and Coke's *Reports,* to be procured for the use of the court.[2]   Law books were exceedingly rare in New England until the latter part of the seventeenth century, when important shipments came into Boston.[3]   Such lawbooks as were to be found were generally located in the libraries of the wealthier lawyers.   A somewhat systematic attempt to build up a good common-law library was made by Judge Sewall at the beginning of the eighteenth century,[4] although down to the American Revolution Judge Edmund Trowbridge of Massachusetts was reputed to have the only fairly complete law library in New England.[5]

The middle and southern colonies were likewise lacking in books relating to the law.   The outstanding colonial library of the middle of the eighteenth century, that of William

[1] Warren, *op. cit.,* p. 39.   Locke's " Constitutions " are also evidential of hostility to lawyers, who are forbidden to plead for fees.

[2] *Mass. Col. Rec.,* II, 212.

[3] T. G. Wright, *Literary Culture in early New England, 1620-1730* (New York, 1920), p. 123.

[4] *Ibid.,* p. 174.

[5] Warren, *op. cit.,* p. 162.

Byrd, the younger, in Virginia, contained only 350 volumes of law and statutes out of a total of 3,625. This condition was partly remedied by the time of the American Revolution.[1]

The shortage of lawyers and the absence of lawbooks is shown by the great infrequency with which English precedents are cited by the colonial courts in the seventeenth century. Where the veneration for the common-law experience was such that the court did not feel free to strike out along original paths, the technical points involved in the lawsuit would be occasionally referred to a prominent English justice for his opinion.[2] In the eighteenth century, however, the courts deferred frequently to the opinions of the English attorney and solicitor-general, and in the reported cases in *Quincy, Dallas, Harris and McHenry,* the *Virginia Colonial Decisions,* and *Jefferson,* the citation of English cases and of the standard abridgments and commentaries is common practice. In addition, the notebooks and correspondence of American lawyers, their own working abridgments, and manuscript treatises testify to the transplantation of many common-law practices.

4. *The Adverse Criticism of the Common Law in England*

Hostility to the technicalities of the common-law system was not confined to the frontier colonies in the New World, where facilities for acquiring a sympathetic understanding of it were extremely limited. A considerable group of lawyers and publicists in England regarded the law with a critical detachment devoid of customary veneration and voiced much dissatisfaction with legal conditions. The flood-tide of pamphlet literature demanding reform is found in the period of the Puritan Revolution, contemporary with the

---

[1] Warren, *op. cit.,* pp. 157, 158, 161.

[2] *Cf.* e. g., Cheesman *v.* Throckmorton (1672) *Virginia General Court Records,* p. 300; Halley *v.* Thorpe (1676) *ibid.,* pp. 451, 517.

most radical experiments in the American colonies.[1]   In large measure, of course, the opposition was of a political character and was directed against the courts of extraordinary jurisdiction; but the attempted reforms under Cromwell are evidence that the hostility was deep-seated. The demand of the Levellers for legal reform was founded on their desire not only to bring the common-law system into accord with the law of God, but to restore local autonomy; hence their wish to reestablish what was affectionately termed the Anglo-Saxon constitution of England.[2]   Professional lawyers attacked the abuse of technical flaws in indictments, and proposed the abolition of imprisonment for debt, the establishment of a registration system for deeds, mortgages, leases and other contracts, and the use of English in legal proceedings.[3]

5. Colonial Reforms in Procedural Law, the Forms of Action, and Evidence

The reformation of English law in England was largely an academic subject confined to pamphlets; in America it was a real reformation espoused by courts and legislatures. In the absence of profound veneration for the common-law system on the frontier of seventeenth-century America, it was to be expected that pleading would be informal in character.   Many of the archaisms of the English procedural law and of the law of evidence were abandoned, and a simplification of legal remedies was effected.   A New Hampshire judge once remarked: "We regard the ignorance

[1] Outstanding examples are cited by Warren, op. cit., pp. 10, 11.

[2] Pease, op. cit., pp. 132-135.

[3] Cf. John Cook, The Vindication Of The Professors & Profession of The Law; so farre as Scriptures and right reason may be judge (London, 1646); John Lilburne, Liberty Vindicated against Slavery (London, 1646), cf. also F. A. Inderwick, The Interregnum (London, 1891), pp. 201-248.

of the first colonists of the technicalities of the Common Law as one of the most fortunate things in the history of the law, since, while the substance of the Common Law was preserved, we happily lost a great mass of antiquated and useless rubbish, and gained in its stead a course of practice of admirable simplicity." [1]

This impatience with the technicalities of the law was voiced as early as 1658 in a Virginia statute, which recited that

Whereas there is and daily doth arise excessive charges and greate delaies and hinderances of justice betwixt the subjects of this collony by reason of small mistakes in writts and formes of pleading, It is therefore for the prevention thereof, enacted by this present Grand Assembly, That all courtes of judicature within this collony shall proceed and give judgement according as the right of the cause and the matter in lawe shall appeare unto them, without regard of any imperfection, default or want of forme in any writt, returne, plaint or process or any other cause whatsoever.[2]

In an appeal which was taken in 1671 from a decision of a county court in Massachusetts, the appellant's attorney claimed that there was a variance in the pleading. The respondents were moved to retort that " if the appellant had been as good a grammarian as his attorney would be thought to be a lawyer, he would have foreborn his simple cavil," and the judgment was affirmed.[3] On the other hand, less than twenty years later an action was nonsuited in a local court in New York on the ground of variance.[4] A Connecticut statute of 1686 restrained the court from reversing a judg-

[1] Bell, J., in B. C. & M. R. R. v. State (1855) 32 N. H. 231.

[2] Hening, Statutes of Virginia, I, 486.

[3] Wood v. Roper (1671) Essex Quarterly Court Records (hereafter Essex), IV, 335.

[4] (1687) Westchester Court Records, p. 42.

ment because of a mere mistake in form.[1]   In some instances, however, technical mistakes in pleading were fatal.[2]   When, in the eighteenth century, common-law practices were more widely accepted, business men frequently expressed impatience with legal technicalities and with the long, involved, and expensive character of lawsuits.[3]

Trespass, " that fertile mother of actions," was used in the colonies for an unprecedented number of remedies.   In its medieval origins the vanquished defendant had to pay damages to the plaintiff for the wrong done immediately to his person, lands or goods, and a fine to the king for the breach of the peace.   The fundamental idea of the trespass action was that it was a remedy for the recovery of damages and not for the recovery of possession.[4]   Therefore, the strange hybrid action of "trespass upon replevin," frequently brought in the county courts of Massachusetts for goods unlawfully taken in distress,[5] was historically unsound, as in such cases

[1] *Conn. Pub. Rec.*, III, 414. In a statute of 1695 resort to common-law writs not among the Connecticut printed forms was permitted. All that was necessary was that the substance of the action be contained in the writ. *Ib.*, IV, 502.

[2] *Cf.* e. g., Belman *v.* Mannerung (1694) *N. C. Col. Rec.*, I, 397, and Butler *v.* Fisher (1699), *ib.*, 522, where a fault in the declaration resulted in a nonsuit. A Connecticut statute of 1711, representative of the more conservative eighteenth-century policy, imposes a fine not exceeding five shillings for every transgression of the rules of pleading set forth by the court. Act of 1711, *Conn. Pub. Rec.*, V, 233, 234. One of the earliest uses of the demurrer in colonial courts is found in Brenton *v.* Coddington (1656), *R. I. Court Records*, I, 19, 20.

[3] Illustrative of this is the correspondence of the New York merchant, John Watts in letters written between 1762 and 1765. *Letter Book of John Watts* (New York, 1927), pp. 108, 246, 331.

[4] G. E. Woodbine, " The Origins of the Action of Trespass," *Yale Law Journal*, XXXIV, 343-344; Pollock and Maitland, *History of English Law* (2d ed., Cambridge, 1899), vol. ii, pp. 166-167, 522, 528.

[5] *Cf.* e. g., Gould *v.* Tod (1664) *Essex*, III, 125, 126; Andrews *v.* Constable of Rowley (1665) *ibid.*, p. 235; Gold *v.* Constable of Rowley (1665) *ibid.*, p. 236; Burrell *v.* Farrar (1666) *ibid.*, p. 345; Lighton *v.* Borman (1666) *ibid.*, p. 346.

trespass was frequently regarded as though it were *rei persecutoria*. Ofttimes it is impossible to tell whether the theory of the action is trespass *de bonis asportatis* or trover. One plaintiff, for example, sues several co-defendants " for coming aboard his bark and carrying her away "; and follows with a second suit " for seven or eight qu. of fish taken away and disposed of illegally and no account given." [1] The very informal nature of the trespass actions which were brought in the colonial courts is more clearly seen in connection with the use of the residuary action upon the case.

a) *The Importance of Case.* The history of early American procedural law illustrates the contention of Maitland that in the continuity of legal history lawyers do not see that there has been a new departure until this has for some time been an accomplished fact; and that " their technical terminology will but slowly admit the fact that a single form of action has become several forms of action." [2] This allusion to the use of trespass *vi et armis* after the reign of Edward I for three different kinds of situations is analogous to the employment in the American colonies in the seventeenth century of trespass upon the case as a remedy in a half-dozen different situations and with little regard for orthodox limitations. At the end of the thirteenth century the power of varying the stereotyped forms of the original writs gave rise to a flexible offshoot of trespass known as trespass on the case, which gave damages in cases stating a ground of complaint analogous to trespass but not equivalent to it under the older precedents, as where the original act was lawful and consequential damage ensued.

While in theory case was a personal action brought to

---

[1] Creford *v.* Browne *et al.* (1664) *Essex*, III, 210 (two actions).

[2] F. W. Maitland, *Equity and the Forms of Action at Common Law*, p. 347.

recover damages, it was used in the colonies to recover sums of money or specific chattels in debt and detinue.[1]   In a Maine action for detinue brought at Saco in 1645, the jury found for the plaintiff one penny damages, a verdict which, from the point of view of the common law, was absurd, for, if the plaintiff had a verdict, he should have had one for the full amount of his claim with interest and costs.[2]   On the other hand, in an action of trespass on the case brought a few years previously in the same court the jury awarded the victorious plaintiff restoration of goods together with damages.[3]

Although by the sixteenth century in England assumpsit, the action for breach of promise, was regarded as distinct from case,[4] in the colonies the action upon the case was used to recover both on express executory contracts and on contracts implied in fact.[5]   Frequently trover actions were brought simply in case and the common-law allegations were ignored.[6]   The most irregular use of the action on the case was as a substitute for the real actions and for ejectment, where the surrender of the realty rather than damages was the gist of the suit.[7]   Thus, actions on the case were brought

---

[1] Cf. e. g., Hall v. Bradly (1667) New Haven Town Rec., II, 200; Clarke v. Hillier (1683) Conn. Pub. Rec., III, 122; Hayward v. Wells (1694) ibid., 125; Stoddar v. Fitch (1697) ibid., pp. 210, 211.

[2] Lander v. Winter (1645) Maine Province and Court Rec., I, 83.

[3] Foxhill v. Cammocke (1640) ibid., p. 44.

[4] Maitland, op. cit., p. 363.

[5] Cf. e. g., Bryan v. How (1666) New Haven Town Rec., II, 169; Bowman v. Welles et al., involving a wager on a horse race (1681) Deale Court Records, pp. 56, 57; Verhoofe v. Groundyke (1682), ib., p. 72.

[6] Cf. e. g., Tod v. Williams[on] (1665) New Haven Town Rec., II, 135; Woolcot v. Woolcot (1685) Conn. Pub. Rec., III, 185, 186.

[7] See infra § c.

for illegally entering upon land,[1] for unjustly detaining land,[2] and in general for the determination of title to realty.[3]

b) *Trover, the Writ of Restitution, and the Appeal.* Trover, the action for damages based on a fictitious loss and finding and subsequent conversion for the use of the defendant, had by the seventeenth century in England come to supplant detinue because it was more extensive in scope and did not involve the wager of law.[4]   In the colonies, however, as late as the eighteenth century no clear-cut distinction was made between the two actions.   Thus in the case of *Train v. Parks* a " plea of the case " for a horse found by the defendant, brought on appeal to the Superior Court of Judicature of Massachusetts in 1723, Robert Auchmuty, counsel for the defendant, urged in his brief on appeal that " this action was a sort of mixt Confounded action between Detinue & Trover for a horse.   The writt according to the plea

---

[1] *Cf.* e. g., Rogers *v.* Rogers (1693) *Conn. Pub. Rec.*, IV, 108; Willson *v.* Willson (1694), *ib.*, pp. 131, 132; Mather *v.* Horsford (1695), *ib.*, p. 152; Rogers *v.* Rogers (1697) *ib.*, p. 231.   *Cf.* also Mason *v.* Leader (1651) Maine Hist. Soc., *Collections, Documentary History*, 2d series, vol. IV (*Baxter MSS.*), p. 55.

[2] *Cf.* e. g., Winthrop *v.* Cullver (1681) *Conn. Pub. Rec.*, III, 88; Newton *v.* Beacham (1683) *ib.*, p. 123; Olcott *v.* Olcott (1683) *ib.*, p. 124; Steele and Standley *v.* Buck (1684) *ib.*, pp. 160, 161; Whitting *v.* Bissell (1684), *ib.*, p. 162; Joanes *v.* Stevens (1692) *ib.*, IV, 71; Seemer *v.* Hancox (1697) *ib.*, pp. 213, *passim*.

[3] Denison *v.* Gallop (1683), *ib.*, III, 123; Cogswell *v.* Cogswell (1701) MSS. Mass. Sup. Crt. of Judicature Records (1700-1714), fol. 60; Peasly *v.* Davis (1702) *ib.*, fol. 86; Winkley *v.* Gunnison (1704) *ib.*, fols. 120, 121; Pierce *v.* Greene (1679) *Newcastle Rec.*, p. 330; Man *v.* Poulson (1680) *ib.*, p. 377; Barentsen *v.* De Witt (1681) *ib.*, pp. 483, 484; Fecoox *v.* La Kar (1694) *N. C. Col. Rec.*, I, 414, 415. See *infra* § (c).

[4] Holliday *v.* Higgs (1605) Noy Rep., p. 12; Vandrinck & Anhers Case (1590-91) I Leon. 221. *Cf.* also William Sheppard, *Actions upon the Case* (London, 1663).

in abatm^t should have been Quashed or abated." [1]   In an action in detinue which came before the Virginia General Court in 1734 [2] for a chest of medicines worth forty pounds, the jury brought in a verdict for 6 d. for the value of the chest and ten pounds damages. Among the exceptions taken to the verdict on appeal, it was claimed that these damages were unreasonable and absurd. Exception was also taken to the declaration on the ground that detinue would not lie for a chest of medicines without setting forth the particular medicines. According to the record, " Randolph for the appellant sayed it would not be good in Trover and that Trover and Detinue were all one and cited Palm. 393. Stile 482. 1 Ven. 114. 2 Lev. 85. 3 Lev. 18. 1 Vent. 317. Sid. 445. Carth. 131." Barradall, for the appellee, pointed out that trover and detinue were not the same, but that the declaration amounted to an adequate description for the remedy of detinue and it would likewise be sufficient for trover. The court held that the declaration was " certain enough."

The declarations in trover were loosely drawn in the seventeenth century and the theory of the actions is not always clear.[3]   In a remarkable action brought in Maine in 1640, the plaintiff sued in trover for the unlawful detention of his land and the jury brought in a verdict in his behalf confirming him in the *title* to the realty.[4]   Even where the

---

[1] MSS. Mass. Sup. Crt. Judic. (1721-1725), fol. 94 and 95 and MSS. files, No. 13,734(3).

[2] Graves *v.* Kennan (1734) *Va. Col. Dec.*, pp. 43, 44.

[3] Two interesting cases are Tayler *v.* Starr (1664) *Ply. Col. Rec.*, IV, 53, where the action sounds like detinue, and Bacon *v.* Billip (1679) " Upland Crt. Rec.," Pa. Hist. Soc., *Memoirs*, VII, 138, 139, where an action is brought by the vendee for conversion of a horse on the theory that property in specific goods passes at the sale.

[4] Cleeve *v.* Winter (1640) Maine Hist. Soc., *Collections—Documentary History*, 2d ser., III (*Trelawney MSS.*), pp. 206, 228, 235 *passim. Cf.* also petition of the defendant to the Councillors for the Province of Maine (1641), claiming that the evidence was insufficient to support an action of trover. *Ib.*, pp. 261, 266, 268.

action is definitely stated as " case sur trover and conversion," the essential allegation of the loss and finding was not included in the declaration.[1]   In the eighteenth century, however, this allegation was generally found.[2]

The machinery of the colonial courts provided an expeditious legal remedy which was analogous to the old appeal of larceny,[3] in that in the single prosecution restitution of property was awarded and there was therefore no necessity for the action of trespass *de bonis asportatis,* the substitute for the criminal appeal which was brought after the criminal prosecution.[4]   Where it appears to be a civil action, it is analogous to the action of trover which supplanted the writ of restitution for larceny[5] as well as trespass *d. b. a.* Throughout the colonies in the seventeenth century cases are found in which an action for conversion is criminal in form and where civil damages are awarded.[6]   In New England and some of the middle colonies larceny was punished by exacting double, treble, quadruple, or even fivefold restitution to the owner in accord with Mosaic and Anglo-Saxon

[1] Wakeley *v.* Stanly (1690) *Conn. Pub. Rec.,* IV, 35.

[2] Blish *v.* Sanderson (1713) *N. C. Col. Rec.,* II, 97, 113, 114; Christopher *v.* Read (1701) MSS. Mass. Sup. Crt. Judic. (1700-1714), fol. 40; Marston *v.* Parker (1702), *ib.,* p. 75; Lane *v.* Lambert (1724) MSS. (1721-1725), fol. 184; Penhale *et ux. v.* Lyon (1724) *ib.,* fols. 182, 183; Stodder *v.* Elms (1724) *ib.,* fol. 188.

[3] *Cf. Mirror of Justices* (Selden Soc., *Publications,* vol. VII), p. 57, c. 16; Hawkins, *Pleas of the Crown,* bk. ii, chap. 23.

[4] YB. 32 & 33 Edw. I. 319; Markham *v.* Cobb (1626) W. Jones 127; Dawkes *v.* Coveneigh (1652) Style 346.

[5] Golightly *v.* Reynolds (1772) Lofft 88.

[6] *Cf.* e. g., Act of 1641, *New Haven Col. Rec.,* I, 48; Hutchinson *v.* Maynard (1679) *Newcastle Rec.,* pp. 307, 308; Boule's case (1687) *Chester County (Pa.) Rec.,* pp. 114, 123; Woodward's case (1696) *ib.,* pp. 393, 393. A judge sitting in Newcastle actually accounted trover a felony. *Cf.* impeachment proceedings against Nicholas More, *Duke of York's Book of Laws,* p. 500.

precedents.[1]   In the southern colonies, where the harsher English punishment was enforced,[2] the owner of the chattels was awarded the writ of restitution which he might bring after the conviction of the felon.[3]

In England larceny above the value of twelve pence was a capital felony; clergy could not be pleaded for larceny from the person, either secretly or by violence, or for larceny from a house or shop in the day-time.[4]   The milder penalties in New England and some of the middle colonies, which laid chief stress upon the restitution of the property, were enforced with much greater effectiveness.   A comparison of the records of the county courts of Essex, Massachusetts, and of Middlesex, England, for the years 1639-1662, reveals that law enforcement in the American jurisdiction, with only brief lapses, was uniformly more successful.   Convictions for these years in Essex County average 82.4 per cent on arraignments for larceny as against 47 per cent for the iden-

---

[1] A few representative instances of each may be cited. *Double restitution: Records of the Court of Assistants* (Mass.) (hereafter *Assistants Rec.*), II, 32, 66, 70, 83; *Essex*, III, 351; *Conn. Pub. Rec.*, I, 203; *New Haven Col. Rec.*, I, 26, 77, 89, 120, 153; *New Haven Town Rec.*, I, 169-173, 421; II, 76, 77; *Grants and Concessions of N. J.*, pp. 234, 235. *Treble: Essex* III, 143, 152, 177; "Records of the Particular Court of Conn.," Conn. Hist. Soc., *Collections*, XXII, 182; *New Haven Town Rec.*, I, 12, 13, 68, 69; II, 153, 154; *Grants and Concessions of N. J.*, p. 79; *Chester Co. (Pa.) Rec.*, p. 596. Eighteenth-century instances of treble restitution are found frequently among the MSS. Records of the Massachusetts Supreme Court of Judicature: MSS. vol. (1700-1714), fol. 28, 32, 44, 64; MSS. vol. (1721-1725) fol. 34, 263. See also Act of 1735, *Conn. Pub. Rec.*, VII, 561. Fourfold: *Conn. Pub. Rec.*, I, 110; Act of 1681, *Grants and Concessions of N. J.*, p. 434; Act of 1654, *Md. Arch.*, I, 344. Five-fold: Act of 1682, *Grants and Concessions of N. J.*, p. 234.

[2] *Cf.* e. g., Shreeve's case (1694) *N. C. Col. Rec.*, I, 40; Act of 1712, *S. C. Stat. at Large* (Columbia, S. C., 1837), II, 496, 505.

[3] Act of 1712, *S. C. Stat. at Large*, II, 458, adopting stat. 21 Hen. 8. c. 11.

[4] Co. Inst. 109; stat. 8 Eliz. c. 4.

tical years in the Middlesex jurisdiction. Of these latter con-victions, sixty-seven culprits pleaded clergy and escaped the extreme penalty; twenty-seven were hanged. The statistics of capital executions give little comfort to the view that the Puritan régime in England accomplished any serious reform in the criminal code.[1]

c) *The Simplification and Expansion of Ejectment.* In England the action of ejectment was evolved because the technicalities of the elaborate real actions led to injustice and oppression and the remedies provided by law for the ejected leaseholders were inadequate. Ejectment was superior since the form of action was always the same and it could be brought in the three great common-law courts. Therefore, by the reign of Elizabeth it practically supplanted the real actions.[2] This remarkable action, by which the court gave judgment to the lessee to recover his term together with a writ of possession, represented in turn accumulated techni-calities and an elaborate fiction—a fictitious lease to a fic-titious plaintiff by the person who was the real claimant, and a fictitious entry and fictitious ouster by a fictitious wrong-doer. In the seventeenth century the consent rule was evolved, as a result of which the tenant agreed to confess at the trial the lease, entry and ouster, and to insist solely upon his title.[3]

Because of its technicalities, ejectment was never a popular

---

[1] *Cf.* statistics of capital executions during the Commonwealth period in Jeaffreson's Introduction to the *Middlesex County Records.* Substan-tial reforms in the criminal law were advocated in the interregnum by Cromwell and Whitelock; but these grievances remained unredressed. Inderwick, *The Interregnum,* pp. 231 *et seq.*

[2] Alden's Case (1601) 6 Rep. 105.

[3] Style's Rep. 368 (1625); Style, *Regestum Practicale or the Practical Register,* pp. 107 *et seq. Cf.* Mansfield, *C. J.,* in Fair Claim *ex Dimiss'* Fowler *et al. v.* Sham-Title (1762) 3 Burr. 1290.

action in New England.   According to Stearns,[1] only two
cases have been found in the Massachusetts records of the
fictitious action of ejectment.   They were brought after the
reorganization of the courts under Sir Edmund Andros, and
in each case there was finally an appeal to the King in
Council.   The Pennsylvania Judicature Act of 1701 required the courts to observe the standards of " Brevity,
plainess and verity, in all Declarations and pleas," and to
avoid " all Fictions and Colour in pleadings." [2]   This statute
reflected the hostility of certain attorneys to the use of the
fiction in ejectment.[3]   One prominent attorney, David Lloyd,
proposed a bill in 1707 to require a real lease, entry and
ouster and to do away with the fictitious proceedings, " a
new practice, allowed only in Westminster Hall, but not in
any Inferior Court in England." [4]   Nevertheless the fiction
remained in force.[5]   In the southern colonies and in New
York the fiction was adopted, although at least in one instance difficulties arose where the parties had agreed to omit
the fictitious names.[6]   The report of the Virginia action of
Bernard v. Stonehouse (1737) [7] contains an elaborate discussion of the precedents justifying the employment of the
fiction.[8]

---

[1] A. Stearns, *A Summary of the Law and Practice of Real Actions*
(2nd edition, n. p., 1831), pp. 352, 353, note. *Cf.* also MSS. Mass. Misc.
Court Files, I, fols. 5-9; *Acts and Resolves*, VII (App. 2), pp. 508, 509.

[2] *Duke of York's Book of Laws*, p. 311.

[3] *Cf.* Lloyd, *Courts of Pennsylvania*, p. 76; *Pa. Col. Rec.*, II, 185.
See also Clayton *v.* Collitt (1691) *Chester Co. (Pa.) Rec.*, p. 242.

[4] *Pa. Col. Rec.*, II, 354.

[5] Carey and Bioren, *Laws of Pa.*, II, 49.

[6] Petition of Wilson, Court of Chancery (1694) *N. C. Col. Rec.*, I,
435, 436.

[7] *Va. Col. Dec.*, II, 61.

[8] Throughout the colonial period, New York under English rule used

With their characteristic hostility to technicalities, the New England colonists effected a more speedy ejectment procedure. In the early period of settlement, the court handled the problem with little regard to orthodox conceptions:

> Upon a complaint of William Tubbs, that Goodwife Thomas, a Welsh woman, that shee dwelleth on his land without his leaue, the Court haue appointed Mr Collyare and Mr Alden to take some speedy course to remoue her unto her owne land.[1]

Such commendable celerity of procedure was not always restricted to New England. A more drastic remedy was adopted in the New York Court of Assizes hearing Long Island cases in 1666, when one Walter Salter, accused of unlawfully dispossessing the plaintiff of his house and lot at Flushing was " committed to prison till Udall [the plaintiff] shall be possessed of said house and lot " and further ordered to pay the plaintiff damages.[2] In general, the English system of real actions was transplanted " practically divested of aid prayers, vouchers, protections, parol demurrers, and essoins, the cumbersome appendages which destroyed it in

the fictitious action of ejectment. *Cf.* Nisi Prius cases: Smith *v.* Baker, More *v.* Dyckman, Duncan *v.* Smith (1694), N. Y. Hist. Soc., *Collections*, XXV, 59; Victor Hugo Paltsits, *Inventory of the Rensselaerswyck Manuscripts* (New York, 1924), pp. 43, 45; Stirling MSS., III, fol. 36, 38 (1762), NYHS. In 1713 the Common Council of New York City ordered "that David Jamison Esqr Recorder of this City do file A Declaration in Ejectment agt some *Casual Ejector* and do what Else may be Proper in the Law to Assert the Right of this Corporation to the Lands and Commons of this City on this Island Manhattans to Low water Marke." *Minutes of the Common Council of the City of New York (1675-1776)*, III, 42 (italics mine).

[1] (1658/9) *Ply. Col. Rec.*, III, 158.

[2] Udall *v.* Salter (1666) Calendar of the Proceedings of the Court of Assizes relating to Long Island, 1665-1672. Extracts from the calendar in the New York State Library, NYPL.

England." [1]   In addition to the frequent use of the action on the case to determine title as well as to secure damages,[2] the New Englanders availed themselves of the statute of 8 Henry VI, c. 9, furnishing a writ of forcible entry to recover possession of land.[3]   Where ejectment was used, it was a simple and direct action, bereft of fictions.[4]   In connection with the Connecticut statute providing for an action of trespass to try title, Francis Fane, standing counsel to the Board of Trade and Plantations, in a report rendered in 1734, observed:

> The method of proceeding in actions of Trespass prescribed by the foregoing Act, in cases where the Defendant justifies or claims title to the land where the trespass is supposed to be committed differs very much from that used in England in the like cases; However, as I do not perceive any inconvenience from this method which has been established by this Act above thirty years, I do not apprehend there is any material objection to the confirming of this Act.[5]

While the fictitious action had been abandoned in New England, it was still cherished in the South in the eighteenth century.   In 1791 South Carolina abandoned ejectment and substituted an action of trespass to try title, in form an action of trespass *quare clausum fregit,* and one in which the court rendered damage, including damage for mesne profits,

---

[1] A. G. Sedgwick and F. S. Wait, "The History of the Action of Ejectment in England and the United States," *Select Essays,* III, 641. *Cf.* also Hett *v.* Tose (1639) Lechford, *Note Book* (Cambridge, 1885), p. 83.

[2] See *supra,* § (a).

[3] Act of 1698, *Conn. Pub. Rec.,* IV, 267; Clement *v.* Wainwright (1695) MSS. Mass. Sup. Crt. of Judic. (1692-1695), I, fol. 197-199.

[4] See MSS. Mass. Sup. Crt. of Judic. (1721-1725), fol. 42 (1722).

[5] Francis Fane, *Reports on the Laws of Connecticut,* pp. 120, 121.

and granted a writ of possession.[1] In turn this action was abandoned for a simple action for the recovery of real property.[2] Other jurisdictions in the nineteenth century destroyed the fictitious nature of the ejectment action, but even in the twentieth century archaic survivals are found.[3]

d) *The Reform of the Law of Evidence.* The technical rules of evidence at common law were likewise largely dispensed with by the colonial courts in the seventeenth century. Especially significant was the disregard of the common-law rules listing various types of experiential incapacity and restricting hearsay evidence within fixed limits. By the seventeenth century in England parties to a suit were disqualified from testifying in their own behalf, and eventually this disqualification was extended to others pecuniarily interested in the outcome of the suit. In the colonies generally this disqualification was disregarded, and, perhaps, proceeding by analogy to the trial by oath, and the wager of law, parties to a suit and those pecuniarily interested gave testimony under oath.[4] In a few seventeenth-century jurisdictions,

[1] *S. C. Stat. at Large*, V, 170. In the preamble it was pointed out that the action of ejectment depended upon a variety of legal fictions, rarely understood except by "professors of the law."

[2] *Rev. Stat. of S. C.* (1783), p. 586.

[3] *Cf.* Townsend *v.* Melson (1911) 26 Del. 79.

[4] Typical cases: Cleeve *v.* Winter (1640) Maine Hist. Soc., *Collections —Documentary History*, 2d ser., vol. III (*Trelawney MSS.*), pp. 206 *et seq.* ("trover") ; Sherman *v.* Keayne (1642) *Mass. Col. Rec.*, II, 12, 51 ; Winthrop, *Journal*, II, 83, 143; How *v.* Cooper (1650) *New Haven Town Rec.*, I, 28; *Ann. Rep.*, N. Y. State Hist., *Bulletin*, II, 399, 400, 403 (1675) ; Test *v.* Morce (1678) *Newcastle Rec..*, p. 114; Shackerly *v.* Salter (1678) *ib.*, pp. 209, 210 (action on the case) ; Lewger *v.* Mottram (1643) *Md. Arch.*, IV, 114; Cox *v.* Thomson (1643) *ib.*, p. 201; Norman *v.* White (1643) *ib.*, p. 257; Hallowes *v.* Percy (1648) *ib.*, pp. 414, 415 (wager of law in debt regarded as the custom of the province) ; Hollis *v.* Nevill (1657) *ib.*, X, 522. See also Thayer, *Preliminary Treatise on Evidence*, part I, p. 33 n.

however, this incapacity was upheld.[1]   In the eighteenth century most jurisdictions introduced the same evidential incapacity in this regard which was imposed by the common
law.[2]   Furthermore, at common law married parties were
disqualified from testifying in behalf of a spouse and could
claim the privilege of refusing to give evidence of marital
facts against a spouse.   Such practices were generally disregarded in the colonies in the seventeenth century.[3]

The English practice of the county courts in admitting
account books of parties was opposed by the common-law
courts on the ground that the party was incompetent to
testify; nevertheless it was generally followed in the colonial
courts.[4]

e) *The Resort to Arbitration.*   It was natural that, in the
colonial jurisdictions where men of legal learning were few
and impatience with the protractions of legal justice in England was general, resort should be had to private arbitration for the settlement of disputes.   The Dutch colonists

---

[1] *Cf.* e. g., Evans *v.* Hickman (1682) *Chester Co. (Pa.) Rec.,* pp. 20
et seq.

[2] Morris *v.* Chamberlayne (1735) *Va. Col. Dec.,* II, 51; Hoghling *v.*
Brinch (*c.* 1755) (New York) is evidential that this rule was not enforced with any degree of unanimity. *Kempe MSS. (C-F),* NYHS.

[3] *Cf. infra,* chap. III.

[4] Wigmore, *Treatise on the Law of Evidence* (2d ed., 1923), vol. iii,
§§ 1518, 1519, and n. For typical examples, *cf.* Marrian, Administrator
of estate of Batt *v.* Lake (1684) *Assistants Rec.,* I, 269, where the court
held that the account book of the deceased was not admissible in evidence.
Townsend *v.* Administrator of estate of Jose (1694) MSS. Mass. Sup.
Crt. of Judic. (1692-1695), I, fol. 105; Garnock *v.* Andrew (1694), *ib.,*
fol. 107; Orian *v.* D'haes (1678/9) *Upland Crt. Rec.,* p. 127; *Hening,
Statutes of Va.,* VI, index, "Book-debts"; *N. C. Col. Rec.,* XXIV, 440
(1756); *Ga. Col. Rec.,* IV, 91 (1738). But *cf.* Jennings *v.* Bayly (1704)
MSS. Book of Minutes of the Mayor's Court, Borough Town of Westchester, 1696-1704 (NYHS), where the suppletory oath to the account
book is not permitted.

used arbitration extensively, and among the Duke of York's laws was the provision that in actions of debt or trespass under five pounds between neighbors, two indifferent persons in the neighborhood should arbitrate and the award was to be conclusive.[1] A Pennsylvania statute of 1683 provided for the annual selection in every precinct of three persons to act as " common peacemakers." [2] A subsequent statute in 1705 provided that parties might refer their claims in contract to persons mutually chosen by them in open court whose award should have the effect of a verdict by a jury. This practice was extended to other forms of legal action, and by 1766 there are records of elaborate decisions by referees resembling decrees in equity in real estate matters. In 1790 Dallas in the preface to his *Reports* states that a very great share of the administration of justice was entrusted to these referees.[3] This widespread use of lay arbitral boards was found throughout the colonies even in the late eighteenth century.[4]

In the words of Sir Henry Maine, " the substantive law is secreted in the interstices of procedure," and in the special studies in this volume it is proposed to show the widespread departures in substantive law which accompanied the procedural reforms effected in the colonial courts in the seventeenth century. A glowing tribute to the facility and economy with which redress might be had in the New England courts as a result of intelligent procedural reforms is paid

[1] *Charter and Laws*, pp. 3, 4.

[2] *Ib.*, p. 128; disallowed by the King and Queen in Council, 1693. See also Pa. Hist. Soc., *Memoirs*, VII, 42. Provision for arbitration of suits not exceeding 20 s. was made in West-Jersey in 1682. *Grants and Concessions of N. J.*, p. 455.

[3] *Cf.* Warren, *op. cit.*, pp. 105, 106.

[4] *Cf.* Act of 1753, *Conn. Pub. Rec.*, X, 201; Archer *v.* Vallentine (1771) MSS. Minutes of the Mayor's Court, Borough Town of Westchester, Oct. 5, 1771, NYHS.

by Jeremiah Dummer in his skillful tract in defense of the New England charters.[1]

C. THE CONSERVATIVE REACTION OF THE EIGHTEENTH CENTURY

The close of the seventeenth century was marked by a conflict in the law between the forces making for change and progress and the forces making for static security and conservation.[2] The compromise which was effected in the eighteenth century was largely a victory for the forces of reaction and brought about the widespread adoption of common-law practices. The basis for this reaction can be found in the changing political, economic and intellectual scene.

1. *The New Imperial Discipline*

By the end of the seventeenth century a new policy of constructive imperialism was introduced which proposed the supplanting of chartered colonies by royal governments, the combination of smaller self-governing or proprietary units into large units of administration, and the strengthening of the executive power at the expense of the representative assemblies.

Furthermore, the new charters reserved for the King in Council the right to disallow colonial legislation and the right to hear cases on appeal from provincial courts. The Board of Trade, which made the recommendations to the Privy Council for or against disallowance, showed in the main considerable tolerance for the experiments in legal

[1] Jeremiah Dummer, *A Defence of the New-England Charters* (London, 1721), pp. 37 *et seq.*

[2] This conflict between static and dynamic security is brilliantly presented in Demogue's *Analysis of Fundamental Notions*, in *Modern Legal Philosophy Series* (Boston, 1916), vol. vii, pp. 429, 470, and in Justice Cardozo's *The Paradoxes of Legal Science* (New York, 1928), chap. I.

engineering effected in the colonies.[1]   Where local usages
and customs differed from those of England, the Board realized the absurdity of applying common-law standards.   On
the other hand, where the colonial law was a limitation of
the royal prerogative or prejudicial to the economic interests
of the mother country or in conflict with fundamental imperial policy, it was generally disallowed.   Statutes which
were carelessly drawn and technically absurd were also for-
tunately a subject for disallowance.   In general, it may be
said that the practice of disallowance was not carried out
with great vigor.   One investigator has compiled statistics
which do not include laws passed in Pennsylvania prior to
1700 nor laws submitted by Maryland between 1691 and
1715 while it was a royal province.   These figures reveal
that of 8,563 acts submitted by the continental colonies, 469
or 5.5 per cent were disallowed by orders in council.   Pennsylvania had the highest percentage of laws disallowed, 15.5
per cent of the total it submitted.[2]   Beginning with 1690
disallowance was more generally applied in the first two
decades than at any other time.

In the New England colonies particularly the claim of the
King in Council to hear cases on appeal was at best grudg-
ingly conceded and in some cases refused.   While the Massachusetts charter of 1691 subjected the laws of that province
to royal disallowance and provided for judicial review before
the privy council, the Connecticut and Rhode Island charters
contained no such provision.   In New York one notable
appeal in the middle of the eighteenth century aroused tre-

[1] E. B. Russell, *The Review of American Colonial Legislation by the
King in Council* (New York, 1915), p. 141.

[2] *Ibid.*, p. 221.   These statistics cannot be accepted at their face value,
for undoubtedly royal disallowance had an appreciable influence in dis-
couraging a good deal of later legislation; a further undetermined influence was the royal governors' instructions denying them power to
approve legislation violative of some standard set forth above.

mendous popular indignation.[1]   The royal charters of New
York and Pennsylvania, indicative of the new imperial policy,
named the King in Council as the court of last resort in
personal actions wherein the matter in difference exceeded in
value £300 sterling.   The unfortunate results of some of
these appeals are considered at length in the next chapter.[2]

2. *The Growth of a Propertied Class*

With the development of the colonies the large-scale accumulation of property was accelerated.   In the south, in the
latter part of the seventeenth century, the plantation conditioned social and economic life.   In the middle colonies
great proprietary estates were founded at the time of settlement.   The English governors in New York issued lavish
patents at small quit rents, none of which were exceeded by
the extravagant grants of Governor Fletcher.[3]   The great
landowners preferred leasing their holdings to tenants to
selling to outright purchasers.   The proprietors of the large
estates and the lawyers were closely affiliated through family

[1] This is the case of Cunningham v. Forsey (1764), in which an appeal
was made from the verdict in an action for assault and battery tried in
the New York Supreme Court. *Cf. Letter Book of John Watts*, p. 307
n., *passim*.

[2] For the general subject of appeals to the King in Council, *cf*. G. A.
Washburne, *Imperial Control of the Administration of Justice in the
Thirteen American Colonies, 1684-1776* (New York, 1923), pp. 182, 183.
Cf. also H. D. Hazeltine, "Appeals from the Colonial Courts to the
King in Council with Especial Reference to Rhode Island," Amer. Hist.
Assn., *Ann. Rep.* (1894), pp. 299-350; A. M. Schlesinger, "Colonial
Appeals to the Privy Council," *Pol. Sci. Qly.*, XXVIII, 279-307, 433-450.

[3] J. H. French, *Gazetteer of the State of New York* (8th ed., New
York, 1860), pp. 49-52; Earl of Bellomont to the Lords of Trade, Aug.
24, 1699, *Docts. relating to the Colonial History of N. Y.*, IV, 553;
C. W. Spencer, "Land System of Colonial New York," in N. Y. State
Hist. Assn., *Proceedings*, XVI, 150-164; P. W. Bidwell and J. I.
Falconer, *History of Agriculture in the Northern United States, 1620-
1860* (Washington, 1925), p. 73.

ties and together created a government by "Junto." Where in matters of property the influence of the "Junto" was conservative, in constitutional matters it served as a weapon of defense against the exercise of strict imperial discipline.[1] In 1764 Lieutenant Governor Colden wrote the Lords of Trade, calling their attention to the "dangerous influence" which the proprietors of large tracts of land exerted in the province and alleging the existence of a legal conspiracy between the judges and the principal lawyers, who together comprised the chief proprietors, to preserve and strengthen their accumulated holdings.[2] The struggle between the proprietors and the non-commoners in many eighteenth-century New England towns testifies to the appearance of an exclusive landholding group in that region, waxing rich on the rise in the value of land as population and settlements increased. The desire to preserve the accumulated property-holdings in the hands of the same families was manifest everywhere during this period in the resurrection of the entail and in the imposition of other restrictions on the distribution of realty.[3] The influence of the propertied class was directed toward the maintenance of stability and conservatism; the rapid growth of business necessitated the resort to the more technical legal system of England.

3. *The Rise of the American Bar*

With the advent of the eighteenth century the number of trained lawyers in the colonies increases markedly. Many of these attorneys emigrated to the colonies; an appreciable number of native lawyers had, by the eve of the American

---

[1] Ralph Volney Harlow, *The History of Legislative Methods in the Period before 1825* (New Haven, 1917), pp. 49 *et seq.*

[2] Colden to the Lords of Trade, New York, Nov. 7, 1764. *Docts. relating to the Colonial History of N. Y.*, VII, 677.

[3] *Cf. infra*, chap. II.

Revolution, received their legal education at the Inns of Court in England.[1]   Among the outstanding New England attorneys who possessed enviable technical equipment might be mentioned John Read, Jeremiah Gridley, and Judge Edmund Trowbridge.   While common-lawyers were now filling positions on the Bench, the majority of Chief Justices in Massachusetts even down to the Revolution were laymen, the most notable being Thomas Hutchinson, who served in that capacity between 1761 and 1769.   The New York bar, while extremely limited in size, contained such competent lawyers as James Alexander, William Smith, Joseph Murray, and John Tabor Kempe.   The outstanding attorneys in the middle and southern colonies received their legal education at the Inns of Court.   Among them may be mentioned the distinguished Andrew Hamilton of Philadelphia, and two other distinguished Pennsylvanians, John Dickinson and Joseph Galloway; Daniel Dulany the elder at the head of the early eighteenth-century bar in Maryland, and Daniel Dulany the younger, at the head of the pre-Revolutionary bar; in Virginia, William Byrd of Westover and Sir John Randolph, and a considerable portion of the highly educated South Carolinian bar, including John Rutledge, received their legal training in England.   The more thorough education in the common law in this period was supplemented by more adequate private libraries of English lawbooks.   Excellent information as to the nature and sources of the provincial law student's education may be found in the " Commonplace Book " of Thomas Jefferson, now located in the Library of Congress.[2]   During the formative years of his

[1] *Cf.* E. Alfred Jones, *American Members of the Inns of Court* (London, 1924).

[2] An edition has been published by Gilbert Chinard (Baltimore, Md., 1926), but, unfortunately for the legal historian, articles 1-694, representing the note-taking of the young lawyer, have only been printed in part.

legal training, Jefferson made extensive briefs of the English printed reports, chiefly of Salkeld and Raymond, and abstracts of Coke's *Institutes*, Lord Kames' *Historical Law Tracts*, Hale's *History of the Common Law*, and of Spelman and Somner. By the end of the provincial era the attorneys in a number of colonies, notably in Massachusetts as early as 1761, formed bar associations and prescribed standards of admission.[1]

4. *The Common Law and the Rights of Englishmen*

The strengthening of imperial discipline and the amplification of mercantilist restrictions were met by stout resistance on the part of the more radical element in the legal profession who were now impelled to a close study of the common law in order to preserve inviolate their historic "rights of Englishmen." Thus, in the declaration of the Continental Congress in 1774 the rights of the colonists are based on "the immutable laws of nature, the principles of the English constitution, and the several charters or compacts."[2] The law of nature, which profoundly influenced the substantive law in the seventeenth century, was now advanced to curb parliamentary excesses.[3] No longer was it completely identified with ecclesiastical concepts; it was now based upon reason and natural equity.[4] But the scriptural basis of the law of nature was not completely abandoned, nor was the political thought of eighteenth-century America divorced entirely from theology. Eighteenth-century New England

---

[1] Warren, *op. cit.*, pp. 83 *et seq.*

[2] *Journals of the Continental Congress, 1774-1789*, edited by W. C. Ford, vol. i (Washington, D. C., 1904), p. 67.

[3] James Otis, *The Rights of the British Colonies* (2d ed., Boston, 1764), pp. 16-17, 61-62, 70, 71.

[4] Carl Becker, *The Declaration of Independence* (New York, 1922), chap. II.

pamphleteers still speak of "those Laws of God that have made it a Sin in any to invade these Rights of a People." [1] The political ideas of John Locke which formed the basis of Revolutionary political theory, were merely an expansion of the political Calvinism which molded New England thought in the seventeenth century.[2]   Nevertheless the resort to the " rights of Englishmen " was more influential even in the Revolutionary Era than the appeal to the " rights of man," and as a result of this process common-law traditions were revived.[3]

[1] John Bulkley, *Conn. Election Sermon*, 1713, pp. 3-30, quoted by Baldwin, *op. cit.*, pp. 38, 39.

[2] Foster, *op. cit.*, pp. 487 *et seq.*   American political writers who accepted Locke, therefore, did not abandon the Scriptural basis of the law of nature.   James Wilson asserted that, in the absence of a specific rule, the judge must be guided by "reason, conscience, and the Holy Scriptures." *Works*, edited by J. de Witt Andrews, I, 121-123.   An interesting discussion of the law of God and the rights of Englishmen (1757) is found in Abram Yates, Jr., MSS. Journals and Copy Books, June, 1754-Sept., 1758.   Yates Papers—Gansevoort-Lansing Collection, NYPL.   *Cf.* also Edward S. Corwin, " The 'Higher Law' Background of American Constitutional Law," *Harvard Law Review* (1928-1929), XLII, 149, 365.

[3] Edmund Burke, in his speech on Conciliation with the Colonies (1775), makes the point that the "untractable spirit" of the colonists, indicated in their devotion to "liberty according to English ideas and on English principles," was inspired in no small part by the widespread study of the law.   Burke's *Speeches and Letters on American Affairs* (London, 1908), pp. 91, 94, 95.

CHAPTER II

Colonial Law Governing the Distribution and Alienation of Land

No other field of the law shows so clearly the constructive results of colonial legal engineering as that of real property. The economic and social requirements of the seventeenth century brought about definite changes in real property law along three lines. In the first place, the primary essential of security was given to landowners by the development of recording systems. Secondly, these systems facilitated the transfer of land; but, by bringing the process of recording under official supervision, they acknowledged the desire manifest by the New England community to preserve its exclusive and homogeneous character. From this desire sprang the exercise of certain restraints upon the alienation of land to new settlers. The third requirement was that property law should respond more readily to the demand for equality of distribution. Thus, in the northern and some of the middle colonies systems of descent for both personalty and realty supplanted the prevailing English rule of primogeniture.

A. THE SECURITY AND ALIENABILITY OF LAND

Early in American colonial history there was evolved a recording system possessing distinctive characteristics. The colonists could not draw upon any general system for the registration of deeds in England, for none had been adopted, although during the Commonwealth a registry system was proposed.[1] Prior practices which undoubtedly influenced

---

[1] Wigmore, Evidence, § 1650.

the colonial experiment were the statutory process of enroll-
ing deeds of bargain and sale;[1] the borough and manorial
practice of going before a court official and acknowledging
a deed; and the local customs by which a registry of deeds
was provided in York and Middlesex.[2]

The characteristics of the most favored colonial system
have been preserved in our recording practices of modern
times. Its essential features have been enumerated by Professor Beale:

(1) The document recorded is a deed, not a memorandum
for a transfer. (2) The deed is operative without record, the
title passing before the deed is recorded. (3) The record is
not a mere device for preserving evidence, but gives legal
priority to the grantee of the recorded deed. In the first
particular it differs from the medieval registry system; in the
second from the continental registry systems and our own
Torrens system of registration; in the third from the recording
system in England under local customs like those of Middlesex
and Yorkshire.[3]

The distinctive system in question evolved first in Massachusetts Bay. While a Plymouth act of 1636 required the
acknowledgment of the deed of transfer before recording,[4]
no provision was made at this time to give priority of right
to the prior record.[5] In 1634 the General Court of Massa-

[1] 27 Hen. VIII, c. 16. *Cf.* Kenelm E. Digby, *An Introduction to the
History of the Law of Real Property*, 5th edition (Oxford, 1897), pp.
366-368.

[2] The reader is referred to J. H. Beale, Jr., " The Origin of the System
of Recording Deeds in America," *Green Bag*, XXIX, 335 *et seq.*

[3] *Ibid.*, p. 335.

[4] Ply. Col. Rec., XI, 12; Brigham, *Compact*, p. 43; act of 1654, *ibid.*,
p. 98; act of 1671, *ibid.*, p. 279.

On the other hand, from at least one case it appears that an unrecorded sale of land was declared void because of the failure to record.

chusetts Bay ordered officials in every town to make a survey of houses and lands, record the results, and deliver a transcript thereof to the General Court. This entry was acknowledged " to be a sufficient assurance to every such free inhabitant, his & theire heirs and assignes, of such estate of inheritance, or as they shall haue in any such howses, lands, or franke-tenements." [1] This measure was followed by a general ordinance of Oct. 7, 1640, providing that by the end of the month, no mortgage, bargain, sale, or grant of houses, lands, rents or other hereditaments should have validity against any other person than the grantor and his heirs, unless it were recorded in the manner specified. Magistrates were empowered to take acknowledgments. The ordinance of 1640 remained in force throughout colonial times; [2] later revisions omitted the express provision against recording the deed in full and provided that the clerk of every county court should be the recorder. [3] The present Massachusetts statute, save for the inclusion among the list of exceptions of " persons having actual notice," is substantially unchanged from the section of the colonial statute granting priority to the recorded deed. [4] The Massachusetts system, with the addition of the practice of acknowledgment

---

The court ordered the vendor to take possession again. Bret *v.* Hall (1652) *Ply. Col. Rec.,* III, 20. *Cf.* Beale, *loc. cit.,* however, who states that there was no idea in Plymouth that the operative act was the entry of the transfer on the public books. Under some circumstances a deedless grant would be recognized. *Ply. Col. Rec.,* VI, 39 (1680). In Massachusetts and under the modern system the vendor is held charged with notice.

[1] *Mass. Col.* Rec., I, 116.

[2] *Laws of 1648,* pp. 13, 14; Whitmore, *Laws of 1660,* p. 141; *Ancient Charters,* p. 86.

[3] *Col. Laws,* ed. 1672, p. 33; *Acts and Resolves,* I, 298, 299; *Ancient Charters,* pp. 303, 305.

[4] *General Laws of Mass.,* 1921, c. 163, § 4.

introduced in Plymouth, was followed generally in New
England and influenced legislation in the middle colonies.[1]

In the southern colonies the Massachusetts system was not
adopted in the seventeenth century. The Virginia act of
1640 [2] differed from the New England practice in that it
made the unrecorded deed void unless possession was delivered. From Maryland practice it appears that priority was
not given to the deed of record.[3]   As a matter of fact, the
records bear witness that in seventeenth-century Massachusetts the practice of investing by " turf and twig " lingered
on alongside the system of registry of title.[4]   Well along in
the eighteenth century the general practice of the colonies
whereby the transfer of a deed of bargain and sale was the
operative act was attacked by conservative lawyers who still
insisted upon the necessity of the formal livery of seisin.[5]

[1] For a leading colonial New England case involving questions of
recordation and acknowledgment, cf. Mohegan Indians v. Conn., MSS.
Chalmers Papers, Conn. I, fol. 54, passim, NYPL; also Conn. Pub. Rec.,
passim.   Cf. also Acts and Laws of Conn. (1769), p. 243; J. T. Hassam,
Suffolk Deeds, Lib. I, 15; Beale, op. cit., p. 338; Duke of York's Laws,
Duke of York's Book of Laws, p. 23.   Among the laws agreed upon in
England for Pennsylvania, 1682, was a provision avoiding all conveyances not recorded against all persons. Ibid., pp. 101, 181.   Subsequent
legislation was necessary to prevent inconveniences arising under this
act.   Laws of 1693, ibid., p. 237; act of 1700, Bioren, Laws of Pa., I,
6, 14, 29, cc. 24, 49, 81.

[2] Hening, Statutes, I, 227.

[3] Cf. Johnson v. Land (1650) Md. Arch., IV, 542; cf. act of 1715, c.
47 § 7.   Herty, Digest of the Laws of Maryland, pp. 159, 160.   The
Jamaica registry act of 1682 seems to include the essential principle of
priority.   Abridgement of the Laws, p. 129.

[4] Cf. e. g., Assistants, I, 388; Essex, III, 206; IV, 119, 228, 295, 317-
319, 340.

[5] Brief of defendant's attorneys, Peter W. Yates and Whitehead Hicks
in Bradt v. Jackson, et al. (c. 1770), an action of ejectment for lands
in the county of Albany, N. Y. MSS. N. Y. Supreme Court (box),
NYHS.

It is not within the province of this study to attempt to present evidence of such restraints upon alienation as resulted from the desire of communities to preserve their homogeneous character. In the typical New England town the proprietors remained a comparatively small and distinct privileged group, generally claiming exclusive rights to the common and undivided lands as against the non-proprietors.[1] The purpose of town restrictions was twofold. In the first place, the towns in this way prevented settlement by unwel·come associates; and secondly, the towns, in imposing restrictions upon the alienation of land, attempted to prevent the accumulation of land holdings in a few hands.[2] This second objective of town supervision found definite formulation in the colonial laws, customary and statute, which aimed to ensure the distribution of property along egalitarian lines.

B. PRIMOGENITURE AND ENTAILED ESTATES
IN COLONIAL AMERICA

1. *The English Experience*

Two primary factors in the growth of the large estate and of the expansion of the influence of the landed aris-

---

[1] *Cf.* R. H. Akagi, *The Town Proprietors of the New England Colonies* (Philadelphia, 1924), p. 156.

[2] *Cf.* W. B. Weeden, *Economic and Social History of New England* (Boston, 1890), pp. 56, 57; Melville Egleston, "Land System of the New England Colonies" in *Johns Hopkins Univ. Studies in Hist. and Polit. Sci.*, iv (Baltimore, 1886), nos. 11, 12, p. 48; C. M. Andrews, "The Influence of Colonial Conditions as illustrated in the Connecticut Intestacy Law," *Select Essays*, I, 434, 435 and fn. The consent of the town was frequently necessary for the sale of lots, and in the case of contemplated sale to non-residents the town reserved the right of preemption. *Cf.* "Springfield Town Records" (1638) in H. M. Burt, *First Century of the History of Springfield* (*Mass.*) (Springfield, 1898-1899), vol. i, p. 164; *R. I. Col. Rec.*, I, 126; P. W. Bidwell and J. I. Falconer, *History of Agriculture in the Northern United States, 1620-1860* (Washington, 1925), p. 54.

tocracy in England were the law of inheritance and the system of entailing estates. In the feudal age the theory of indivisibility of baronies and military fiefs enters England with the Norman Conquest and with it the law of primogeniture or the succession of the eldest son to the entire real property of the father. Very slowly the rule was extended from the lands of military tenants to include socage tenure.[1] In order to build up a territorial family and to make it impossible for descendants to lose or alienate the land, the practice of entailing estates was introduced. The statute *De donis conditionalibus,*[2] 1285, was designed to check free alienation of property by the donee or any subsequent holder in the line, in grants where, not general heirs or assigns were named, but certain specified heirs were parties with the donee. The estate tail came to form an essential element in the strict settlement. Although by the middle of the fifteenth century the courts had developed a collusive procedure which defeated the obvious intention of the statute, the effects of the system of entails, which in fees tail general or male followed the rule of primogeniture, were to act as a restraint upon the alienation and widespread distribution of realty.

2. *Factors conditioning American Real Property Law*

As early as 1623 William Bradford stated that the attempt to establish a system of community property in the colony of Plymouth had failed and that therefore every family was assigned a parcel of land " according to the proportion of

---

[1] Bracton, *Lib.* VII, c. 3; Digby, *op. cit.*, pp. 95-100. *Cf.* also 22 & 23 Vict. c. 35 § 19.

[2] Although the date of the Statute of Westminster, II, c. 1, the cornerstone of entailed estates, commonly known as *De donis*, is 1285, it appears that it was not until 1312 that the courts held that the issue to the fourth degree as well as the donee were restrained from alienating in a grant, *A* to *B* and the heirs of his body. Belyng *v.* Anon. YB. 5 Edw. II (1312) Selden Soc., *Publications*, XXXI, 176.

their number for that end." [1] Thus the early ideal of the small peasant proprietor nurtured in rural America was given actuality. Communistic experiments, and, by implication, European feudal practices were abandoned at the beginning of New England settlement. Throughout the seventeenth and eighteenth centuries there was a fundamental colonial interest in the widespread distribution of land, and, it seems fair to conclude, in the words of one writer, that " political democracy came to the United States as a result of economic democracy." [2]

In New England the topography and soil conditioned the small freehold and the compact settlement. In general, allotments of land before 1700 produced fairly even distribution, although equality was far from being attained. In order to secure a rough measure of equality, the fields were frequently minutely subdivided after the fashion of the English manor. The investment of the settler in the original enterprise and his ability to use the land were the two criteria of distribution.[3] Efforts were made by the towns to check the tendency toward the concentration of land, evident even before 1700, by passing orders requiring the consent of the town to the sale of lots,[4] and by prohibiting the accumulation of two or more home lots.[5] This sentiment in opposition to the accumulation of large estates was not confined to New England. In 1742 the President and Assistants for the

[1] Bradford, *History of Plimoth Plantation* (Commonwealth edition), pp. 162, 163.

[2] J. F. Jameson, *The American Revolution considered as a Social Movement* (Princeton, 1926), p. 41.

[3] Bidwell and Falconer, *op. cit.*, pp. 52, 53.

[4] *Cf.* also *supra*, § 1.

[5] Rusdorp, Long Island, Town Order, Weeden, *ibid.*, I, 57; "Springfield Town Records" (1638) in H. M. Burt, *First Century of the History of Springfield*, I, 164.

county of Savannah, Georgia, opposed the claims of a creditor to the estate of a decedent debtor on the ground that it
would be "destroying the Trustees Good Intentions to
Suffer any Lotts within the Town to be Monopoliz'd." [1]   In
1733 William Alexander, in a memorial to the Governor of
New York, presented a forceful argument in favor of small
estates and fees,[2] and as late as 1784 a correspondent of
Joseph Reed expressed the opinion that "nothing can be
more dangerous to any state than to permit large Tracts of
Land to be possessed by single Individuals, which inevitably
introduce vassalage, and internal weakness;" he alluded to
some unfinished tracts "on the necessity of establishing some
agrarian Laws in America to prevent monopolies of Land." [3]
By the end of the eighteenth century the general recognition
of the value of widespread distribution of realty led to the
breakdown of the survivals of the manorial system in the
middle colonies and the South.[4]   This was accomplished by
remedial legislation enacted along broad lines.

3. *Partible Descent and the Survivals of Primogeniture*

As a result of this legislation, the rule has obtained generally in the United States for over a century that, on the
death of an intestate seised of real property in fee simple,

[1] *Ga. Col. Rec.*, VI, 29.

[2] MSS. William Alexander (Stirling) Papers, I, fol. 3, NYHS.

[3] London, Old Jewry, Aug. 3, 1784. MSS. Reed Papers, VII, fol. 128,
NYHS.

[4] For material concerning the manorial system in colonial America,
cf. e. g., J. H. French, *Gazetteer of New York* (8th ed., Syracuse, 1860) ;
E. H. Hall, *Philipse Manor Hall at Yonkers, N. Y.* (New York, 1912) ;
N. Y. Col. Docts., XIII, 471 ; *Papers of the Lloyd Family of Lloyd's
Neck*, 2 vols. (New York, 1927) ; *Grants and Concessions of New
Jersey*, p. 16; John Johnson, "Old Maryland Manors," *Johns Hopkins
Studies in Hist. and Polit. Sci.*, I (Baltimore, 1883), no. 7. Cf. also
Julius Goebel, Jr., *Some Legal and Political Aspects of the Manors in
New York* (Baltimore, 1928).

such property descends to his or her children equally, subject to the varying rights of the surviving husband or wife. In England, on the other hand, it has only been since the new Administration of Estates Act, which went into effect on January 1, 1926, that descent to the eldest son in fee simple has been abolished.[1] The attitude of this country early in its history may be attributed to the social philosophy in the colonies and to an experience which has been unfavorable to the preservation of primogeniture.

Early and effective criticisms of the English rule of descent were contained in tracts published in 1683 and 1685 for the purpose of attracting settlers to East Jersey. One of them stated that

Both the Gentrie and Commonaltie of our Countrey being very fruitful, and the Law giving to the Elder Brothers all their Fathers Estates, and that of the younger being but small. It is known how they are for most part put upon the Rack for a comfortable Lively hood, the session-house is not able to contain the hundred part of them: Where sometimes also the elder Brothers will have their share, and six or seven advocates make, for most part the Lives of all the rest, but a miserable and tedious Drudgery, so that they are either forced to go abroad upon their Shifts, whence few or none of them ever return; or otherwise, if they stay at home, hang upon the hand in a most slavish and sordide manner, which is a great Debasement to the Spirits of many, and a defeating of good Improvements they might make in the Creation, for by Birth and Education being equal till they come to be Men, then their Spirits are spoiled by so great inequality afterwards.

Now these younger Brothers having but a thousand or five hundred Acres of Ground in a Forraigne Plantation, with a hundred lb. starling to stock it, which the most ordinary of their Portions might reach to, might by a very moderate Industry

[1] Administration of Estates Act (1925), 15 Geo. V, c. 23, § 45.

live as comfortably as their Elder Brothers at home, and provide their Children better: and each of those would not want
enough of the Commonality to go alongst with them upon the
Encouragements they might receive to be their Servants.[1]

The corrective legislation in the middle and southern colonies found its inspiration in the practice of New England.
In that region generally, as will be detailed below, from the
very beginning of its settlement, prior to specific legislation,
partible descent was a custom observed in the administration
of an intestate's estate. Subsequent legislation merely confirmed the custom of distributing the estate of the intestate
to all the children equally, saving a double share for the
eldest son. Rhode Island, in this, as in much else, was the
black sheep of the New England flock, and, except for an
interval of ten years, from 1718 to 1728,[2] land descended to
the eldest son,[3] although there is considerable evidence in the
seventeenth century of uncertainty and lack of unanimity.[4]

[1] "A Brief Account of the Province of East-New Jersey in America:
Published by the Scots Proprietors" (Edinburgh, 1683), in Whitehead,
East Jersey under the Proprietary Governments (2d ed., 1875), p. 324.
Cf. also "The Model of the Government of the Province of East-New
Jersey in America" [by George Scotland] (Edinburgh, 1685), in *ibid.*,
p. 389.

[2] *R. I. Col. Rec.*, IV, 238, 417; *R. I. Col. Laws* (1719), pp. 95, 96;
Early Records of the Town of Providence, Will Book No. 2, p. 93.
Prof. Channing intimates that in the Narragansett country, the region of
large estates, land seems to have been more or less equally apportioned
among the heirs. "The Narrangansett Planters," *Johns Hopkins Univ.
Studies*, vol. iv (Baltimore, 1886), no. 3, p. 16.

[3] *In re* Estate of Thomas Patey (1704) *Early Records of the Town of
Providence*, X, 77.

[4] William Harris to Sergeant Steele, Aug. 15, 1768: " Some Collonyes
they give yᵉ Eldest Son a duble portion (to any of yᵉ younger) & to yᵉ
younger equail partes but in this Collony of Rhode Island each towne
hath a Councill & yᵉ sᵈ Councill from theyr townes (intestates) make
wills according to theyr pleasures & done according to theyr interests &
afaction or disafactions & yᵉ sᵈ councills Chose ever year & mostely

Pennsylvania, following Massachusetts, provided for divisible descent but preserved a double portion for the eldest son.[1] Prior to the Revolution legislation was not enacted in New York and the southern colonies establishing the system of divisible descent, and in these regions primogeniture was the rule of inheritance. The voluminous real estate papers of New York colonial estates,[2] and the statutes of descent in Maryland, Virginia, and the Carolinas[3] bear testimony to the establishment of the rule. Therefore the New England practice of assimilating realty and personalty was looked upon with hostility in those jurisdictions. In 1683 the first colonial assembly of New York resolved:

That from hence forward Noe Lands Within this province

changed as often & likewise as often alltered ye maner of intestates childeren & heirs proportions of theyr partes in lands & goods, & yet (in this collony) ye laws of England acknowledged though not soe much put in performance prayeth a clear answer in writing." R. I. Hist. Soc., *Collections*, X, 249, 250.

[1] Act of 1693, § 13; act of 1697, § 4, *Charter to William Penn*, pp. 231, 264-266. In 1683 the council voted that the eldest son be allotted half of the intestate's estate. *Pa. Col. Rec.*, I, 48. The inequitable nature of this discrimination is discussed by Franklin, *Works* (Bigelow edition), VIII, 421.

[2] *Cf.* e. g., Interrogatories to be administered *in re* Taylor Estate (c. 1740-1750), MSS. James Alexander Papers, I, NYHS; covenant of Cortlandt Skinner (1757), *loc. cit.*, V, NYHS. In the Articles of Capitulation on the surrender of New Netherland, the Dutch were permitted to "enjoy their own customs concerning their inheritances." O'Callaghan, *Documents relating to the Colonial History of New York*, II, 251. The Dutch law of descent in America was in accord with the law of Aasdom, providing for divisible succession. *Ibid.*, I, 620. *Cf.* also order of the Council of War, Fort Willem Hendrick, Aug. 18, 1672, *ibid.*, II, 576.

[3] Act of 1639, *Md. Arch.*, I, 60, 61; act of 1642, *ibid.*, pp. 157, 190, 191; act of 1705, Hening, *Statutes of Va.*, III, 362, act of 1748, *ibid.*, V, 455; N. C. Col. Rec., XVII, 146; act of 1762, c. 8, *ibid.*, XXIII, 586; act of 1766, c. 3, *ibid.*, p. 665; J. S. Bassett, "Landholding in Colonial North Carolina," *Law Quarterly Review*, XI, 163 and statutes cited; act of 1712, *S. C. Stat. at Large*, II, 524.

shall be Esteemed or accounted a Chattle, or personall Estate of Inheritance according to the Custome and practice of his Majesties Realme of England.[1]

Supplementary evidence, such as judicial decisions and will books, indicate clearly that the eldest son had landed rights superior to the other children and was regarded as heir-at-law.[2]   In tribute to this rule, Henry William Parker, known as the "eldest son of Georgia," was granted as his birthright in 1750, five hundred acres of land.[3]   Feudalism renascent is exemplified in records such as this from the Court Leet and Court Baron of St. Clement's Manor in Maryland, 1672: "We present that upon the death of Mr. Robte Sly there is a Reliefe due to the Lord and that Mr. Gerald Sly is his next heire who hath sworne fealty accordingly."[4] This affords interesting comparison with the provision of the Massachusetts Body of Liberties of 1641, abolishing feudalism and all its incidents.[5]   Along with the recognition of primogeniture in these jurisdictions went the accompanying conservative English real property practices, such as the barring of the half blood from inheritance,[6] the recognition

---

[1] *N. Y. Col. Laws*, I, 114.

[2] Comment by Barton, editor, *Va. Col. Dec.*, I, 163; *dicta* in Powell *et ux. v.* Turner (1738) *ibid.*, II, 78; Anon. (undated) *ibid.*, p. 360; Anderson *et ux. v.* Logan (1741), *ibid.*, p. 151. *Cf.* also e. g., Pelletreau, *Early Wills of Westchester County* (1664-1784), pp. 15, 78, 79, 85, 86, 116, 161; McIntosh, *Lower Norfolk and Norfolk County Wills* (1637-1710), pp. 174, 196, 197.

[3] *Ga. Col. Rec.*, VI, 322.

[4] "Records of the Court Leet and Court Baron of St. Clement's Manor, 1659-1672," in *Johns Hopkins Univ. Studies*, I, no. 7, p. 38.

[5] *Mass. Col. Laws, 1660-1672* (Whitmore ed., 1889), p. 35.

[6] Evans *v.* Evans (1665) *Va. Gen. Crt. Rec.*, p. 503. *Cf.* especially the important legal opinion of William Fitshugh contained in a letter to Major Robert Beverley, Sept. 11, 1679, *Va. Mag. of Hist. and Biog.*, I, 19, 20.

of survivorship in joint tenancy,[1] and the adjudging of a grant to "a man and his children" a fee tail.[2]

In regions where primogeniture never gained a strong foothold it is important to bear in mind that partible descent gained recognition as a custom. In other regions, primogeniture was destroyed by legislation. The first attack upon primogeniture appears to have taken place in Rhode Island in 1718,[3] but the results were not tangible. The American Revolution was a fillip to renewed legislative efforts. The Jeffersonian offensive in Virginia in 1776 [4] bore immediate fruit. Georgia in 1777,[5] North Carolina in 1784,[6] Virginia in 1785,[7] Maryland [8] and New York in 1786,[9] South Carolina in 1791,[10] Rhode Island in 1798,[11] all, under the influence of the back-country party, abolished primogeniture; and during the same period the New England group of states, together with Pennsylvania, which had preserved the Mosaic double portion for the eldest son, dispensed with this special endowment, and by statutes provided for equal division among the children.[12]

[1] *Md. Arch.*, IV, 49; Evans *v.* Evans (1665) *Va. Gen. Crt. Rec.*, p. 504.

[2] Sharp *v.* Hatcher (1679) *Va. Gen. Crt. Rec.*, p. 520. But *cf.* decision (1668) that "by a devise ... the fee passes although the word heirs be omitted." *Ibid.*, p. 511.

[3] *R. I. Col. Rec.*, IV, 238, 417; *R. I. Col. Laws* (1719), pp. 95, 96.

[4] Jefferson, *Writings* (H. A. Washington's ed., 1853), I, 43, 139.

[5] *Ga. Col. Rec.*, XIX, part 2, p. 455.

[6] *N. C. State Rec.*, XXIV, 572-577.

[7] Hening, *Statutes at Large*, XII, 148.

[8] *Md. Laws* (Maxcey, 1871), II, 16: "Whereas the law of the descents which originated with the feudal system is contrary to justice, and ought to be abolished ..."

[9] *N. Y. Laws* (Greenleaf, 1792), I, 206.

[10] *S. C. Stat. at Large* (1839), V, 162.

[11] *R. I. Laws, 1798*, p. 287, estates tail being specifically excepted.

[12] *Mass. Laws*, 1801, I, 124; *New Hamp. Laws*, V, 384; *Pa. Laws*, 1810, III, 143.

4. *Entails and the Accumulation of Realty*

The practice of entailing estates in the American colonies was unfavorable to the widespread distribution of realty, and, more specifically, to the prosperity of the egalitarian system of partible descent. In this drama of the law, primogeniture and entailed estates are the twin protagonists. From Maine to Georgia the practice of entailing land was extensive in the colonial era. An analysis of the wills probated in York County, Maine, 1640 to 1760, reveals that the use of the entail steadily increased and became by no means uncommon in the second quarter of the eighteenth century.[1] In the other New England colonies the practice of entails appears at the very beginning of settlement.[2] The manorial and plantation systems of the middle and southern colonies were naturally adapted for the fee tail, which was in very extensive use in those regions. It is estimated that the act of 1776 destroying entails in Virginia released from entail at least half, and possibly three-quarters, of the entire " seated " area of the state.[3] The confiscation of the great Loyalist estates carried out by the state legislatures brought about the subdivision of vast entails, among which may be mentioned the properties of Sir William Pepperrell in Maine, the Philipse estate in New York, and the estate of the Penn family, proprietaries of Pennsylvania.

---

[1] *Maine Wills, 1640-1760*, edited by W. M. Sargent, *passim. Cf.* especially the strict entail in the will of Humphrey Chadburne (1667), *ibid.*, p. 48, and the elaborate entail in that of Sir William Pepperrell (1759), *ibid.*, pp. 846, 847.

[2] Will of George Willis (1644) *Conn. Pub. Rec.*, I, 469; Providence wills, 1682-1703, in *Prov. Rec.*, VI, 64, 140, 170, 217; 1722, *ibid.*, XV, 202, 205, 208.

[3] Jameson, *op. cit.*, p. 58.

5. *The Effect of the Statute De Donis in America*

The practice of entailing realty found legal support in theories as to the effect of the statute *De Donis* in the English colonies. A restrictive view was adopted, but too late in colonial history to curb materially the growth of entails in the seaboard colonies; in the new states, where entails had never obtained a foothold, this modified view was often employed by the courts to work immunity from medieval property statutes.

During the colonial period, the view among English legal authorities as to the effect of British statutes as well as of the common law in the colonies seems to have been gradually modified. In *Blankard v. Galdy* [1] the question was raised as to the extension of a Parliamentary statute to Jamaica. The court held that where the English people gained territory by discovery and settlement " all the Laws in Force in England, are in force there "; but in the case of a conquered country, such as Jamaica, the laws of England were not operative " until declared so by the Conqueror or his Successor." " In such cases where the Laws are rejected or silent, the conquered Country shall be governed according to the Rule of Natural Equity." Bermuda erroneously, in its case, followed the law expounded in *Blankard v. Galdy* with resultant serious difficulties. In 1740, the preamble of an act, entitled " An Act to Prevent Law Suits," recited rather pathetically that " estates in tail have heretofore been granted in persuasive opinions from eminent counsel from England in 1684, that the Statute de Donis of 13 Edw. I, not being in force here, real estates could not be entailed here, but are estates in fee; but this opinion has been recently contradicted by the most eminent lawyers at home in 1736, who have informed us that not only the Statute de Donis, but all the laws of England prior to the settlement of these

[1] 2 Salk. 411 (1694).

islands are in force here, and that no entails can be docked but by fine and recovery according to the law of England." [1]

Blankard v. Galdy was reaffirmed in no uncertain terms in 1722,[2] and accepted by Blackstone in a famous passage.[3] On this principle, *De Donis* would not extend, among other colonies, to Jamaica, Granada, Canada, Nova Scotia,[4] and in strictness to New York — which in fact was a conquered province, although the legal theory is *contra* [5]—except by specific enactment, or usage and acquiescence. The other American colonies, with the possible exception of New Jersey, would presumably embrace the common law and statutes of England prior to colonization. The end of the colonial era finds the Attorney and Solicitor-General curtailing this extension and taking into consideration the effect of colonial charters, actual practice and local legislation.[6]

[1] Dill, "Colonial Development of the Common Law," (1924) *Law Quarterly Review,* XL, 234, 235. An interesting sidelight on the constitutional argument raised by the Americans in the 18th century was that in the early part of the century, where the question was one of the tenure and distribution of property, colonial advocates found the conquered nation analogy potent (Conn. Hist. Soc., *Collections,* V, 489; Mass. Hist. Soc., *Collections,* VI, 495, 496) ; after 1760 the great constitutional lawyers on the colonial side still cited Blankard *v.* Galdy, but denied that the colonies had been conquered by England. *Cf.* James Wilson, "Considerations on the Nature and Extent of the Legislative Authority of the British Parliament," (1775) *Works* (1896), II, 529, 533 *et seq.*; John Adams, *Works* (1851), IV, 158, 170.

[3] Anon., 2 P. Wms. 75, 24 Eng. Rep. 646. *Cf.* also earlier case of the Earl of Derby, 2 Anderson, 116 (1597). Statutes would not extend to the Isle of Man unless specifically named.

[3] 1 Bl. Comm. Introd., § 4.

[4] Howard, *Laws of the British Colonies,* I, x, xi.

[5] *Cf.* J. W. Pirrson, *The Dutch Grants, Harlem Patents and Tidal Creeks* (New York, 1889), pp. 2 *et seq.* and cases cited; but *cf.* Reynolds *v.* Swain (1839) 13 La. 193.

[6] Opinion of R. Henley and C. York, May 17, 1757, George Chalmers, *Opinions of Eminent Lawyers on Various Points of English Jurisprudence chiefly concerning the Colonies* (Burlington, 1858), pp. 209, 210.

The Massachusetts law of 1651, providing that no estate tail should pass without the words " to the heir or the heirs male of his body, lawfully begotten forever," [1] impliedly adopts *De Donis*. In Maryland, Dulany and the tide-water party desired to introduce all the British statutes in bulk and claimed the extension of the statute *De Donis*.[2] One opponent, Eversfield, urged that the common law bound the colonists only so far as it was tacitly approved by the legislature, and submitted that equal division of real as well as personal property was a rule more reasonable than that of the common law.[3] *De Donis*, however, has been held to have extended to Maryland.[4] In the Act of South Carolina of 1712 " to put in Force in this Province the several statutes of the Kingdom of England or South Britain, therein particularly mentioned," chapters 11, 12, 19, 34, 37 and 40 of the Statute Westminster II were adopted,[5] and because of the omission of chapter 1, the statute *De Donis* has been held never to have extended to that colony, and a grant, *A* to *B* and the heirs of his body, is a conditional fee, which becomes capable of being alienated as a fee simple on the birth of issue to *B*.[6] In Iowa, although the legislative restriction against entailed estates appears to have been removed by statute, entails have been regarded as " entirely foreign to the genius and policy of our institutions," and the

[1] *Mass. Col. Laws, 1660-1672* (Whitmore, 1889), p. 140.

[2] *Rights of the Inhabitants of Maryland to the Benefit of English Laws* (1728), pp. 30, 31.

[3] Sioussat, "English Statutes in Maryland," *Johns Hopkins Studies in Hist. and Polit. Sci.*, XXI, 523, 524.

[4] *Cf.* letter, Chase to Tilghman, *J.*, referred to in Kilty, *Report of All Such English Statutes as Existed at the Time of the First Emigration by the People of Maryland Found Applicable to their Circumstances and Such Others as have since been Introduced* (1811), Introd., vi, vii, 211.

[5] *S. C. Stat. at Large* (1837), II, 401.

[6] Mattison *v.* Mattison (1902) 65 S. C. 345, 43 S. E. 874.

curious result reached in an opinion noteworthy for its liberal tenor is that the more archaic conditional fee survives [1]—a policy directly contrary to the view expressed in the English Law of Property Act of 1922, in which fees simple conditional subsisting on January 1st, 1926, for want of a custom to entail in enfranchised lands, are converted into entailed interests.[2]

6. Early American Opposition to Entails

Just as primogeniture proved inapplicable to American conditions, so the attempt to restrict alienation by entailing estates was very early found adverse to colonial interests. The opposition to both sprang from the same feeling that they would nurture and perpetuate an undesirable social and political class.

In their criticism of early experiments with entailed estates the colonists pointed clearly to conditions which also made primogeniture undesirable. In Georgia, the details of settlement were left by charter to the trustees, who promptly resolved that their land grants should be entailed.[3] A typical deed would grant fifty acres in tail male to the settler.[4] It was believed that small military fiefs could in this way be erected, which would be of defensive value in a semi-military frontier settlement: the trustees further believed that free alienation would result in rapid accumulation of lots in the hands of a few men. The colonists thought differently, and

[1] Pierson et al. v. Lane (1882) 60 Iowa 60, 14 N. W. 90. In Mississippi, De donis has been held not to extend; but conditional fees cannot be created. Jordan v. Roach, 32 Miss. 481, 617, 618 (1856).

[2] Law of property Act, 1922, 12th Sch., para. 8 (ii); Wolstenholme and Cherry, Conveyancing Statutes (11th ed., London, 1925), vol. i, p. 350.

[3] Ga. Col. Rec., V, 675.

[4] J. R. McCain, Georgia as a Proprietary Province (Boston, 1917), pp. 228, 229. The earlier deeds were for 500 acres in tail made (1732). Ga. Col. Rec., II, 14, 15.

prolonged strife ensued. For a time the trustees continued adamant, and proceeded to make grants of five-hundred-acre tracts to gentlemen adventurers. The colonists alleged that credit from outside business men was withheld because they were not able to show fee-simple estates.[1]   One colonial argument against entails was that

not only are parents incapable, for want of credit to provide for themselves, being necessitated to dispose of their servants for want of provisions; but if they could, only their eldest son could reap the benefit; their younger children, however numerous, are left to be fed by Him who feeds the ravens. . . . Are not our younger children and daughters equally entitled to our bowels and affections? And does human nature end with our first-born, and not extend to the rest of our progeny and more distant relations.[2]

In 1739 the Earl of Egmont stoutly declared that " we would never suffer the people's property to become a bubble in exchange alley." [3]   Yet within a year the situation in the colony caused his conversion, and in 1740 he records in his Journal:

I was very urgent for altering the Tenures, thinking that there was an absolute necessity for it: I shew'd that for want of it, Inhabitants were daily withdrawing themselves: That the only End of the strictures of our Tenure was to keep the Inhabitants in the Colony, but seeing it has had a quite contrary effect, we must change our measures, or the colony would be entirely abandon'd, which would bring a lasting reproach on us. That if we refused to give the Inhabitants all the ease & liberty possible, consistent with the safety of the Province, it would be better for us to surrender our Charter: for we should be accused of suffering the Colony to perish by our own willfullness

[1] Journal of the Earl of Egmont, Jan. 16, 1739. *Ga. Col. Rec.*, V, 93.
[2] Tailfer, Anderson and Douglas, "A True Historical Narrative of the Colony of Georgia," (1741) Ga. Hist. Soc., *Collections*, II, 228.
[3] Journal of the Earl of Egmont, Nov. 5, 1739. *Ga. Col. Rec.*, V, 246.

& mistakes.   That I saw no inconvenience would arise from
suffering the people to alienate their lands in their life time, or
to annex other lands by marriage or gift (which were things the
people desired), but I was not for allowing any person to add
to his possessions by purchase.   That no Man could sell, but
another must buy who would be ty'd up to the same conditions
& covenants as he lay under who sold.   That it is certain the
silk will never come to any thing but by a number of Inhabitants, and therefore we should take care above all things to keep
those who are yet remaining, & to invite others to return.[1]

The appeal of the trustees to the verdict of posterity was
soon dropped, for after 1735 they gradually trimmed their
sails, and, in 1750, the Common Council enlarged all grants
already made to absolute inheritances and determined to
create future grants in fee simple.[2]

Likewise in Bermuda the possibility of the extension of
the statute *De Donis* to include most of the property on the
island was faced with alarm, and brought forth decisive
legislative action.[3]   In North Carolina one petitioner urged
that " the respective Governments in the Colonies have
always discouraged the Intail of Lands which were not improved, as the Quit Rents and Provincial Taxes could not
be properly collected from such Lands, and also that the
owners of such Lands could enjoy little or no benefit from
them," and cited the colony law of 1749,[4] empowering the
tenant in tail to convey by deed if the land was less than £50
in value.[5]

---

[1] *Ga. Col. Rec.*, V, 379.

[2] McCain, *op. cit.*, p. 244.   In the act of 1741 half of the entail was
reserved for the eldest son.   *Ga. Col. Rec.*, II, 394, 395.   Accumulation
of realty was restricted to 2,000 acres in 1742.   *Ibid.*, V, 646, 647.   The
final act was dated Mar. 19, 1750.   *Ibid.*, II, 500.

[3] *Acts of Legislature of Bermuda, 1690-1902* (1923), I, 4, 5.

[4] Act of 1749, c. 4, § 2.

   N. C. Col. Rec., VI, 745-747.

A cause of great hardship to tenants in tail was the expense and the protracted and technical character of the proceedings by which entails could be alienated. In general, the fine and the common recovery were not popular in the colonies. In a number of jurisdictions the courts of law were empowered to levy fines and common recoveries.[1] Due to the fact that these common recoveries were frequently drawn, suffered, and executed defectively, supplementary legislation was necessary to protect titles.[2] Nevertheless, the skillful attorneys of the eighteenth century favored perpetuating the English fictitious actions.[3] In Virginia an act of 1705 forbade the docking of entails by fine and common recovery. Thenceforward, an act of the legislature was necessary in order to release an estate from an entail;[4] and the private laws and resolves of all the colonies contain many of these legislative enactments.

Entails were frequently docked by the colonial legislatures on the ground of mistake,[5] or that an entail had proved economically harmful to small property, often poorly located,[6] or that the present value of the property would not warrant improvements,[7] or to satisfy creditors, a common ground

---

[1] *Cf.* e. g., *Acts and Laws of R. I.* (Newport, 1767), p. 112; Carey and Bioren, *Laws of Pa.*, I, 306, 307 (1750).

[2] *Cf.* e. g., Maryland Act of 1766, c. xxi.

[3] *Cf.* James Alexander *in re* entail of estate of Cornelia Livingston (1740), MSS. James Alexander Papers, I, IV, NYHS. The procedure was exceptionally complicated. *Cf.* letter of Joseph Murray to James Alexander, Mar. 15, 1750. MSS. James Alexander Papers, V, NYHS.

[4] Hening, *Statutes at Large*, III, 320.

[5] *New Hamp. Prov. Laws*, II, 545, 546, 556, 557, 702, 703; IV, 316, 317.

[6] *Mass. Acts and Resolves*, I, App., pp. 81, 82; V, 199, 613; VI, 43, 89-91; VII, 198, 717; Hening, *Statutes at Large*, VII, 514; VIII, 57, 285, 289.

[7] *Mass. Acts and Resolves*, VI, 79, 80, 81, 161, 162; Hening, *Statutes at Large*, VII, 455.

for enlarging the proprietary interest in an estate,[1] or to clear title,[2] or to provide for the younger children.[3]   Generally, but with little consistency, the interests of the remainderman or the heir were protected.[4]   In Virginia land or slaves of equal or greater value were always settled to the same use. This type of legislative relief, though expensive, elaborate, and at times dilatory,[5] was generally preferred to resort to the courts.[6]

As a result of the unfavorable colonial experience, the legal profession by the close of the colonial period was in-

---

[1] *New Hamp. Prov. Laws*, II, 85. *Cf.* petitions of inhabitants of Lancaster and Chester Counties, Pa., stating that "some in Possession of entailed Estates falling into Decay by the Hand of Providence, are reduced to Streights, being cast into Prison for their Debts, the Creditors lose their Money, and the Debtors Children enjoy the Estate, without paying any Part of their Parents Debts: that others being prevailed on to be bound for such Debtors, imagining the Lands in their Possession were entirely their own, have after the Death of these Debtors been obliged to sell their own Lands to pay such Debts, to the Ruin of their own Children; while the Debtors Children...come into full and free Possession, without being accountable to their Parents Sureties..." *Votes and Proceedings of the House of Representatives of the Province of Pennsylvania* (Philadelphia, 1774), IV, 126-132. *Cf.* also Willys *v.* Hull (1694) MSS. Mass. Sup. Crt. Judic., I, fols. 91, 92; *Mass. Acts and Resolves*, IV, 42, 43 (1758); Hening, *Statutes at Large*, VIII, 163, 218, 280; *Acts of Barbados*, Nos. 220, 364, 372, *Abridgement of the Laws*, pp. 258, 259.

[2] *N. C. Col. Rec.*, VI, 383, 384.

[3] Hening, *Statutes at Large*, VII, 157, 159; VIII, 27, 57, 218, 464.

[4] *N. C. Col. Rec.*, VI, 745-747; *Mass. Acts and Resolves*, I, App., pp. 89-91; II, 285; IV, 110, 135; VI, 673; *New Hamp. Prov. Laws*, II, 574, 575.

[5] For procedure, *cf. N. C. Col. Rec.*, V, 818.

[6] Judge Sewall, Diary (August 23, 1712) in Mass. Hist. Soc., *Collections*, VI, 361: "The Gov[r] speaks with some earnestness that we should not give the Ordinary Court the go-by, in taking off Entails; it was in their power to take off Entails." *Cf.* Chalmers, *Opinions, etc.*, for strict English supervision of legislative action in docking entails.

clined to look with disfavor upon the institution of the fee tail. There was a disinclination to extend entails to personalty,[1] and a marked tendency to construe grants liberally in favor of the fee simple.[2] The legislation in Virginia, culminating in 1776 in Jefferson's successful attempt to abolish entails and supplant " an aristocracy of wealth " by an " aristocracy of virtue and talent," [3] is typical of this changing attitude. In 1734, in recognition of the great financial burden which the act of 1705 imposed upon the poor man by compelling him to resort to the legislature for relief, a Virginia statute provided that entailed estates not exceeding £200 could be barred by a deed of bargain and sale after an inquisition had been made by the sheriff.[4] An act of 1765 empowered the tenant in tail to make a lease of his land for twenty-one years or for three lives or any lesser term, saving the interests of the remaindermen and the heir.[5] The act of 1776, declaring tenants of lands or slaves in tail holders in fee simple,[6] recites in its preamble that the policy

[1] Blackwell v. Wilkinson (1768) 1 Jefferson (Va.) 73, where Mason observes : " The inconveniences attending the entailing of lands have been loudly complained of ; but how much greater are those attending entails of slaves."

[2] Dudley v. Dudley et al. (1762) Quincy (Mass.) 12, where Otis says : " For however Estates Tail were once favoured and praised by us in the Statute De Donis, yet Ld. Coke tells us they were convinced of their Mistake, and exclaims in pretty full terms. Co. L. Wood, Inst. And here the Reason is greater than in England, for here all Estates are partable."

[3] Jefferson, *Writings* (H. A. Washington, ed., 1853), I, 36, 37 ; Hening, *Statutes at Large*, IX, 226.

[4] Hening, *Statutes at Large*, IV, 398-400 ; V, 414, 415. In North Carolina a simplified procedure was authorized for entails not exceeding £50. *N. C. Col. Rec.*, XXIII, 315, 316.

[5] Hening, *Statutes at Large*, VIII, 183.

[6] *Ibid.*, IX, 226, 227.

of making gifts in tail "tends to deceive fair traders, who give a credit on the visible possession of such estates, discourages the holder thereof from taking care and improving the same, and sometimes does injury to the morals of youth by rendering them independent of and disobedient to their parents." Noted southern statesmen and advocates were, by the end of the century, converted to the Jeffersonian viewpoint in regard to the need for free alienation and widespread distribution of realty. "When property is made inalienable," wrote Bozman, "it is like so much coagulated blood in the virus of an animal, which does not circulate. It is politically unwholesome." [1]

7. Survivals of Primogeniture in Entailed Estates

The legislation designed to destroy entails and primogeniture was never completely effectual. An analysis of the statutes and the modern cases reveals that today in some jurisdictions entailed estates descend to the eldest son. This situation, it is true, is not very widespread, for in the vast majority of American states, in emulation of the example of Virginia in 1776, there is legislation aimed at the abolition of entails. [2] One group by statute abolished the fee tail by making it a fee simple in the first taker. [3] There is a

---

[1] "Observations on the Proposed Bill, entitled 'An Act to declare and explain the Law in certain cases therein mentioned.'" Harrison, Bozman, pp. 30 et seq. Cf. also speech of Charles Pinckney in behalf of the ratification of the federal Constitution by his own state (1788), Jervey, Haynes, pp. 21, 22.

[2] These statutes have sought to accomplish their end in various ways and have been subjected to various interpretations. Cf. Columbia Law Review (1915), XV, 618, 619.

[3] Ala. Civ. Code (1923) § 6901; Ariz. Rev. Stat. (1913) §§ 4668-9; Calif. Civ. Code (Deering, 1923) § 763; D. C. Ann. Code (Torbet, 1919) § 1012; Ky. Stat. Ann. (Carrol, 1922) §2343; Minn. Gen. Stat. (1913) § 6654; N. Y. Real Prop. Law § 32; Mich. Comp. Laws (1915) § 11521; Ga. Ann. Code (Park, 1914) § 3661; Va. Code Ann. (1924) § 5150;

second group of a few states in which entails are preserved
by statute merely for the life of the donee in tail or are
made life estates in the first donee with remainder in fee
simple either to his children,[1] or to the person to whom at
common law the estate would pass at his death.[2]   In this last
event, it might be presumed that the common-law descent to
the eldest son would be invoked; but under such a statute,
in Arkansas and Illinois, the courts regard all the children
of the tenant in tail as his " heir at law." [3]   There is a third
group without legislation on the subject, and logically the
statute *De Donis,* the corner-stone of fee tail, would be in
force; but the few courts in which the question has been
raised seem to be divided.[4]

In a fourth group of states—to a consideration of which
this investigation is directed—the fee tail subsists, but the
tenant in tail is permitted to convey the property in fee

W. Va. Code (Barnes, 1923) § 1446; Wis. Stat. (1921) § 2027. In some
of these states, as in New York, a remainder in fee on what at common
law would be a fee tail is valid as a contingent limitation on a fee and
takes effect on the death of the first taker without issue living.

[1] Mo. Rev. Stat. (1919) § 2267; Gray *v.* Ward (1911) 234 Mo. 291,
136 S. W. 405; Same *v.* Krischel, 136 S. W. 408 (Mo. 1911); N. J.
Comp. Stat., Cum. Supp. (1918-1920) art. 57, § 11; Ohio Gen. Code
(1923) § 8622; Conn. Gen. Stat. (1918) § 5082.

[2] Ill. Rev. Stat. (Cahill, 1923) c. 30, § 6; Colo. Ann. Stat. (Mills, 1912)
§ 815; Ark. Dig. Stat. (Crawford and Moses, 1921) § 1499.

[3] Cooper *v.* Cooper (1875) 76 Ill. 57, 59; Kochersperger *v.* Drake (1897)
167 Ill. 122, 47 N. W. 321; Wheelock *v.* Simons (1905) 75 Ark. 19,
86 S. W. 830; Dempsey *v.* Davis (1911) 98 Ark. 570, 136 S. W. 975.

[4] Thus, the New Hampshire court in Jewell *v.* Warner (1857) 35 N. H.
176, held that the omission of the words " fee simple " in the statute of
descent of 1789 impliedly abolished fee tail; and see Stimson, *American
Statute Law* (1886-1892) § 1313. But in Ewing *v.* Nesbitt (1913)
88 Kan. 708, 129 Pac. 1131, the court held that in the absence of statute
entails exist. The court regarded the omission from the Laws of 1859
of § 5 of the Stat. Kan. Terr. 1855, c. 26, converting fees tail into
estates for life, as repealing it by implication.

simple, usually by ordinary deed.[1]   In Massachusetts the statute provides that " a person seised of land as tenant in tail may convey such land in fee simple by a deed in common form, as if he were seised thereof in fee simple; and such conveyance shall bar the estate tail and all remainders and reversions expectant thereon." [2]   This statute does not abolish entailed estates, and, in the event of the failure of the tenant in tail to convey in fee simple, the land is subject to the common-law rules of primogeniture as they had evolved by 1312 in the interpretation of the statute *De Donis* with its associated evils.   This was the law in New Jersey before 1820, in Pennsylvania before 1855, in New Hampshire apparently before 1857, and is the law in Massachusetts and Maine at the present day.   In the few remaining jurisdictions where fees tail survive it appears that they descend according to the general laws governing intestate succession.

The persistence of primogeniture is not to be explained by current economic and social tendencies.   The investigator, challenged by its survival, is compelled to turn to an examination of its historic antecedents.   In order to gain a clear understanding of the colonial attitude toward the distribution of land, the descent of entailed estates and the general practice of entailments in the colonial period must be considered.   It is proposed to summarize below the general evidences of a colonial doctrine of the descent of entails from the earliest period of American history, to consider as an analogy the similar problem in gavelkind tenure in England, and to show how the rule of partible descent evolved out of new social and economic conditions.

---

[1] Mass. Gen. Laws (1921) c. 183, §§ 45, 48; but not by will, c. 191, § 1; Me. Rev. Stat. (1916) § 10, p. 1115; *In re* Tillinghast (1903) 25 R. I. 338, 55 Atl. 879; Whittaker *v.* Whittaker (1868) 98 Mass. 364; Caulk's Lessee *v.* Caulk (1902) 19 Del. 528, 52 Atl. 340.

[2] Mass. Gen. Laws (1921), c. 183, § 45.

8. *Colonial Attitude toward the Descent of Entailed Estates*

Instead of finding in our historical material an evolutionary development of an American doctrine of the descent of entails, the investigator encounters three distinct strata of judicial pronouncements, superimposed upon one another in a sort of geological formation, for there is no apparent logical connection between the views of the separate centuries. But each is explicable on historical grounds. The seventeenth century in New England witnessed a conscious attempt to depart from the archaisms of English property law and to cultivate with solicitude a more democratic tenure and rule of succession to satisfy the desire of a frontier community for an equitable property distribution in the family. As indicated elsewhere, the eighteenth was marked by a development on some scale of groups of large landowners, exercising a more conservative influence, and by stricter imperial discipline. In the early nineteenth century the most important materials of the preceding periods were not as yet available in printed form. In adjudicating the question two centuries of American law were overlooked, and what was thought to be the law of England was employed by the courts in the delusion that the colonists had themselves obediently observed it.

The Quincy Reports of late provincial Massachusetts were not published until 1865, so that unfortunately in none of the principal nineteenth-century cases did the courts have an opportunity to examine the decisions and valuable opinions of opposing counsel, which are given at length. In the middle eighteenth century the courts were of the opinion that the law had been well settled. Thus, in *Baker v. Mattocks*,[1] it appeared that Samuel and Constance Mattocks were donees in tail; their eldest son inherited the property and

[1] Quincy 69 (Mass., 1763).

conveyed it in turn to one of his younger sons. The plaintiff, grandson of the conveyor (eldest son of the eldest son) sued on a writ of formedon in the descender. The court admitted that there were a good many other descendants of the original donee besides the parties to this case; " and if it shall appear to the court upon the whole that the said Samuel and Constance, the donees, took an estate in tail, and that the said estate tail is not made partible by the law of this Province, then the jury find for the appellant." The court held that the province statute of 1692, by which land descended to all the children, did not extend to estates tail, but left them as at common law.[1] Cushing, *J.*, in a dissenting opinion, was obviously impressed by the arguments of Fitch and Gridley in favor of partible descent, to the effect that " the Tail is only cut out of Fee Simple, it is only excluding others to whom it would otherwise descend." [2] The learned justice urged as " the Manner and Construction of the Law at Home: when Fee Simple is partible, so are Estates Tail; and where Fee Simple descends to the eldest son, so does Tail." Hutchinson, *C.J.*, leading conservative and Loyalist in New England, in an opinion, noteworthy for its liberal tenor, was likewise impressed.[3] Both conceded, however, that such an interpretation would be opposed to current practice. With some historic irony, Otis, New England radical, arguing with Thacher for the plaintiff, found in the law of nature no particular inherent right of descent; but maintained that primogeniture should be respected in the light of common-law precedent.[4]

[1] Benjamin Lynde, Chambers Russell, and Peter Oliver, *JJ.*, in favor; John Cushing, *J.*, and Thomas Hutchinson, *C. J.*, dissenting.

[2] *Ibid.*, pp. 69-71.

[3] Editor Quincy notes that Judge Trowbridge, in an opinion given in the will of Shute Shrimpton Yeomans, who died in 1769, took the same view of the law as the dissenting justices.

[4] Generally Otis could find a justification for all liberal tendencies in

This decision pays not the least deference to the strong propaganda in New England in the revolutionary era for effecting greater economic equality. By the eve of the Revolution New England sermons were not infrequent which urged the equitable division of property and free tenure of land in order that " the landed interest " might not be " engrossed by a few." [1]

The admission of the dissenting judges in *Baker v. Mattocks* that the rule they favored was opposed to the practice then current seems almost conclusive proof that up to that time the weight of authority in Massachusetts had been in favor of descent to the eldest son in fee tail. Unfortunately, the Quincy Reports only include the years from 1761 to 1772, and there are no earlier printed reports for the province. Among the law papers of John Adams there is, however, a valuable opinion rendered on this subject by the leading and most erudite member of the New England bar, John Read, in *Banister v. Cunningham.*[2] In this case, Thomas Banister in 1708 gave property to his three sons to be equally

the law of nature. *Cf. The Rights of the British Colonies* (2d ed., Boston, 1765), pp. 46, 49, 70, 71. In Banister *v.* Henderson, Quincy 119, 140 (Mass., 1765) Otis took occasion to criticize entailed estates, and regarded cross remainders as "big with the great Confusion and Injustice—inconsistent both with Law and Common Sense," and three years before the principal case, we find him asserting in Dudley *v.* Dudley *et al.* (1762) Quincy 12: "The Law will not admit an Inheritance contrary to the known Law of the Country; and this being contrary to the Law descends as a Fee Simple...here all Estates are partable." *Cf.* also Barradall, *J.,* in Edmondson *v.* Tabb (1741) *Va. Col. Dec.,* II, 362, 363.

[1] Phillips Payson, *Election Sermon,* Boston, 1778; Samuel Webster, *Election Sermon,* Boston, 1777; James Dana, *Election Sermon,* Hartford, 1779; Ezra Stiles, *Sermon,* New Haven, 1783, Benjamin Trumbull, *A Discourse, Delivered at the Anniversary Meeting Of the Freemen Of the Town of New Haven, April 12, 1773,* New Haven, 1773; cited by Baldwin, *The New England Clergy and the American Revolution,* p. 128.

[2] Quincy 156 (Mass., 1745).

divided among them; and if any of the three died without
heirs lawfully begotten in wedlock, he devised his share to
the surviving sons or son. On the death of the third son
without issue, the second son mortgaged part of the property
to Cunningham. Read in his opinion held that the Cunningham estate was void, as the mortgagor only had one-half of
the estate in tail. In answer to the question: " To whom
doth this Pasture fall,—to John the eldest son surviving, or
to the four Children of Thomas equally?" he asserted, to all
the children by the province law, " and they must join suit."

. . . The fullest Words of Limitation to make an Intail, as
in a Gift to *A* and his heirs of his Body begotten, have no ten-
dency to alter the Course of Descent, but only to limit whose
Issue shall Inherit, and so how long the Inheritance shall en-
dure; and when that Issue is spent, the Estate reverts to the
Donor. Lit. Ten. §§ 18, 19. the Statute of Westminster 2,
c. 1, makes no Intail but of such Estates as were Fee Simple
Conditional at common law and confirms them according to the
Will of the Donor, but makes no alteration of the Course of
Descent. Co. Lit. 18, 19.

He then submitted the gavelkind and borough English anal-
ogies, which proved such effective weapons in his brief in
the appeal to the Privy Council in *Clark v. Tousey.*[1]

Despite the dicta of Hutchinson and Cushing as to current
practice, the question seems to have been by no means disposed of in the first quarter of the eighteenth century. On
December 10, 1723, the Council passed a declaratory resolve
in connection with chapter 14 of the Statute of Descent of
1692, to this effect:

In Council: Upon a Question moved upon the Law of this
Province made in the fourth year of King William & Queen
Mary Entituled An Act for the Settlement & Distribution of

[1] *Cf. infra*, pp. 109, 114.

the estates of Intestates, Whether such estates as are or may be entailed by an entail General; Viz. To the Heirs of the Body lawfully begotten,—are, by Vertue of the said Law, subject to the Same Division or Distribution, as estates in Fee Simple Intestate, & ought accordingly descend to & be Divided among all the Children of the Tenant in Tail, Saving only to the Eldest Son a double Portion? Resolved in the Negative. In the House of Representatives Read, & Resolved that the Resolving of this question will not be of any service to the Province.[1]

The private acts of the Massachusetts legislature indicate much inconsistency in this regard. In the petition of the younger children of Nathaniel Saltonstall in 1723 to dock the entail of their deceased father, the eldest son made his consent a matter of record.[2] Again, in 1712, a petitioner speaks of his " only Brother William Clarke, the next heir in Taile to the Premises." [3] On the other hand, it would not be correct to assume that the eldest son was invariably favored by the General Court. In a significant case in 1742, the legislature passed a private act, purporting to partition the descent of a fee tail. The entail of the deceased was docked and his wife empowered to convey in fee simple; one-third of the proceeds of which sale was to be paid to the two sons, John and Francis, in these proportions: "Two third Parts of the said Third to the said John, & the other Third to the said Francis; And the remaining two third be in the same proportion forthwith, or as Occasion shall require, applied to defray the charge of the said John & Francis's Education." [4] The Privy Council on May 28, 1746,

---

[1] *Mass. Acts and Resolves*, I, 107 (abridged report) ; *Records of the Governor and Council*, XII, 101 ; *Journal of the House of Representatives*, V, 279, 284. The House dealt similarly with another resolution by the Council in 1726, *Ibid.*, VII, 166, 173.

[2] *Acts and Resolves*, VI, 158.

[3] *Ibid.*, pp. 79, 80.

[4] *Ibid.*, pp. 161, 162.

disallowed this act, asserting that it gave " power to dispose of *an estate entailed belonging to an infant* without a proper and due regard to justice and equity, and has not the suspending clause required by article 17 of the Governor's instructions." [1]

The reason for this extensive legislation is revealed in the engrossed minutes and among the file papers of the Superior Court of Judicature. In 1721 Gurdon Saltonstall, Governor of Connecticut, brought a plea of review of an action of trespass and ejectment from the Inferior Court of Pleas held at Salem. He claimed judgment on the ground that he was " eldest son and *one* of the heirs in Tail Lawfully begotten " of Nathaniel Saltonstall who died seised of a fee tail, and as such was entitled to two-fifths of the entailed parcel of land. In his brief on appeal, the defendant, Rev. Rowland Cotton, urged the confirmation of the judgment on the ground that a fee simple conditional, not a fee tail, was created by the deed of Richard Saltonstall in 1664, because " the Statute De Donis or the Statute of Entayles does not reach New England, and because an entail does not come within the statute concerning intestates estates." The appellee further declared that " he never heard of any such opinion of the Court and former Jury That the Appellant had a right to 2 parts; nor believes he shall ever hear so." [2] His prophecy was ill-timed, for the court decided against him on both points, holding that Gurdon Saltonstall was entitled to two-fifths or a double share of the land entailed.[3]

In the same year the court reached a similar decision in *Leach v. Herrick et ux.,*[4] where an entail was divided in

[1] *Acts of the Privy Council, Col. Ser.*, III, App., p. 848.

[2] Suffolk Files, No. 26654.

[3] Saltonstall *v.* Cotton (1721) MSS. Mass. Sup. Crt. Judic. (1721-1725), fol. 8; Suffolk Files, No. 24746.

[4] MSS. Mass. Sup. Crt. Judic. (1721-1725), fol. 13. Also Same *v.*

nine parts, the eldest son receiving a double portion, and each of the seven daughters a ninth of the estate. The court appears to reverse itself three years later in *Manchester v. Willcox,*[1] where judgment was affirmed for the appellee, the eldest son and heir claiming under a fee tail male, but it is by no means clear that his attorney Blagrave based his cause of action on this point of law,[2] or that it was determining with the court.

While it is manifest that in the early eighteenth century the law as to the descent of entails was not settled, but was at best debatable, an examination of the seventeenth-century stratum reveals a well-settled formation. Sullivan,[3] writing without the benefit of the *Acts and Resolves* or the *Quincy Reports,* declared unequivocally that, despite the common-law rule of descent in entails, " every son of an intestate is equally an heir male by our statute." Earlier, in commenting on the act of 1651, providing for the use of the words " heirs of the body " in a deed in order to create an entailed estate,[4] he expressed a contrary view, asserting that " inheritances in Fee Tail were continued, according to the common law, or rather according to the statute *de donis,* while fee simple estates were partible inheritances."[5] Neither text-writer nor court can fairly be charged with notice of the original collection of Massachusetts law, the Body of Liberties (1641), which was not " discovered " until 1843. The provisions in point are:

Preston *et ux.* (1721) *ib.,* fol. 32. Ireland *et ux. v.* Allen (1722-1723), *ibid.,* fols. 85, 86, 112, is an instance where the eldest son takes by purchase and not by descent, and it is therefore a consistent ruling.

[1] MSS. Mass. Sup. Crt. Judic. (1721-1725), fol. 220, 221 (1724).

[2] Suffolk Files, No. 17957 (2, 5).

[3] *History of Land Titles in Massachusetts* (Boston, 1801), p. 161.

[4] *Mass. Col. Laws, 1660-1672* (Whitmore ed., 1889), p. 140.

[5] *Op. cit.,* p. 77.

81. When parents dye intestate, the Elder sonne shall have a doble portion of his whole estate reall and personall, unless the Generall Court upon just cause alleadged shall Judge otherwise.

82. When parents dye intestate *haveing noe heires male of their bodies* their Daughters shall inherit as copartners, unless the Generall Court upon just reason shall judge otherwise.[1]

Here, in the earliest colonial law dealing with the problem, the basis for the statute of 1692, there is no distinction between estates tail and fee simple; and, further, the drafters, by the words " heires male of their bodies," mean all male children, and not the eldest son. The code of 1660 likewise provides the same method of distribution for realty and personalty and does not differentiate among inheritable estates. Even though the Statute of Descent of 1692, providing for equal distribution to all the children, saving a double portion to the eldest son, specifically refers to " fee simple " estates, nevertheless it is a rule of statutory interpretation that where a new act is couched in general affirmative language, and the previous law can well stand with it, the old and new laws may stand together.[2]

Plymouth, when a separate colony, apparently found the question important enough to warrant legislation, and in 1685 it was " ordered and declared that all Lands heretofore Intailed, and that shall be entailed hereafter, shall descend and enure as by the Law of England the same ought to do." [3] This declaratory resolve was fated to have a brief authority of six years, for under the second charter of Massachusetts in 1691, Plymouth was joined with the Bay Colony. The declaration would seem to be authoritative for all entails

[1] *Mass. Col. Laws, 1660-1672* (Whitmore ed., 1889), p. 51; *Laws of 1648*, pp. 54, 55. (Italics mine.)

[2] Craies, *Treatise on Statute Law* (3rd ed., London, 1923), p. 308.

[3] Brigham, *Compact and Charter*, p. 299.

created before that year; this explanatory legislation is probably a reflex of the new conservative influence resulting from the passing away of frontier conditions, and evidenced by the employment of entails,—a curiosity in the earlier period,—and by the curtailment of the earlier statutes designed to establish the liberal course of descent practiced in Kent.

The deeds and the will books of Maine, New Hampshire, and Rhode Island indicate that the eldest son was recognized as the heir-at-law in an entail.[1] The famous Mason entail of the major portion of the colony of New Hampshire, created by a devise of John Mason in 1625, descended according to the rules of primogeniture.[2] In those colonies in which primogeniture was the customary rule of descent, there is no real problem; entails followed the common-law course of descent.[3]

C. THE CUSTOMARY CHARACTER OF AMERICAN LAND TENURE

If the fee tail is placed in the general setting provided by our American land tenure, the anomalous character of primogeniture in entails will be more apparent. Gavelkind tenure in England has afforded precedents of value for the determination of American land tenure and more particularly of the rule for the descent of entails. The approach has been from two angles. 1. Gavelkind has been cited in analogy to the New England tenure and rules of partible succession.

---

[1] *Maine Wills*, p. 72 (1676); pp. 688, 689 (1733); *Providence Records*, VII, App., pp. 221-223 (1702); XI, 68 (1689); XI, 68 (1702).

[2] *New Hamp. State Papers*, XXIX, 88; and see genealogical table in Belknap, *History of New Hampshire* (Dover, N. H., 1862), vol. i, p. 253. *Cf.* also Atherton in New Hamp. Hist. Soc., *Collections*, III, 163.

[3] Typical examples are provided by the will and codicil of David Jones of Queens County, N. Y., 1768, and by the course of descent of the entailed devises of the Penn proprietaries. Thomas Floyd-Jones, *Thomas Jones and his Descendants: The Floyd-Jones Family* (New York, 1906), pp. 29, 34 *passim*.

2. It has been urged that gavelkind was literally extended to this country by the charters.

1. The analogy to English gavelkind was at an early period suggested by counsel, Strange and Belcher, for the respondents in *Phillips v. Savage* (1737) in their appeal to the King in Council. " As the rules of descent in England differ and clash with one another, it is impossible," they asserted, " but that the rule of descent in America should vary from some rule or other of descent here." The analogy was raised again by Read in *Banister v. Cunningham,* by Gridley in *Baker v. Mattocks,* and by Rand in his adverse comment on the findings of law in *Hawley v. Northampton,*[1] and was accepted by Justice Lowrie in *Price v. Taylor.*[2]

What is the situation where gavelkind land, in which partible descent obtains, is entailed? The answer is found in Robinson, *Gavelkind,* that when a man dies seised of gavelkind lands in tail, " the sons will inherit together as heirs of the body, because the estate-tail is part of the old fee simple." [3] A careful examination of the English cases shows that it is well settled that where fee simple is partible in intestate succession, fee tail observes the same rules. The pertinence of the analogy to the New England situation will

[1] 8 Mass. (Rand's ed., 1864) 45; 9 *ibid.*, p. 518 n.

[2] 28 Penn. St. 95 (1857).

[3] (5th ed., 1897), pp. 94 *et seq.* A stronger instance of the rule is in borough English. In 1660, in Anon., 2 Dyer, 179b, in a fee tail in borough English, "all the Board of Serjeants Inn thought that the younger shall have it by descent notwithstanding the words aforesaid." Accord, Roe *ex dem.* Aistrop *v.* Aistrop (1788) 2 Bl. Rep. 1228, where the court held it was "a mighty clear case." Apparently, according to Robinson in his first edition, May *v.* Milton (1556) Dyer, 133, pl. 5, laid down the same rule for gavelkind. Doe *ex dem.* Long *v.* Laming (1760) 2 Burr. 1100 (*per* Mansfield), does not enforce the rule, when, in accord with Archer's Case, it is the manifest intention of the donor to alter the descent in gavelkind by giving to females as well as males.

be apparent when it is shown that partible descent was the common law of New England.

The analogy of American entails to gavelkind entails could not be drawn were we to accept the view of Tiffany [1] that " on the death of the tenant in tail the land passes to the next heir of the body of the original donee; but such heir, though he takes because he is the heir of the body, takes not by descent, but as a substitute purchaser from the original donor, *per formam doni,* as it is expressed." According to this view, the statutory changes of the general course of descent would not affect the succession of fee tail, since it could only have such effect by altering the " well understood meaning of the term ' heirs of the body.' " The great weight of authority in English law renders this view untenable; [2] it is clearly established that in fee tail the heirs take by descent. [3]

2. Numerous colonial charters raise the question as to the literal extension of gavelkind tenure to many of the American colonies. The Massachusetts Bay charters are typical. Thus the charter of 1629 grants land " To the sole and proper use benefitt and behoofe of them the saide Councell and their successors and assignes forever: To be holden *of* our saide most deare and royall father (James I) his heires and successors *as of his mannor of Eastgreenewich in the County of Kent in free and common Soccage,* and not in Capite nor by Knights' service." [4] Two questions arise: (1) Whether this charter established gavelkind tenure, " the

[1] Tiffany, *Real Property* (2d ed., Chicago, 1920), vol. i, pp. 73, 74, and citations.

[2] For succinct statement, see Goodwright *v.* Wright (1717) I P. Wms. (Chanc.) 397; see also George *v.* Morgan (Pa., 1851) 4 Harris 85; Goodman *et al. v.* Russell (1841) 14 Conn, 210; Harkness *v.* Corning (1873) 24 Ohio St. 416.

[3] Shelley's Case (1581) 1 Co. Rep. 104a; Spence, *Equitable Jurisdiction of the Chancery* (London, 1846), pp. 141, 142.

[4] Poore, *Federal and State Constitutions,* I, 926.

common law of Kent," with its rules of divisible succession;[1] and (2) whether the colonists themselves thought it did and acted accordingly.

In regard to the first issue, opinion is sharply divided. While a long list of writers are inclined to believe that gavelkind was extended either by charter or specific legislation,[2] Professor Cheyney[3] maintains that Greenwich was employed

---

[1] Randall *v.* Writtall (1674) 3 Keb. 214, 215; Robinson, *op. cit.*, p. 44, note 88; Lambard, *Perambulations of Kent* (Chatham, 1826), p. 538; Co. Lit. § 265; Somner, *Treatise of Gavelkind* (2d ed., London, 1726), p. 44. The Anglo-Saxon custom of partible descent has as a general rule been confined to the county of Kent, although Vinogradoff shows that gavelkind, though later contended to be distinctly Kentish, seems to represent the original mode of hereditary succession of free folks. Vinogradoff, *Growth of the Manor* (3d ed., New York, 1920), p. 141. Incidents: (1) Equal division among all sons or representatives, and in default, among all daughters or representatives; (2) in dower, wife gets a life estate of one-half instead of one-third of lands of which her husband was seised of an estate of inheritance during coverture; (3) husband has merely a life estate in one-half of wife's property, is not dependent on birth of inheritable issue, and is defeated by second marriage of the tenant. Littleton, *Tenures*, Bk. III, c. ii, p. 305; Lambard, *op. cit.*, p. 535; Co. Lit. 33b; Robinson, *op. cit.*, pp. 128, 129, and note 88. For the advantages this custom afforded the occupier of the soil over against the lord, *cf.* M. Neilson, "Custom and the Common Law in Kent," *Harvard Law Review* (1924-1925), XXXVIII, 482.

[2] Atherton, New Hamp. Hist. Soc., *Collections*, III, 156, 159; W. Brigham, "The Colony of New Plymouth and its Relations to Massachusetts" in *Lectures delivered in a course before the Lowell Institute . . . on subjects relating to the Early History of Massachusetts* (Boston, 1869), pp. 173, 174; Hoar, Amer. Antiq. Soc., *Proceedings* (1883-1885), pp. 351 *et seq.*; Adams, "Constables," in *Johns Hopkins Studies in Hist. and Polit. Sci.*, I, 3, 4; Washburn, "Tenure of Lands in New England", Mass. Hist. Soc., *Proceedings*, XIII, 114-121; Palfrey, *History of New England*, II, 20; Ballagh, "Introduction to Southern Economic History —Land System," Amer. Hist. Assn., *Annual Report* (1897), p. 108; Sidney S. Rider, *The Meaning of the Phrase "The Manor of East Greenwich in our County of Kent," in the charter of Rhode Island in 1662* (n. p., n. d.).

[3] "Manor of East Greenwich, *Amer. Hist. Rev.*, XI, 29-35.

customarily in the charters merely because " it was the most usual dwelling-place of the king at that time," and that for the colonists it was a mere empty name. Egleston [1] contends that the words " as of the manor of East Greenwich," were used, " not with reference to the customs of that manor, or of the County of Kent (gavelkind, etc.), but simply to negative the otherwise necessary inference that the grant was to be held *in capite,* or, to speak more accurately, *ut de corona."* His sole authority is *Lowe's Case,* [2] which merely holds that whenever it is unclear as to the tenure of land held of the king, the presumption shall be that the land is held *in capite* and by knight's service. This case does not explain the employment of the words, " as of the manor," etc., in the Massachusetts charter, for there follows a specific denial that the land is held *in capite* or by military tenure. To accept Egleston's interpretation would be to render the phrase superfluous.

Robinson [3] would seem to challenge the power of the crown to endow grants of land with gavelkind prerogatives or those of ancient customs. On the other hand, Bacon, writing of the royal prerogatives, asserts: " The King may create any corporation or body politick, and enable them to purchase, and grant, and to sue, and be sued; and that with such restrictions and modifications as he pleases." [4] And if we view the colonial charters with Hobbes as " donations of the Soveraign; and not Lawes, but exemptions from Law," [5] there is some ground for regarding the " Kent

---

[1] " Land System of the New England Colonies," *Johns Hopkins Studies in Hist. and Polit. Sci.,* IV, 448.

[2] Bacon, *Works* (ed., 1730), IV, 113-120.

[3] *Op. cit.,* p. 44. " The tenure guideth not the descent, but the tenure and the nature together doe governe it." Lambard, *op. cit.,* p. 394.

[4] *Works* (ed., 1730), IV, 93.

[5] *Leviathan* (Lindsay's ed.), p. 154.

charter " series as containing exemptions from the inapplicable rule of primogeniture.[1]

However much we may discount the legal value of the reference to Kent in the charter, there is considerable evidence that in a number of colonies the conviction existed that gavelkind tenure was in force.   In Plymouth, on November 15, 1636, it was enacted " that inheritance do descend according to the comendable custome of Engl. hold of Est Greenwch." [2]   Then, with characteristic inconsistency, perhaps due to lack of information, there follows on the heels of this gavelkind provision this clause: " That if the husband die the wife shall haue a third *pt* of his land, during her life, and a 3[d] of his goods to be at her owne disposing." Dower in gavelkind, however, would have given the wife a one-half interest.   The provision was reenacted in 1664.[3] The popular reverence for the tenure of Kent is revealed in an examination of the Plymouth Colony Deeds, where, in numerous instances, land is granted in fee " to be holden of his Majestie as of his Manor of East Greenewch in the County of Kent in the Realm of England." [4]

Massachusetts Bay was also a supplicant at the shrine of Kentish customs.   John Winthrop, negotiator of the charter

---

[1] As late as 1867 we find Mr. Justice Gray maintaining that the reference to Kent in the charter transplanted the tradition that " no one was ever born a villein in Kent," and set up an old custom incompatible with the system of hereditary slavery. Jackson *v.* Phillips (1867) 14 Allen 560, 561.

[2] *Ply. Col. Rec. (Laws)*, XI, 12, 13; Brigham, *Compact and Charter*, p. 43.

[3] *Ply. Col. Rec. (Laws)*, XI, 187: "It is enacted by the Court on Authorities thereof That Inheritances shall descend according to the commendable custom tenure and hold of East Greenwich." Sullivan, *op. cit.*, does not appear to have a clear understanding of these acts.

[4] *Ply. Col. Rec. (Deeds)*, XII, 92, 93 (1642); 93, 94 (1643); 96-100 (1644); 105 (1645); 118, 119, 170, 190, 191 (1649); 192, 193, 200, 201 (1650); 209 (1651); 217 (1649).

of 1629, was a great admirer of Lambard and was well versed in that author's *Perambulations of Kent* (1576).[1] The Kent analogy is employed in the habenda of Massachusetts colonial deeds.[2] In 1678, in answer to the objections of the Attorney-General to manifest departures from English law, specifically in the privilege traitors and felons enjoyed in disposing of their estates by will, and the refusal to work forfeiture of goods, the General Court asserted: " We conceive it to be according to our patent and of its original, vizt, that of East Greenwitch, according unto which, as wee conceive, notwthstanding the fathers crime, yet the children are to possesse the estate." [3] This was a specific allusion to the liberal gavelkind doctrine: " The father to the bough; the son to the plough." [4]

Again, in Connecticut, when a later Winthrop appealed to the General Court against the distribution of his father's real property by the probate court, he asserted bitterly: " I was insulted by an adverse attorney, *who trumpt up gavelkind uppon me* (wch has so long been out of date by Act of Parlem^t & wch ye Charter knew nothing of,) and made a long flourish of words how I was but a coeheir, &C." [5] On the other hand, in the tentative instructions drawn up for the agent, Belcher, in *Clark v. Tousey* in 1728, Bracton is cited by the colony as authority for the view that " a Custom as our law has been in England," [6]—an allusion to gavelkind.

[1] R. C. Winthrop, *Life and Letters of John Winthrop*, I, 41-43. Winthrop's copy of the 1596 edition of Lambard with his father's annotations is in the library of the Massachusetts Historical Society.

[2] *Suffolk Deeds*, XIV, 69, 70 (1686).

[3] *Mass. Col. Rec.*, V, 199; Hutchinson, *History of Massachusetts*, I, 447.

[4] Littleton, *loc. cit.*, note 93.

[5] Mass. Hist. Soc., *Collections*, 6th ser., V, pt. vi, 427, 428; *cf.* also p. 488.

[6] Conn. Hist. Soc., *Collections*, V, 427 (in Gov. Law's handwriting).

William Harris, the alert Rhode Island planter, in a letter to Sergeant Steele, dated August 15, 1678, pertinently queries whether the charter reference to Greenwich establishes gavelkind descent. " Here is great need of A resolution in ye s^d case for here is noe certayne knowledge of ye full & certain meaning of ye s^d words." ¹ A deed and will disposing of Harris's property show that he was convinced that gavelkind was in force.² Francis Brinley, on the death of Harris, rendered an ambiguous opinion on the gavelkind instructions contained in the secret codicil of Harris's will, expressing his disbelief that gavelkind tenure obtained in East Greenwich.³

The Kent reference in the charter was utilized by conservatives and liberals as a fiction to attain some desired end. A striking instance was the barring of the entail of the vast Mason estates in New Hampshire by a common recovery in the Court of Common Pleas at Westminster, in which over 700,000 acres of land were alleged to be " In New England in America in the Parish of Greenwitch," and a writ was issued to the sheriff of Kent " to cause him to give full Seizin of the Manor." ⁴ This procedure was undoubtedly illegal.⁵ Nevertheless, if the Kent fiction could arbitrarily be asserted by the English courts for their own purposes, there would logically seem to be no reason why by the same

¹ R. I. Hist. Soc., *Collections*, X, 249, 250.

² *Records of Providence*, XIV, *Deed Book No. 1*, p. 60; *ibid.*, VI, 48-56.

³ Francis Brinley to Mrs. Susanna Harris, R. I. Hist. Soc., *Collections*, X, 356, 357. *Cf.* also *Pa. Arch.*, 2d ser., VII, 735.

⁴ *New Hamp. State Papers*, I, 145-147.

⁵ The Earl of Athol *v.* the Earl of Derby held that the Court of Chancery could not by any decree bind the Isle of Man, nor could any sheriff execute a writ. 1 Cases in Chancery 220, 221 (1673). Same issue raised in Benedict Calvert's Lessee *v.* Sir Robert Eden *et al.* (Md., 1789) 2 H. and McH., where Hargrave, Dulany and Hall agree.

process it could not be effectively employed in the colonies to provide a more democratic tenure.[1]

With the evidence at hand, it is difficult to draw conclusions as to how general the impression was that literal English gavelkind was introduced by the charter provisions; in the later colonial era the use of these words probably indicated nothing more than sentimental attachment. On the other hand, it is submitted that some form of divisible descent had always existed as a custom in the succession to fee simple realty from the beginning of New England settlement, although, as was indicated at the beginning of this study, no such custom was found in the southern colonies, where primogeniture was the rule. Many of the New England colonists came from Kent;[2] they generally felt that feudalism and its survivals were inapplicable to their frontier conditions; in the North, wealth, and, later, aristocracy were in large measure based on the ownership of increasable commodities of commerce rather than land. These conditions would be important factors in the growth and thriving of an indigenous "gavelkind" in New England soil.

In Massachusetts, prior to 1641, the law of nature, illuminated by Old Testament texts, was the rough, equitable rule administered by the courts. The early equality among male heirs, with a double portion to the eldest son, was based upon this idea of fundamental equity. In Chapter 4 of the first proposed draft of laws for the Bay Colony, entitled "Moses his Judicialls," (c. 1636) the rule is laid down:

[1] "Sometimes we are told, that our estates are by our charters all in the manor of East Greenwich, and therefore all in England; and yet have we any right to vote among the voters of East Greenwich? Can we trade to the same ports?" Franklin, *Works* (Sparks ed., 1844), IV, 220.

[2] For list of Kentish emigrants to New England, *cf.* Hoar, in Amer. Antiq. Soc., *Proceedings* (1883-1885), p. 369.

V. Inheritances are to descend naturally to the next of the kinne, according to the law of nature delivered by God.   Numb. 27, 7, 10, 11.

VI. If a man have more sonnes than one, then a double portion to be assigned and bequeathed to the eldest sonne, according to the law of God, unlesse his owne demerit doe deprive him of the dignity of his birthright.   The like for personall estate. Deut. 21. 17; 1 Chro. 5. 1.[1]

The early Lancaster town records, in a passage concerning the distribution of land, speak of that " equallitie which is the rule of God." [2]   Peter Oliver, Chief Justice of Massachusetts, declared in 1773, in the course of a conversation recorded by Ezra Stiles, that the descent of property in Massachusetts was " neither according to England in general or Co. of Kent, but Mosaic.   He said by Common Law the Estates of Felons went to the King, in Kent to the children, in New England to the children; so that the Common Law . . . would not apply to New England in this Case." [3]

In England the law of succession, whether primogeniture, ultimogeniture, or gavelkind, developed from the customary practices.[4]   Up to the time of Bracton, gavelkind and primogeniture were the two dominant customs struggling for supremacy.[5]   As early as Edward I, in the final conquest of Wales, English law was compelled to acknowledge that the rule of primogeniture could not be forced upon

---

[1] " Hutchinson Papers," Prince Soc., *Publications*, II, 191. For a similar attitude on the part of one of the founders of New Haven, *cf.* John Davenport, *A Discourse about Civil Government in a New Plantation whose Design is Religion.* Cambridge, 1663.

[2] Hurd, *History of Worcester County*, I, 6.

[3] *Literary Diary of Ezra Stiles* (New York, 1901), vol. i, p. 331.

[4] Vinogradoff, *Historical Jurisprudence*, I, 368 and n.

[5] Reeves, *History of English Law*, I, 30, 78, 227; Pollock and Maitland, *History of English Law*, II, 260-274.

the Welsh tribesmen.[1] The Statute of Wales declared that " Whereas the custom is otherwise in Wales than in England, concerning succession in an inheritance, inasmuch as the inheritance is partible among the heirs male, and, from time whereof the memory of man is not to the contrary, hath been partible, our Lord the King will not have the custom abrogated." Primogeniture was ultimately established as a general custom of the realm by the deliberate encouragement of the judges.[2]

In like manner in New England partible succession was rooted in customary practice. As early as 1627 a visitor at Plymouth found that " in the inheritance they place all the children in one degree, only the eldest son has an acknowledgment for his seniority of birth." [3] This is evidence that prior to the first statute of distribution in 1636, in which the custom of Kent was introduced, land was being distributed partibly. The statute of 1636 was modified by later legislation to be in accord with the customary practice of descent in Massachusetts.[4] In that colony, in 1640, a year before the adoption of the Body of Liberties, we find the Court of Assistants distributing the realty of an intestate to his six children, reserving a double portion for the eldest son.[5] The Body of Liberties was analogous in many respects to a char-

---

[1] Seebohm, *Tribal System of Wales*, pp. 51, 52.

[2] C. K. Allen, *Law in the Making* (Oxford, 1927), pp. 82-83. Holdsworth, *Hist. Eng. Law* (2d ed., 1914), III, 140-143, points out that the principal became definitely established after the social reason for it—i. e., the military convenience, had ceased to operate. *Cf.* also 1 Bl. Comm. 68-79. In Scotland succession developed from Scottish customary practices. Erskine, *Principles of the Law of Scotland* (Edinburgh, 1764), p. 7.

[3] Cited by A. W. Calhoun, *Social History of the American Family* (Cleveland, 1917), vol. i, pp. 121, 122.

[4] Laws of 1685, Brigham, *Compact and Charter*, p. 299.

[5] *Assistants*, II, 97.

ter of liberties of thirteenth-century England, in that it was regarded more in the light of a reaffirmance of customs and privileges than as an enactment of new law.[1]   For more than twenty years, asserts Professor Andrews,[2] the intestacy law " existed as a custom " in Connecticut " in no way binding on the people."   " I have observed," writes Lieutenant Governor Law, " the law to be of no ancienter date than 1699 and our old law book, dated in 1682, prescribes no rule excepting the righteousness and equity lodged in the breast of the County Court." [3]

The weight of evidence proves that contemporaries in New England looked upon this native gavelkind as a custom. The English courts have established certain attributes as indispensable to the recognition of a local custom; they have decided that the custom must be immemorial, reasonable, or at least not unreasonable, continuous, undisputed, certain or clear, compulsory, not against an act of Parliament, nor against divine law, although it may be contrary to common law.[4]   In the voluminous correspondence between the colonial authorities and their home agents in the two Connecticut cases of *Winthrop v. Lechmere* and *Clark v. Tousey,* and the Massachusetts case of *Phillips v. Savage*—all involving the determination of whether primogeniture extended to the

---

[1] Frequent 17th century instances of administration by the probate court of realty and personalty in accord with this provision are found: e. g., *Essex*, I, 112, 270, 387, 442, 443; VII, 170.

[2] *Op. cit.*, pp. 266, 267.

[3] " Talcott Papers," Conn. Hist. Soc., *Collections*, V, 119; also *ibid.*, pp. 122-123, 144, 392-394; *ibid.*, II, 225, 244-245. See October Orders of 1639, *Conn. Pub. Rec.*, I, 38.

[4] Co. Inst. 110b; Bracton, *L.* 1, pt. 2 and I, 3, pt. 2; Sowerby *v.* Coleman, L. R. 2 Ex. 96 (1867); Simpson *v.* Wells, L. R. 7 Q. B. 214 (1872); Blewett *v.* Tregonning, 3 A. & E. 554 (1835); Stewart's comment in 1 Bl. Comm. (Sharswood's ed., 1862), pp. 78, 79; *contra, ibid.*, Introd., pt. 3, *Doctor and Student*, I, 6.

respective colonies—there is frequent iteration by the colonists that these recognized attributes are possessed by their law of divisible succession.   Thus, in 1728, Law writes to Belcher:

'Tis true that our Law is of so antient standing (as I presume you are furnish'd with copies of Record to evince) that one would think it to have the like foundation with the general and particular customs in England, which are unalterable by any thing, short of an Act of Parliament, and it does not appear by the Act of the King and Council that it might not have been supported by its antiquity . . . [1]

Again, in New Hampshire, in 1751, in reviewing the claims to the Allen property therein, it is related that the law of intestate succession, giving a double portion to the eldest son, was " our Law by which every Estate has been ever Settled." [2]   In 1740, Talcott, the Connecticut governor, wrote to Francis Wilks, with regard to *Clark v. Tousey*:

It is now 104 Yeares Since our predecessors Settled in this Colony, who upon all occasions (in their Courts of Probate) Settled Reale Intestate Estates amongst the Children of the Deceased ancestor, the eldest son having a double portion, which practice or Custom, when we procured a Charter of King Charles the 2d was presently enacted into a Law . . . and from the time of our Settlement heare, which was in 1636, unto the time that the King declared our sd Law void, there had elapsed above 90 Yeares, in which time almost all the Real Estate in the Colony had been settled according to the above named Law; for the Inhabitants of the Colony, seeing that our Assembly had made a Law so well calculated for the good of the Colony, rested therein, and there was but few persons that settled theire estates by will: So that the admitting the eldest Son as heire at

1 Conn. Hist. Soc., *Collections*, IV, 122.

2 *New Hamp. State Papers*, XXIX, 285.

Law will make such confutions and alterations in this Governt that will certainly end in our ruin.[1]

With all seriousness, after a century it was affectionately hailed as a custom existing " beyond the memory of man." [2] Nevertheless it is clear that before the statute of 1699, the validity of the custom had been challenged unsuccessfully on several occasions.[3]

The chief test which the English courts have imposed is that the special custom must be reasonable, or at least not unreasonable, in order to be enforced; [4] the " error " of being contrary to the general rule would not imply unreasonableness *per se*.[5] A reasonable custom, the colonists asserted, was their intestate succession.

. . . We would represent to your Majty that so far as we have learn'd, the law of England is divided into three several species or kinds, the statute law, the common law, and reasonable cus-

---

[1] Conn. Hist. Soc., *Collections*, V, 244, 245.

[2] *Ibid.*, IV, 143 *et seq.* In England this expression, of course, was used in a restricted and technical sense.

[3] As early as 1687 the issue was clearly raised in the case of Thomas Wells, eldest son, claiming as heir at law. The decision in his favor was reversed in 1690 and this order was confirmed by the Court of Assistants the next year. *Conn. Pub. Rec.*, III, 396, 400, 435. The custom was again disputed by Josiah Talcott, in 1691 (as governor he became a staunch defender of the practice), *ibid.*, IV, 48; by Philip Lewes in 1692, *ibid.*, p. 70, and by Major Palmes in 1698. Palfrey, *History of New England* (Boston, 1883), vol. iv, p. 491. *Cf.* also Andrews, *op. cit.*, p. 439, n. 4, for the complaint of Dudley of Massachusetts in 1693. In the seventeenth century the practice of giving the eldest son a double portion was not always adopted. Compare Estate of Wakeman (1645), *Conn. Pub. Rec.*, I, 135, with Estates of Brundish (1640), *ibid.*, p. 45; and of Dewey (1648), *ibid.*, p. 168.

[4] Tanistry Case (1608) Davies, 78-115; Jethro Brown, " Customary Law in Modern England," *Columbia Law Rev.*, V, 561.

[5] Parker, *J.*, in Johnson *v.* Clark (1908) 1 Ch. 311, 312.

toms, all of which are liable to an alteration. And we would with the greatest prostration request your Majty, that when we find any rules of law needful for the wellfare of your Majesties Subjects here, which is not contrary to and *agrees well with some one of the Tryangles of the law of England, as it then is, or heretofore has been,* when England might have been under the like circumstances in that particular, which we are when we make the law, that it might not be determined to be contrary to the law of England. . . . [1]

Again:

. . . And as ancient Customs take place in England against ye Rule of ye Comon Law and are irreversible by anything short of an Act of Parliament, unless they are judged to be unreasonable and mischievous, so this Custom which has been more serviceable for ye promoting ye Settlement of this Colony and enlarging his Majties Dominion than ye Rule of the Comon Law would have been, as is manifest by the greater Increase of ye people in this and the neighboring Colonies where this Custom has prevailed, beyond ye Increase of the people, where ye Rule of the Comon law has taken place, as in N. York and other Provinces, on many other accounts under more enduring circumstances . . . [2] Since the reason obtained for the law in Boston to be different from the Comon Law of England, we hope we may have leave to mention the ancient maxim, the like reason, the like Law, and that is all we ask for.[3]

The requisite that the rule be reasonable would to the Puritans be synonymous with the principle that it be in consonance with their idea of the law of nature as manifested by the law of God. *Blankard v. Galdy* is the basis of the

[1] Conn. Hist. Soc., *Collections,* IV, 143 *et seq.; ibid.,* V, 421, 422. *Cf.* also *ibid.,* pp. 244, 245.

[2] *Ibid.,* p. 421, draft of address to the King, signed by Talcott.

[3] *Ibid.,* p. 429.

contention that, in a conquered country, prior to the conqueror's assertion of the law, natural equity, providing equal division of an intestate's property to all his children, saving a double portion to the eldest son, should rule. The preamble to the proposed gavelkind act of Connecticut of 1731 declares that such a rule " immediately became a Custom." [1] In the instructions to the home agent in *Clark v. Tousey,* the colonial government thought it " obvious " that in a new and unpopulated country " where Mankind are more wanted than land to subdue & Cultivate yᵉ Earth and Defend its Inhabitants, as was and still is the Case of Connecticut," their ancestors had chosen wisely in not following the common-law rule of descent. [2]

In the dispute over its intestacy law, Connecticut alleged that partible descent was the continuous and uninterrupted usage of the colony. Winthrop, in his appeal to the Privy Council to reverse the holding of the General Court in favor of partible descent and to give him his father's entire realty, rather than a mere two-thirds, maintained glibly that partible descent was " obsolete, made in yᵉ infancy of yᵉ Province." [3] Counsel for the respondents were unprepared with data to

---

[1] Conn. Hist. Soc., *Collections,* IV, pp. 441, 442. *Cf.* also draft of suggestion by Lieut. Governor Law to Wilks, *ibid.,* IV, 261.

[2] *Ibid.,* V, 489 *et seq.*

[3] He alleged further that " the first Govʳ, the appellants grandfatʳ, on receiving the Charter, was obliged to swear before a Maʳ in Chancery, that he and his successors would observe and keep the comon law of England," whereas it is no secret that the early Winthrops in both colonies were instrumental in developing the new practice and in ignoring the common law. Brief in Appeal to the Privy Council, written by Sir Philip York (afterwards Lord Chancellor Hardwicke), Attorney-General, and Charles Talbot (afterwards Lord Chancellor), Solicitor-General, 1727. Mass. Hist. Soc., *Collections,* 6th ser., V, 478. *Cf.* also, Paris to Allen, 1737, Conn. Hist. Soc., *Collections,* V, 78; and memoranda of the respondents: " 2ᵈ obj. Never put in use & obsolete. Not prepared wᵗʰ instances, nor any c. v." Mass. Hist. Soc., *Collections,* 6th ser., V, 495, 496.

meet this plea; and the appeal was sustained. But when
Clark v. Tousey, a test case, arose fifteen years later, Connecticut was found far better equipped with historical evidence. " There Cant be an Instance produced that the Eldest son Excluded the rest as heir at Law," wrote Governor
Talcott to Francis Wilks in 1740.[1] The brief for the
" American " custom of partible descent is asserted by the
respondents in *Phillips v. Savage*:

Descents must be governed by the circumstances of every
country, so that the rules about them will always be as different
as the state and situation of the country itself; and therefore
the only essential invariable requisite, is, that the descent be
fitting, and *reasonable, beneficial to the community, notorious,*
and *established.*   And the law in question reaches every branch
of this rule; for that it is fitting, reasonable and beneficial, appears as well from what has been just before urged, as from
the acquiescence and satisfaction of the whole collective body
of the Province for near a century under it without appeal; for,
even after such a long tract of time, the appellant stands alone
in his complaint.   That it is notorious and established can't be
contested, after so many confirmations of the law, and such
extensive practice and experience of it.[2]

The ultimate decision in favor of the intestacy law in the
action of *Phillips v. Savage,*[3] carried by appeal from the
Superior Court of Massachusetts to the King in Council,

[1] Conn. Hist. Soc., *Collections,* V, 343, 490.

[2] Mass. Hist. Soc., *Proceedings,* V, 78.

[3] As a matter of law, the decree of the King in Council in this case
did not rule on the usage and continuity of the custom, but merely asserted that " it appear'd to Their Lordships that, from that time (1692),
it had been the constant usage for the several judges of the court of
probates, &c. to cause the estates of all persons dying intestate to be
distributed pursuant to the tenor and according to the directions of the
said several acts of Assembly." (Feb. 15, 1737). *Ibid.,* XIII, 100-103.

and the dismissal of the suit of *Clark v. Tousey* on a technical ground, settled the question. The experience of the legal advisers of the home government in dealing with these colonial property practices served them in good stead in handling the Canadian situation. In the report undertaking to interpret the Proclamation of 1763, the French law in use in connection with titles, alienation and descent of realty was recognized.[1] Hillsborough wrote Carleton in 1768 that " it never entered into Our Idea to overturn the Laws and Customs of Canada, with regard to Property, but that Justice should be administered agreeably to them, according to the Modes of administering Justice in the Crts of Judicature in this Kingdom, as is the Case in the County of Kent, and many other parts of England, where Gavel-kind, Borough-English, and several other particular customs prevail, altho' Justice is administered therein according to the Laws of England." [2]

1. *The Descent of Entails under Customary Tenure*

When the attributes of divisible descent in New England are recognized as those of custom, it is clear that under the circumstances, and in accord with the prevailing doctrine of English law, the descent of entailed estates should have followed the customary descent of fee simple. In Rhode Island, where this issue was raised several times in the seventeenth century, it appears that the gavelkind rule was strictly enforced. In 1667 the council of the Town of Providence ordered that the property of an intestate be distributed, saving the widow's right, to her son,

---

[1] Ordinance of Nov. 6, 1764. Shortt and Doughty, editors, *Documents relating to the Constitutional History of Canada, 1759-1791* (Ottawa, 1907), p. 166; and report of Attorney and Solicitor-General, April 14, 1766, *ibid.*, p. 177. But *cf.* Carleton to Shelburne, Quebec, Dec. 24, 1767, *ibid.*, p. 202.

[2] Whitehall, Mar. 6, 1768. *Ibid.*, pp. 207, 208.

to have & hold for him & his Lawfull begotten & borne children if it please God to give him: & if he dye haveing no child then liveing then ye s^d howse & landes shall desend to his sister Hope; & if shee die first & leave a lawfull borne child it shall then decend to her s^d child, or children, according to the Law of the Charter to witt of Gavellkind land.[1]

In a conveyance executed in 1672, William Harris, the early Rhode Islander, entailed his grants to his children, specifying that the entails were to descend " according to ye Teanure of Gavillkind y^t is to say Equally to ye males of theyr Body lawfully Borne, & if neither males nor male, then to desend to ye Females or Female lawfully Borne of them or Either of them." [2] In his significant will, written six years later, Harris elaborately expounded the doctrine of partible descent in fee tail, calling upon the New England charters and Lambard's *Perambulations of Kent* for authority.[3] In this document the land is entailed to the fourth generation according to the custom of gavelkind.[4]

Unfortunately, in some jurisdictions where fee tail sub-

[1] Estate of Power (1667) *Prov. Rec.*, VII, 30-34.

[2] *Ibid.*, XIV, 60.

[3] *Ibid.*, VI, 48-56.

[4] This restraint on alienation to the fourth generation finds a parallel in the early cases interpreting the statute *de donis*. Cf. Belyng *v.* Anon (1312) 5 Edw. II, Selden Soc., *Publications*, XI, 176. The courts were apparently influenced (1) by the *fidei commissa* of Roman law, for Justinian's 159th Novel restrained fidei-commissary substitutions to that number of degrees, including the party who instituted the substitution (*cf.* Butler's notes on Coke's *First Inst.* [ed., 1809], 191a; with which compare Gibbon's criticism in *Decline and Fall of the Holy Roman Empire*, note 154 to chap. XLIV) ; and (2) by popular customs. Cf. Seebohm, *Tribal System of Wales*, p. 73. Modern Maltese law provides an entail that seems to be absolute to and including the fourth degree, after which it becomes alienable. C. M. Updegraff, " Interpretation of ' Issue' in the Statute De Donis," *Harvard Law Review* (1925-1926), XXXIX, 200 at p. 212.

sists, the courts have not followed this doctrine, and, when the question arose in the last century, it was treated virtually as one of first impression. I have discussed these modern cases at length elsewhere.[1] In Massachusetts, in Maine which follows the law as it existed in Massachusetts prior to its separation from the Bay State, and in Pennsylvania (as to all property conveyed by deed or devised by will prior to the Act of 1855 which converted fees tail into fee-simple estates), entails, as a result of these modern decisions, descend according to the common-law rule of primogeniture. The courts in these jurisdictions narrowly interpreted the statutes of descent which specifically refer only to fee-simple estates, holding that entails were expressly excluded from the general course of descent.[2] On the other hand, when the same question arose in New Hampshire and Connecticut, the courts, in complete accord with public sentiment and the colonial position on the question of intestate succession, repudiated primogeniture in entails.[3] In construing the statutes of descent, the courts of Massachusetts and Pennsylvania gave no intimation of having observed a fundamental rule of statutory interpretation, — that the historic background of the enactment should be taken into consideration.[4] Hence, instead of interpreting the statute of descent as " a

---

[1] *Cf.* my " Primogeniture and Entailed Estates in America," *Columbia Law Review*, XXVII, 47 *et seq.*

[2] The leading modern cases are: Davis *v.* Hayden (1813) 9 Mass. 514; Corbin *v.* Healy (1838) 37 Mass. 514; Goodright *v.* Morningstar (Pa., 1793) 1 Yeates 313; Price *v.* Taylor (1857) 28 Pa. St. 95, 105, and Williams and Wife *v.* Leach *et al.* (1856) 28 Pa. St. 89, *contra* favoring partible descent, but overruled in Guthrie's Appeal (1860) 37 Pa. St. 9, 10, 21.

[3] Jewell *v.* Warner (1857) 35 N. H. 176; Larabee *v.* Larabee (Conn., 1793) 1 Root 555. *Cf.* also Swift, *A System of the Laws of the State of Connecticut* (Windham, 1795), I, 247.

[4] *Cf.* Heydon's Case (1584) 3 Co. Rep. 7 (b).

judicial creation in the light of social demands," [1] these courts have disregarded both the demand and the policy behind the statutes.

It is manifest that entailed estates and primogeniture were in disaccord with colonial life and with the statutes and judicial practices which borrowed their substantive content directly from customary usage.[2]   In Massachusetts, the Act of 1692,[3] following the policy of the Liberties of 1641, provided for divisible descent in intestate succession and the assimilation of realty and personalty for that purpose; thus serving as a model for later colonial legislation.[4]   To its intrinsic merit, the English Real Property Act of 1925 bears tribute,[5] and the modern legislation which has as its social object the liquidity of land.   In England, the descent of entailed peerages to the eldest sons has been challenged on the ground that eldest sons have shown politically anything but a monopoly of hereditary virtue.   In this country, by the beginning of the federal era, primogeniture had been repudiated, and the widespread adoption of such characteristic colonial legislation as the abolition of survivorship in joint tenancies,[6] and the levy of execution on the property of a

[1] *Cf.* M. R. Cohen, " The Process of Judicial Legislation," *Amer. Law Review*, XLVIII, 161, 183.

[2] This view that custom suggests the rules of law but is not law *per se* is ably presented by John Dickinson, " The Law behind Law," *Columbia Law Rev.*, XXIX, 113-146.

[3] *Ancient Charters*, pp. 230-232.

[4] The New Hampshire act of 1703, with exactly the same wording as the Massachusetts act, was disallowed in 1706. *New Hamp. Prov. Laws*, I, 566, 567, 646; II, 295. The law was reenacted in 1718 in disregard of the home authorities. *Ibid.*, II, 241, 295. *Cf.* also act of 1699, *Conn. Pub. Rec.*, IV, 307; *Laws of Penn,* (Franklin ed, 1742), App. 5; *ibid.*, p. 60.

[5] Administration of Estates Act, 15 Geo. 5, c. 23, §§ 1, 45.

[6] Brigham, *Compact and Charters*, pp. 75, 279; *Mass. Perpetual Laws* (1784), I, 162.

deceased debtor,[1] was evidence of the liberal trend in property law. It is significant that the philosophers of the Cotton Kingdom, convinced that conservatism was the best weapon for self-preservation, advocated, prior to the Civil War, the creation of entails and the re-introduction of primogeniture.[2] It was a far cry from Jefferson to Fitzhugh, and the American states did not propose to heed it; it was a devious road from the Body of Liberties to the line of modern cases maintaining the English rule of descent in entailed estates in some jurisdictions, but the courts have followed it and have not realized in which direction they have traveled.[3]

This study cannot be concluded without mentioning the telling argument against too great distribution of realty which has been drawn from modern agricultural experience. In Canada, partible descent worked such excessive subdivisions that a royal edict of 1745 was necessary to restrict

---

[1] *New Hamp. Prov. Laws*, II, 293; *Mass. Acts and Resolves*, I, 68, 69 (1692); *ibid.*, II, 42, 43 (1716); 150, 151 (1719); Brigham, *Compact*, pp. 33, 282. In explaining the differences between the North Carolina act of 1716, § 12, subjecting the lands of fugitive debtors to the payment of their debts, and the English rule, Governor Burrington states "that Lands in England being improved to a great yearly value may by the annual income on an extent pay the Debt but Lands here are generally of little yearly rent and the Benifit of them is the accruing Improvements of the Occupyer which on extent in the end he must loose the Benefit off would be too hard." *N. C. Col. Rec.*, III, 182.

[2] Fitzhugh, *Sociology for the South* (Richmond, Va., 1854), pp. 189-193. An interesting analogy was the abortive proposal of de Peyronnet during the Restoration regime of Charles X in France for the partial reintroduction of primogeniture. For the popular reaction, *cf.* A. de Lamartine, *Histoire de la Restauration* (n. p., 1851-2), vol.. viii, pp. 58-60.

[3] Since January 1, 1926, the analogous problem as to the descent of entails in England is likely to be raised The Administration of Estates Act, abolishing descent to the heir-at-law, does not affect entailed interests. §§ 1, 45 (2). Hence entails will descend according to the general rule of descent prevailing before 1926. Law of Property Act (1925), 15 Geo. 5, c. 20, §§ 130-134. For general effect, *cf.* Sanger, " Estates Tail under the New Law," *Cambridge Law Journal*, II, 212.

this practice. The disregard of this edict when Canada came under British control was the subject of much criticism by the attorney-general.[1] Similarly the establishment of egalitarian inheritance in France has resulted in the division of agricultural lands into relatively small holdings, and in this way has prevented the effecting of greater economies by large-scale production, and the opportunities for experimentation presented thereby.[2] A similar situation exists in India.[3] In Roumania alienation and subdivisions of the land of the peasants have been restricted within definite limits in order to avoid the undesirable effects resulting from equality under the civil code.[4] Recent studies indicate that the large plantation and the tenant-farmer are supplanting the smaller freehold in the New South; that agricultural experience favors the large plantation organization in that region;[5] and that throughout the United States there has been in recent years an appreciable increase in the total acreage operated by tenants.[6] Whether these agrarian readjustments will necessitate a change in our rules of succession is a problem for the future.

[1] Correspondence and reports of Francis Masère, 1769-1774. Shortt and Doughty, *op. cit.*, pp. 241, 262, 373, 374. *Cf.* also W. B. Munro, *The Seignorial System in Canada* (New York, 1907), pp. 83, 84.

[2] *Cf.* M. Augé-Laribé, *L'évolution de la France agricole*, p. 103.

[3] Aubrey O'Brien, "The Welfare of the Indian Agriculturist," *Nineteenth Century* (Sept., 1928), pp. 322-331.

[4] Ifor L. Evans, *The Agrarian Revolution in Roumania* (Cambridge, Eng., 1924), pp. 38, 39, 123 *et seq.*

[5] *Cf.* C. O. Brannen, *Relation of Land Tenure to Plantation Organization with developments since 1920.* Fayetteville, 1928.

[6] L. C. Gray, "The Trend in Farm Ownership," Amer. Acad. Pol. Sci., *Annals*, CXLII, 20-26.

CHAPTER III

Women's Rights in Early American Law

A. THE COLONIAL CONCEPT OF MARRIAGE IN RELATION TO THE LEGAL POSITION OF WOMAN

THE new legal rights which married women acquired to a greater or lesser degree throughout the colonies evolved out of the revised concept of the institution of marriage which resulted from the Protestant Revolution and out of the different economic and social conditions of colonial America. The concept of marriage and its celebration which was held throughout the colonies in the seventeenth and eighteenth centuries bore closer affinity to the attitude of the continental reformers and of the civil law than to the prevailing doctrines of the Anglican Church. The Reformation view of marriage as a civil contract based on the mutual consent of the parties was directly opposed to the belief of the medieval church that marriage was a sacrament valid but not spiritually complete, without the public blessing of the church, and lying within the jurisdiction of the ecclesiastical courts. The notion of mutuality basic in the civil marriage lay at the root of the substantial advance in the position of the wife in seventeenth-century American law.

The policy behind the colonial marriage legislation seems to have been threefold: firstly, to expedite the marriage of the parties and to obviate breaches of the contract to marry *in futuro*; secondly, to see that the marriage covenant was kept, to punish its traducers, and to enjoin matrimonial society upon wedded couples whose affections for each other had grown tepid; thirdly, in cases of a breach of the covenant, manifested by various types of conduct, to dissolve the contract in order to prevent its desecration, and to make possible new matrimonial engineering upon happier and more lasting foundations. In order that marriage might be given a fair trial, its reciprocal rights and duties were vigorously asserted by the courts. (1) The courts clearly recognized the right of both the husband and the wife to the consortium of the other spouse, and to that end enjoined compulsory cohabitation upon couples whose mutual indifference had led to their separation, and ordered wife-deserters to return home. (2) The courts throughout the colonies took practical steps to compel recreant husbands to support their wives and children, and, in the south, an action for alimony independent of the suit for judicial separation was frequently brought. (3) The married woman was protected from the personal abuse, the cruelty, and the improper conduct exercised toward her by her husband. This attitude of humane paternalism over marriage was without precedent at common law. Richardson's *Pamela* regarded marriage as " a kind of state of humiliation for a woman." While such a description was no doubt a fair estimate of the condition of most married women of her day in England, it would not be applicable to the American colonies.

Material relating to the problem of marriage and divorce in colonial law has been reserved for a subsequent study. But it may be sufficient to suggest here that the acceptance of the marriage contract as a reciprocal agreement helped materially to raise woman from the state of legal subordination which was her position in England. A significant analogy may be found in the Roman law. Under the Roman Republic the institution of the marriage by *usus,* or the free marriage, developed alongside the formal marriage with *manus,* and rapidly ousted its rival. As the reciprocal nature of the matrimonial contract was stressed in the free marriage, the legal position of the Roman matron was materially improved. Under the Empire she was virtually her own mistress. Practically independent of her father, she was legally independent of her husband, and could bring suit and hold and dispose of property freely.

At common law the married woman's general incapacity to contract and the absence of her right to sue in tort or to be sued as a feme sole was due to the lack of her proprietary capacity. In the American colonies the proprietary capacity of the married woman was measurably enlarged, and with it came an enlargement of her contractual and tortious rights and liabilities. The bases for this change in the legal status of women may be found in the changing economic and social conditions in colonial America. The origin of the common-law restrictions against the property rights of married women can be traced to the feudal system; in medieval England this system supplanted the practices of community property which obtained among merchants. Married women's proprietary rights and their rights to make contracts persisted merely as local custom in some of the commercial boroughs.[1] With the advent of the commercial revolution the relative significance of real property declined. In America, particularly in New England, commercial enterprise contributed materially to regional prosperity, even though the colonies were primarily agrarian in interest. The commercial revolution stamped its impress more speedily upon American legal economics than upon that of England, where the conservative policy of the common-law courts remained centuries behind economic progress.

As a result of the new economic conditions in the colonies, women, both married and single, were attaining a measure

---

[1] Holdsworth, *History of English Law*, III, 524, 525, and *cf. infra*, § 2, *Married Woman's Contractual Capacity*.

of individuality and independence in excess of that of their English sisters. Women acted in their own interest and in behalf of their husbands in conducting mercantile establishments and in supervising landed estates. These factors brought about the obsolescence of the concept of the unity of husband and wife in marriage to form one legal personality, which, for all practical purposes, was the husband.

In some of the trading communities in England the wife acting as a merchant was regarded as a feme sole.[1] The individual and virtually independent conduct of mercantile and other establishments by married women progressed during the eighteenth century, as the *Sessions Papers* of Old Bailey, summarized by Miss George,[2] indicate. In New England and the middle colonies there are numerous instances where married women and widows conducted important business establishments in the colonial period: Mary Spratt, later the wife of James Alexander, Anne Waddell, Mrs. Mary Smith, Mrs. Robert Sanders, and Ann Elizabeth Schuyler are a few illustrations chosen from the province of New York. Martha Smith, widow, of St. George's Manor, Long Island, was a leading entrepreneur in the whale fishery. Women partnerships, and partnerships of women and men, are frequent, one instance being the firm of Robert Charles and Mary Jackson in Boston.[3] Mrs. Dexter, in her investigation of the subject, concludes on the basis of rather limited evidence that in the eighteenth century there were more women merchants and dealers proportionally than there were in this country in 1900.[4] Special tribute to the impor-

---

[1] *Borough Customs*, Selden Soc., *Publications*, I, 227, 228; II, cxii.

[2] M. Dorothy George, *London Life in the XVIIIth Century* (New York, 1925), pp. 427 *et seq.*

[3] *Boston Evening Post*, March 26, 1744.

[4] Elizabeth A. Dexter, *Colonial Women of Affairs. A Study of Women in Business and the Professions in America before 1776* (Boston, 1924), p. 37.

tance of the legal problem raised by married women in business is paid in the colonial statutes " concerning feme-sole traders," [1] discussed hereafter.

Doubtless the important position which colonial women occupied as landowners accounts for the expansion of legal devices to increase their proprietary capacity. Notable and fairly representative examples may be chosen: Mrs. John Davenport, wife of the minister of New Haven, looked after the extensive property interests of John Winthrop the younger when political business kept him in England.[2]   In Maryland, Margaret Brent supervised her own manor and conducted her own court baron. According to the record, at one of its sessions in 1659 " a tenant appeared, did fealty to the lady, and took seisin of a message of thirty-seven acres by delivery of a rod," as was the custom of the manor.[3] Mistress Brent, aside from important landed interests which she had in her own right in Maryland, was the executor of the estate of Governor Leonard Calvert. The Maryland Provincial Court Records are replete with real property actions which she carried on in her own name. In the records of the Maryland Land Office is found a query of Mistress Brent in regard to a claim to escheat.

At a court held at St. Mairies, 7th December, 1648, came Mrs. Margaret Brent and required the opinion of the court concerning . . . the tenements appertaining to the rebels within his

[1] Act of 1718, c. 226. Carey and Bioren, *Pa. Laws*, I, 116, 117. *Cf.* also Amy Hewes, " Early Eighteenth Century Women," *Commonwealth History of Massachusetts* (New York, 1928), II, 355-417, especially p. 372.

[2] Mass. Hist. Soc., *Collections*, 4th ser., VII, 492 *et seq*. Colonial women frequently were landladies and collected rents. *Cf.* e. g., MSS. Memoranda Book of Anna Hooglandt, 1729-1738, containing a record of accounts received on lands and rents in New York, NYHS. A typical instance of a lawsuit brought by a colonial landlady on a contract for rent is Jansen *v.* Ellekesen (1654) Fernow, *Rec. Amst.*, I, 174.

[3] Cited by Dexter, *op. cit.*, p. 98.

Manors, whether or no their forfeitures belonged to the Lord of the Manors. The resolution of the court was that the said forfeitures did of right belong to the Lord of the Manors by virtue of his Lordship's Conditions of Plantation.[1]

In New England there are instances where land grants were made by the courts to married women whose husbands were living.[2] Generally women who were heads of families received their proportion of planting land.[3] A further instance of the extreme social pressure exercised in behalf of the marital career was the discrimination against spinsters in the distribution of property. Thus, in the early period of its history, Salem authorities granted so-called "maids lotts," but, as Governor Endicott notes, the town soon manifested a desire to avoid " all presedents & evill events of graunting lotts vnto single maidens not disposed of." In accord with this new policy, Deborah Holmes was refused land, " being a maid," but the Governor in his magnanimity granted her a bushel of Indian corn, assuring her that it " would be a bad president to keep hous alone." [4]

In addition to cases where women acted as independent entrepreneurs, they were frequently authorized to represent their husbands in assertion or defence of the latter's legal and economic interests. Throughout the colonies married women constantly acted as attorneys for their husbands, often in their husbands' absence, both suing on their hus-

[1] " Landholder's Assistant," quoted by Kilty, *Laws of Maryland*, I, 104.

[2] Grant to Sarah, wife of Thomas Haward, Jr. (1667) *Ply. Col. Rec.*, IV, 159. According to the record the husband appears to have been alive the next year (1668), *ibid.*, p. 193.

[3] *Salem Town Records*, I, 21-27.

[4] *Salem Town Records*, I, 28, 32, cited by Herbert B. Adams, " Village Communities of Cape Anne and Salem," *Johns Hopkins Studies in Hist. and Polit. Sci.*, IX, X, 35.

bands' contracts [1] and tort claims, [2] and defending their husbands' suits. [3] While this practice prevailed throughout the colonies, it was most common in New Netherland. Wives were often required to present in court letters of attorney from their husbands. [4] In a few New Amsterdam cases, where it appeared that the plaintiff or defendant whose wife was acting as his attorney was in town, he was required to appear in person. [5] The most celebrated instance when a woman acted as a colonial attorney is that of Mistress Margaret Brent, whom Governor Leonard Calvert of Maryland

[1] Estate of William Snelling (1679) *Assistants*, I, 153; Peacock *v.* Pen (1684) *ibid.*, p. 273; Hundlock *v.* Hubbard (1685) *ibid.*, p. 294; Craford *v.* Savage (1666) *Essex*, III, 330-333; Morgen *v.* Vis (1653) Fernow, *Rec. Amst.*, I, 136; Kraey *v.* Kuyper (1654) *ibid.*, p. 149; Steendam *v.* Leeck (1651) *ibid.*, p. 261; Jacob and Hans *v.* van Couwenhoven (1654) *ibid.*, p. 234, both wives appearing for plaintiffs; Antony *v.* Michiel *et al.* (1668) *ibid.*, VI, 146; Jochemsen *v.* Turcq (1669) *ibid.*, p. 203; Aldrits *v.* Dircksen (1678/9) Pa. Hist. Soc., *Memoirs*, VII, 128 (Upland Court).

[2] Joung *v.* Taylor (1680) *Newcastle Rec.*, p. 438.

[3] Jansen's case (1653) Fernow, *Rec. Amst.*, I, 112; Withart *v.* Smith (1655) *ibid.*, p. 399; Van Couwenhoven *v.* Stoffels (1666) *ibid.*, VI, 11, 27; Schout *v.* Vervilen (1666) *ibid.*, p. 39; Sharp *v.* Smedes (1666) *ibid.*, p. 46; De Wit *v.* Schol (1667) *ibid.*, p. 81; Smedes *v.* Jansen (1667) *ibid.*, p. 96; Goosens *v.* Carpyn (1667/8) *ibid.*, p. 110; Gerrits *v.* Barentsen (1667) *ibid.*, p. 72; Hussey *v.* Hammond (1658) *Md. Arch.*, XLI, 73; Low and wife *v.* Kitching (1694[5]) *N. C. Col. Rec.*, I, 443.

[4] Meggs' case (1652) *New Haven Town Rec.*, I, 104; van Borsum *v.* van Beeck (1654) Fernow, *Rec. Amst.*, I, 248; Schellinger *v.* van Dincklagen (1655) *ibid.*, pp. 296, 297; Heath *et ux. v.* Blydenburgh (1699) Supreme Court of Judicature, New York Hist. Soc., *Collections,* XXV, 160, 173, 176; Williams *v.* Tallent (1679/80) *Newcastle Rec.*, p. 374.

[5] Schrick *v.* Rapaeje (1653) Fernow, *Rec. Amst.*, I, 109; Planck *v.* Teunessen (1653) *ibid.*, p. 50; Tomasen *v.* Paulisen (1654) *ibid.*, p. 188. In Rapalje *v.* Clyn the plaintiff was represented by his wife. The defendant maintained that he had " no question with the woman, but with her husband." Nevertheless the court gave judgment for the plaintiff. *Ibid.*, p. 338.

appointed in 1647 as his executor. The Archives are replete with records of her suits. In one case, notable in the early annals of woman suffrage, the archives tell us that on January 21, 1648,

. . . came Mrs. Margarett Brent and requested to have vote in the howse for herselfe and voyce allso, for that att the last Court 3d Jan. it was ordered that the said Mrs. Brent was to be looked upon and received as his Lps. Attorney. The Govr. denyed that the sd. Mrs. Brent should have any vote in the Howse. And the sd. Mrs. Brent protested against all proceedings in this present Assembly unless she may be present and have vote as aforesd.[1]

The situation presented in the Maryland courts where women frequently acted as attorneys soon aroused the conservative authorities to enact a measure calculated to suppress these ultra-modern activities. In 1658, by proclamation, husbands were forbidden to appoint their wives as their attorneys in their absence, but were requested to appoint " some other Attorney " in their stead.[2]

The emergence of the colonial woman as a distinct personality led to a demand on her part for greater political and social recognition as well as for greater rights at law. In the columns of the *New York Journal* for January 21, 1733 is found this interesting letter to its editor, the famous Zenger:

Mr Zenger,

We, the widdows of this city, have had a Meeting, and as our case is something Deplorable, we beg you will give it Place in your *Weekly Journal*, that we may be Relieved, it is as follows.

We are the House keepers, Pay our Taxes, carry on Trade, and most of us are she Merchants, and as we in some measure

[1] *Md. Arch.*, I, 215.
[2] *Md. Arch.*, XLI, 233.

contribute to the Support of Government, we ought to be Intituled to some of the Sweets of it; but we find ourselves entirely neglected, while the Husbands that live in our Neighborhood are daily invited to Dine at Court; we have the Vanity to think we can be full as Entertaining, and make as brave a Defence in Case of an Invasion and Perhaps not turn Taile as soon as some of them.

The consequences attendant upon this derisive complaint do not appear on record. One result of the granting of Georgia lands in tail male at the time of settlement was that women were deprived of any inheritable interest in the property of the colony. This defect contributed to the series of complaints which were discussed in a previous study and which culminated in the abolition of the practice of making entailed grants. According to a remarkable alteration in the tenure ordered for Georgia in 1739, the eldest daughter, if unmarried and not possessed of any land in her own right, was to succeed where the tenant died intestate without male heirs. General Oglethorpe, who disliked these orders, neglected to carry them out.[1] After much controversy, and as a result of considerable agitation in the colony, the trustees in 1740 resolved that previous restrictions confining devices which could be made to daughters to less than five hundred acres be amended to permit the accumulation of as much as two thousand acres.[2]

Women were not successful in aspiring, if they in fact had the aspiration, to political and social equality. The New England town meeting gave preference to men in seating,[3] and the colonial franchise was everywhere denied women

---

[1] Journal of the Earl of Egmont, *Ga. Col. Rec.*, V, 210, 211.

[2] *Ga. Col. Rec.*, II, 338; Journal of the Earl of Egmont, Aug. 23, 1739, *ibid.*, V, 216, 217.

[3] *Cf.* e. g. (1674) *New Haven Town Rec.*, II, 319.

" sole or covert." [1]   In rights at private law, colonial women fared much better.

B. THE MARRIED WOMAN'S PROPRIETARY CAPACITY

At common law the husband had extensive control over his wife's possessions.   He was entitled to the sole administration of all her property.   The personalty which he reduced to possession became his own.   He had the administration and usufruct of his wife's realty.   While he could not affect the substance of such property, he was entitled to the income and profits and was not required to account for the same.[2] In the sixteenth and early seventeenth centuries a good deal of dissatisfaction was manifest by women of the wealthier classes, and their relatives, with the inequitable restrictions imposed by the common law.   Efforts to ameliorate this undesirable condition were made by the Court of Chancery in this period.   In the first place, though the decisions are not uniform, Chancery recognized the device of a contract entered into before marriage.[3]   In the second place, use was made of the machinery of the trust, by means of which a proprietary capacity could, where the court deemed it fair and reasonable, be conferred on a married woman.[4]

In seventeenth-century colonial America equitable jurisdiction was assumed by the " common-law " courts, and ante-nuptial contracts were recognized.   These settlements were viewed as prudent provisions for the maintenance of the woman regardless of the changes of fortune in her husband's affairs.   In 1667, " upon a motion of marriage betwixt John Phillips, of Marshfield, and Faith Dotey, of Plymouth," the

---

[1] *Cf.* e. g., act of 1699, Hening, *Statutes at Large of Va.*, II, 172.

[2] Pollock and Maitland, *History of English Law*, II, 401-403.

[3] Avenant *v.* Kitchin (1581-1582) Choyce Cases 154; Palmer *v.* Keynall (1637-1638) Ch. Rep. 118.

[4] Flecton *v.* Dennys (1594) Monro, *Acta Cancellaria*, pp. 656-659, and cases cited by Holdsworth, *Hist. Eng. Law*, V, 314, 315.

parties entered into a contract, which, in addition to securing
for Faith a one-third interest in John's estate upon his decease, provided

. . . That the said Faith Dotey is to enjoy all her house and
land, goods, and cattles, that shee is now possessed of, to her
owne proper use, to dispose of them att her owne free will from
time to time, and att any time, as shee shall see cause.[1]

The power of disposition sanctioned in this pre-nuptial contract was not clearly recognized by the Court of Chancery
in contemporary England;[2] it was patently in derogation of
the common law. The only secure method of conferring this
power of disposition upon a married woman was by means
of the trust.[3]   On the other hand, the common law had upheld an agreement between a man and a woman if the obligation arose only after the determination of the marriage.[4]
In the colonies this hesitancy vanished.   Following the Plymouth precedent, the General Court of Connecticut in 1673
allowed £200 to be set aside from the estate of Thomas
Fairchild, to satisfy the pre-nuptial obligations owing to his
wife.[5]   Likewise after the dissolution of the marriage, the
pre-nuptial property arrangement was upheld by the Connecticut assembly.[6]

A seventeenth-century Long Island agreement illustrates
that in the ante-nuptial contract the woman often drove a
sharp bargain.   This contract was drawn up between Captain
Elbert Elbertz Stoothoff and Saartje Roelofs in 1683, and
it provides in part

---

[1] *Ply. Col. Rec.*, IV, 163.

[2] Holdsworth, *op. cit.*, V, 311, 312.

[3] Bannister *v.* Brooke (1619) Tothill 158.

[4] Smith *v.* Stafford (1618) Hob. 216, dissenting Hobart; Clark *v.*
Thomson (1620) Cro. Jac. 571; Lupert *v.* Hoblin (1657) 2 Sid. 58.

[5] Petition of Fayrechild (1673) *Conn. Pub. Rec.*, II, 198, 199.

Petition of Wolcott (1774) *ibid.*, XIV, 387, 388.

. . . that the aforesaid bridegroom, for the support and maintenance of this marriage and to the advantage of the family, shall bring in such goods as he, the party appearing by the blessing of God has acquired, nothing thereof being reserved, but shall have no common ownership, in the estate and property of the aforesaid future bride, and shall also bring in whatever he shall obtain and acquire hereafter; and that the future bride, for the support and maintenance of this marriage, shall not bring in anything, but that she, with her two children, Rachel and Anna, shall be cared for and supported out of the estate and property of her future bridegroom as to board and clothing, as is otherwise honorable and befitting. Wherefore it is provided and stipulated, that the property, movable and immovable, present and future, nothing excepted, shall be held in common ownership with the estate and property of the aforesaid future bridegroom, but that she shall hold and control her goods separately, either by herself or others; and dispose thereof as she shall see fit, without the future bridegroom having or claiming any guardianship, power or administration over the property of the future bride, against her will or desire; but that the same property, with that added and acquired, shall remain to her forever and as an inheritance, and at her demise to her child or children and the legal successors thereof. And on account of the aforesaid stipulated condition a list of the goods of the future bride shall be made and signed by them both and entered on the minute hereof. . . . Further it is expressly stipulated and provided that as to all debts and obligations contracted before the date of this marriage by one of the parties hereto, their persons and property shall not be claimed, molested or attached, much less sold under execution directly or indirectly, in any manner, inasmuch as all community of debts and property between the two aforesaid contracting parties is most expressly prohibited and excluded hereby . . [1]

---

[1] Stoothoff Papers, Long Island Historical Society; cited by Frederick Van Wyck, *Keskachauge, or The First White Settlement on Long Island* (New York, 1924), pp. 738-740.

A similar degree of caution was exercised by a Maryland widow, whose second husband, prior to the nuptials, agreed " not to lay any Clayme to or Intermeddle with all or any part of the Estate " of her deceased first husband. Provision was made that she be permitted to control this property for the benefit of her children by her first marriage.[1] Ante-nuptial contracts of this character were widely employed.

The legality of an ante-nuptial contract was upheld in the late provincial period in Massachusetts by the Governor and Council. In 1762 Elizabeth Keith of Easton brought suit against her husband on a pre-nuptial contract and petitioned for a divorce from bed and board on the ground of his cruel conduct. She alleged that her husband endeavored " by threats and perswasions " to rescind the agreement. Before judgment the parties submitted to a new agreement, according to which, after providing for yearly alimony to be paid Elizabeth and allowing her the household goods she brought with her at her marriage, the contract specifies that her husband " shall be intirely free from any other demand, from the said Elizabeth except what arises from the original contract made before their intermarriage, which contract is to remain good," saving minor modifications. A decree in accord with this separation agreement, and based on the ante-nutial contract, was rendered.[2]

Because of the illusion which the law nurtured concerning the complete unity of husband and wife, contracts between married parties were proscribed at common law, just as conveyances between husband and wife were disallowed.[3] In

[1] Contract between Peter Godson and Jane Moore (1654) *Md. Arch.*, X, 395, 396.

[2] Keith *v.* Keith (1762) MSS. "Divorce," fol. 24-26, Suffolk Court (Boston, Mass).

[3] *The Lawes Resolutions of Womens Rights: or, the Lawes Provision for Woemen* (London, 1632) (hereafter *Lawes Resolutions*), pp. 120-123.

conformity with this view, it was held in Chancery that there could be no contract between husband and wife,[1] that neither could sue the other,[2] and that after marriage no variation of any settlement made before marriage could be effected by agreement.[3] It is none the less clear that in the American colonies in the seventeenth century post-nuptial contracts were upheld.

The post-nuptial contract in most frequent use was the separation agreement. In 1686, Dorothy Clarke of Plymouth, who had unsuccessfully sought a divorce from her husband on the ground of his impotence, placed on record in court an agreement made with her spouse, which reads in part as follows:

July ye 10th, 1686. Whereas Mrs Dorothy Clarke hath exhibited a complaint unto the Court against her husband, Nathaniel Clarke, in order to a divorce, and prosecuted the same att his maties Courts held at Plimouth in June & July, 1686, and she not having made out her charge, as may appear by Court records, that soe they still remaine husband and wife. There being such an uncomfortable difference between the said Clarke and his wife, and fearing least they should ruine each other in their estates, have mutually agreed to a settlement in that respect untill the law otherways determine or they agree themselves. The conditions of the agreement betweene themselves are these following, vizt: that the new house is in the sd Nath Clarkes possession as his and his wives estate, she having liberty to live in part of the sd house to the quantity of half if she please, and he, the sd Clarke, to have all the estate that he brought with him to be dd up to him, sd Clarke, excepting what he hath disposed of by her or said Clarke, & one lhld of

[1] Stoit *v.* Ayloff (1632-1633) 1 Ch. Rep. 60.

[2] Simpson *v.* Simpson (1627-1628) Tothill 97.

[3] Dockwray *v.* Poole (1609) Tothill 98.

rum in Clarkes hands for the finishing of the new house, and three barrells of cyder for his own drinking, or at his dispose. The sᵈ Nathˡˡ Clarke is not to be charged with any obligation, bond, or debt, &c, that she, the sᵈ Dorothy, hath already or shall make, contract, and to save harmles the sᵈ Clarke from the matters of administration of the estate of her late husband, Edio Gray, and that she deliver up to the sᵈ Clarke his bond given to her before marriage. And the sᵈ Dorothy is not to be charged with any obligation, bond or debt, that he, the sᵈ Clarke, hath already, or shall make, or contract . . . [1]

The legality of such a post-nuptial agreement was attacked in a suit brought in 1674 by Mistress Hallet of Jamaica, New York, against her husband, for the non-performance of a contract providing for a yearly payment to the wife. The contract was the consequence of their mutual disagreement and refusal to cohabit. Hallet's offer to cohabit with his wife being rejected, he alleged that the contract was "voyd & contrary to Law." The Court of Sessions at Jamaica regarded the case as "of extraordinary Concernm't," and referred it to the Governor. That official directed that Hallet appear and state "his Reasons why he makes not good his covenant & to do Justice therein." [2] A definite holding on the point at issue does not appear.

Similarly in Maryland in 1656, after attempts on the part of the judiciary to effect a reconciliation between husband and wife had failed, there was placed on record at court an agreement between the parties for the separate control of their property and for the payment by the husband in tobacco of amounts received by him on accounts due his wife. On her part, the wife freed her husband of any duty of further maintenance. The equitable character of this agreement was

[1] *Ply. Col. Rec.*, VI, 190, 191, 203.

[2] Hallet *v.* Hallet (1674) New York State Hist., *3d Annual Report*, pp. 252, 257.

recognized by the court, which had instructed the arbitrators who had effected the contract " to find what might be done in a way of Equity." [1]

A resident of Providence in 1691 attacked the legality of such a contract when it was pointed out to him that the agreement he had made with his wife gave her the power of disposition over his estate. The husband therefore had placed on record in court his declaration that the contract was null and void, " as it also legally is in it selfe," he observed parenthetically.[2]

A second use for the post-nuptial contract was as a basis of reconciliation by a married couple. In token of such reconciliation and to obviate further marital strife, a Rhode Island husband promised his wife to bequeath her his realty upon his death. This property she was to have " dureing her remaineing a widdow;" upon her re-marriage, she was merely to retain a third interest. He further promised not to sell or mortgage his realty without her consent and to bequeath to her his chattels, including his sailing vessels. She in return promised to give back any beds beyond one which she might have disposed of in her absence from her husband.[3]

A much more elaborate working business and social agreement was drawn up by a reunited couple at Eastville, Northampton County, Virginia, in 1714. From the post-nuptial contract it appears that John Custis and his wife Frances, having had a disagreement, are inspired with hope and faith that they may renew " perfect love and friendship " by bond and covenant. First, therefore, it is stipulated that " the sd Frances shall return to the sd John all the money, Plate and

---

[1] Post-nuptial agreement between Cannady and his wife (1656) *Md. Arch.*, X, 471.

[2] Instrument of Ephraim Pierce (1691) *Early Records of Providence,* IV, 83.

[3] Contract of George and Rachael Potter (1669) *ibid.*, V, 9.

other things what soever that she hath from him or removed
out of the house upon oath and may be obliged never to take
away by herself or any other anything of value from him
again or run him in debt without his consent, nor sell, give
away or dispose of anything of value out of the family without his consent, upon the condition that the plate and damaske
linen " shall not be given away or otherwise disposed of by
the said John during her life, but be delivered to his children
" by the said Frances immediately after her decease." It is
further agreed that " Frances shall henceforth forbear to
call him yᵉ sd John any vile names or give him any ill language." Neither shall he give her any, but that they are
" to live lovingly together and to behave themselves to each
other as a good husband & good wife ought to doe. And
that she shall not intermeddle with his affairs but that all
business belonging to the husband's management shall be
solely transacted by him, neither shall he intermeddle in her
domestique affairs but that all business properly belonging
to the wife shall be solely transacted by her." After settling
his debts, John gives bond in the sum of £1,000 that he will
keep " true and perfect accounts of all the profitts and dis-
bursements of his whole Estate," and that he will " produce
the same accounts yearly if it be required upon oath." After
deducting necessary expenditures on the plantation, he prom-
ises further " freely & without grudging " to " allow one
full moity . . . . of his whole estate " to his wife annually
for personal and household expenses and for the education
of the children, so long as she remains peacefully with him.
In addition, the husband stipulates a definite weekly allowance of victuals, which, if exceeded, is to cease and the
" bond to be voyd." [1]

In the late provincial era, despite conservative tendencies
appearing in other branches of the law, the validity of sep-

[1] *Va. Mag. of Hist. and Biog.*, IV, 64-66.

aration agreements continued to be upheld. Thus, in the libel which Ann Vansise of New York City brought against her husband Cornelius before the Governor and Council of Massachusetts in 1764, for restitution of conjugal affection and maintenance, there was submitted in evidence a separation agreement between the parties, according to which Vansise had promised his wife annual alimony of £10 sterling. The Governor and Council, upon perusal of the agreement, ordered that the parties be separated from bed and board, and that the financial terms of the contract be carried out, including payment of the four years in which the husband was in arrears.[1] In the case of *Richardson v. Mountjoy*,[2] a Virginia court held in 1739 that, although ordinarily a feme covert could not convey property by deed in her own name, in the instant case, a separation agreement between husband and wife had conferred that power, and hence the conveyance in question was valid.

The separation agreement and other types of post-nuptial contracts clearly served a useful purpose in protecting the economic interests of a married woman and her children without necessitating recourse to a divorce action with its attendant unpleasant publicity. The spectre of " public policy," which the courts of the nineteenth century mysteriously summoned forth because they did not like separation agreements and felt that judicial supervision in matters of marriage dissolution was being supplanted by private judgment, held no horrors for the colonial judiciary. In England, it was not until 1879 that equity, spurred on by Sir George Jessel, recognized that economic and social conditions had changed, and clearly upheld such agreements.[3]

[1] Vansise *v.* Vansise (1768) Suffolk Court MSS., "Divorce," fol. 44, 45. See also Keith *v.* Keith (1762) MSS. *ibid.*, fols. 24-26.

[2] (1739) *Va. Col. Dec.*, II, 207.

[3] Besant *v.* Wood (1879) 12 Chancery Div. 604. For a scathing criticism of this decision, *cf.* Bishop, *Marriage, Divorce, and Separation*, § 1265.

A remarkable expansion of the proprietary capacity of the married woman in the American colonies was effected by the liberal policy of the colonial courts in regard to the transfer of realty. In England, at common law the married woman could only convey her real property by the fictitious suit known as the fine or common recovery, in which the husband was required to unite with her in the action. The economic pressure in the American colonies which favored free alienation of land was manifest in the substitution of a more facile method of conveyancing. By the close of the provincial period, the American colonies, recognizing the advantage of speedy alienation of realty, permitted, either by statute or local usage, the conveying of the real estate of a married woman by a deed executed by husband and wife, the separate examination and acknowledgment of the wife by the court being customarily required in her own interest. In the earlier colonial period there was no uniformity in this regard; at least four legal methods were pursued in conveying the estates of married women. (1) In one jurisdiction the husband had complete control over his wife's property and alone could execute the conveyance. (2) In several, conveyance by the archaic fine or common recovery was in use. (3) More generally the validity of a joint deed executed by husband and wife was upheld. (4) Finally, the wife occasionally executed the conveyance alone, and frequently, where she was living separately from her husband, she was endowed by the court with the complete proprietary capacity of a feme sole.

(1) In Connecticut the theory of the legal unity of husband and wife, and of the merger of her existence in his, was recognized by giving the husband an absolute instead of a limited title to the real estate of the wife. It is indeed difficult to correlate this policy with the liberal attitude of the Connecticut courts in other matters affecting the interests

of women and with the progressive adjudication on other property questions generally. The court in *Fitch v. Brainard* [1] set forth an apologia decidedly unsatisfactory as measured by modern standards, observing that

They who could declare to the world, as prefatory to their first code of laws, " we have endeavored not only to ground our capital laws on the word of God, but also all our other laws in the justice and equity held forth in that word, which is a most perfect rule " (preface to Statutes, ed. of 1672), would not be likely to swerve from the maxims of unity and subjection attached by sacred writers to the matrimonial vow. They had not then the art of refining upon the institution of marriage, which they might have since learned in England, and which has wrought up a system of separate property, separate management, and separate residence, at once the cause and effect of licentiousness,

the court concludes in derogatory vein with this allusion to Chancery practice.

The preamble of the Connecticut act of 1723 for " preventing the sales of the real estate of heiresses without their consent," is descriptive of the archaic state of the law existing prior to that time:

Whereas in the first settlement of this Colony land was of little value in comparison with what it now is, by which means it became a general custom with the real estate of any person which either by descent or by will became the estate of his daughter, whether they were seized of it at the time of their marriage or whether it descended or came to them during their coverture, became thereby the proper and sole estate of their husbands, and might be by him alienated or disposed of without the knowledge or consent of such wives; and a great number of estates having been thus settled and so remain at this day:

[1] (1805) 2 Day 163, 194. The case actually stands for the proposition that a will, executed by a feme-covert, devising real estate to her husband, is void.

And whereas by reason of the present value, usefulness and security of real estate, the suffering of such a custom any longer to obtain would be attended with much inconveniency and wrong, altho for the time past the custom which has obtained ought to be holden good :

it is therefore provided " that for the future, any real estate whereof any woman at the time of her marriage is seised as her estate of inheritance, or does during such coverture become so, either by descent or otherwise, shall not be alienable by her husband's deed, without her consent, testified by her hand and seal to such deed, and acknowledgment of the same." [1]

(2) The New York lawyers, possessing the more technical equipment of the eighteenth-century legal profession, introduced into that colony the elaborate conveyancing devices of contemporary England. The fine or the common recovery was occasionally resorted to by cautious persons.[2] Among the law papers of James Alexander are numerous instances in which the New York attorney has occasion to detail the necessary procedure in levying a fine, and in which he cites Coke [3] as authority for the rule requiring the separate examination of the wife on a fine before the puisne judge.[4] But in the colonies generally, even in the conservative south, the fine and the common recovery were abandoned in favor of the joint deed.[5]

---

[1] *Conn. Pub. Rec.*, VI, 425; Adams *v.* Kellogg (1787) Kirby 441; Fitch *v.* Brainard (1805) 2 Day 163, 190. For the later form of this statute and the wife's power under it, *cf.* Stafford Savings Bank *v.* Underwood (1886) 54 Conn. 2.

Manchester *v.* Hough (1828) 5 Mason (U. S.) 67.

[3] 1st. Inst., 121a.

[4] MSS. James Alexander Papers, IV, fol. 5, 8, NYHS.

[5] *N. C. Col. Rec.*, XXIII, 35; Hening, *Stat. of Va.*, II, 317; Davey *et ux. v.* Turner (1764) 1 Dallas (2d ed., Phila., 1806) 11-14.

(3) The married woman's property was customarily conveyed by the simple procedure of a joint deed executed by husband and wife. Massachusetts deeds of the seventeenth century afford innumerable instances of this practice. To John Read, the eminent New England lawyer of the first half of the eighteenth century, is attributed the perfection of this liberal conveyancing reform.[1] Reference to the copious evidence of this practice is made by the federal court in *Manchester v. Hough*.[2] " From an early period in the history of New England," the court observes, " the right of a feme covert to convey her real estate by deed with the assent of her husband was recognized and has been constantly enforced by courts of law. It now constitutes a part of the common law of New England." In its decision, the court upholds a joint conveyance made by husband and wife prior to the enabling statute. New York deeds of the late eighteenth century are also evidential of this usage.[3]

The Pennsylvania action of *Davey et ux. v. Turner*,[4] which arose in 1764, involved the validity of a joint conveyance by husband and wife of the lands of which the wife was seised in fee prior to her marriage. The property was transferred to two trustees and their heirs for the use of the wife, for and during their joint lives, and after the decease of either of them, to the survivor and his or her heirs. The validity of the deed was challenged on the ground that it was an improper substitute for the fine, that, by the Statute of Uses, it vested the legal estate immediately in the husband, and therefore was a conveyance from wife to husband, and that the consideration of marriage and a trifling sum of money was inadequate. In support of the deed, the defend-

---

[1] Fowler *v.* Shearer (1810) 7 Mass. 14.
[2] (1828) 5 Mason (U. S.) 67.
[3] *Cf.* e. g., De Peyster MSS., III, fols. 55, 57, 115 (1792-1798), NYHS.
[4] (1764) 1 Dallas (2d ed., Phila., 1806), pp. 11-14.

ant cited the famous maxim, *communis error facit jus,* buttressed by many authorities; Coke on Littleton (112) was submitted as authority for the equitable conveyance. A special verdict found " that for fifty years and upwards it had been the constant practice and usage of the province of Pennsylvania in cases where Baron and Feme have been desirous to settle, sell and dispose of the estate of the Feme, for the Baron and Feme to join in a deed or deeds." After advisement, the court unanimously upheld the conveyance, and stated that the maxim above cited could not " operate more properly than in this case." [1] Six years later the legislature, in order to dispel all uncertainty raised by *Davey v. Turner* and a subsequent decision, passed a statute confirming the joint conveyance of husband and wife, and reciting in its preamble that this method of transfer had been " the custom and usage ever since the settlement " of the province.[2]

In the southern colonies the fine or common recovery either became obsolete shortly after settlement or was never adopted for this purpose. The Maryland case of *Hammond's Lessee v. Brice* [3] upheld the validity of a joint conveyance made subsequent to the act of 1715, c. 47, as a result of which the fine passed into disuse. The Virginia statute of 1674,[4] which bears testimony to the substitution of the joint conveyance by husband and wife in that colony for the fine or recovery under the English system, and which upheld the validity of such transfers of realty, formed the basis for the North Carolina statute of 1715 [5] and the Georgia enactment of 1760.[6]

[1] *Cf.* also Lessee of Lloyd *v.* Taylor (1768), 1 Dallas 17, where the court follows Davey *v.* Turner.

[2] Act of 1770, Carey and Bioren, *Laws of Pa.*, I, 495, 496.

[3] (1769) 1 H. and McH. 322.

[4] Hening, *Statutes at Large*, II, 317.

[5] *N. C. Col. Rec.*, XXIII, 35.

[6] *Ga. Col. Rec.*, XVIII, 417.

To protect the married woman from the undue influence which her husband might conceivably exert upon her in exacting her signature to the conveyance of her inheritable estate, the colonial courts resorted to a private examination of the married woman by a judicial officer to determine whether the transfer was effected of her own free will. The pattern for this inquisition was the fine at common law. The colonial courts and legislatures were emphatic in their insistence upon this prudent method of judicial supervision.

About 1686, James Lloyd of Long Island, New York, asked Nicholas King, a New York attorney, to get a legal opinion in England on the accepted method of conveying to himself an interest in Queens County realty belonging to his wife. King, when in London, consulted the noted Sergeant Pollexfen, who informed him that a fine or recovery levied in that country would have no legal recognition in the colonies; but that in lieu thereof, a conveyance in which the wife joined, supplemented by a private examination before a judge, would effect a valid transfer.[1] It appears that subsequently a transfer of certain Lloyd interests in New York was acknowledged by Lloyd's wife before a New York judge then resident in Massachusetts. Henry Lloyd wrote in 1717 to Robert Auchmuty of Boston for legal advice, and that attorney gave it as his opinion that " the Judges Power is not ambulatory but Local & the Acknowledgment Coram non Judice." Therefore, the acknowledgment should have been taken in New York.

North Carolina attempted to cope with a similar problem. Where married women who were residents of neighboring colonies, held estates of inheritance in North Carolina, a good deal of irregularity in the form of the conveyance resulted. " In such cases," recites the preamble of the act of 1751,[2] " conveyances have been made by the Husband, with

[1] MSS. Lloyd Papers, NYHS.

[2] Act of 1751, c. 3. *N. C. Col. Rec.*, XXIII, 358, 359.

the Wife's Consent, and Sometimes by both, and at other times by the wife only, and afterwards ratified and confirmed by the Husband." To clear titles of estates conveyed in this manner, the statute provided for the personal acknowledgment of the husband and wife before the Chief Justice or the county court where the land was located, and for the private examination of the wife. Where the married woman was resident in another jurisdiction, or too ill to attend court, the clerk of the county court was empowered to issue a commission to receive the acknowledgment of her deed and to conduct a private examination, the results of which were to be certified and registered. An earlier Virginia statute of 1734 had made a similar provision in cases where the wife was infirm and unable to travel,[1] and an act of 1776 included a provision for holding a private examination of non-resident wives.[2]

Statutes provided that the private examination was requisite to the effecting of a valid conveyance;[3] and judicial decisions and legal opinions expounded the rationale of this provision. In a brief written in the late provincial period Joseph Galloway discusses the legality of the conveyance of Mercy Masters, who had never submitted to a separate examination, and who died leaving a son as heir-at-law. The basis for such examination is stated as follows:

. . . By the Law of God, as well as that of the English Gover(t) a wife is enjoined to be Obedient and Subject to her Husband. Hence all Acts of the Feme that has a Tendency to the Disposition of that Part of her Estate in which the Law

[1] Hening, *Statutes at Large*, IV, 400, 401; similarly, act of 1748, *ibid.*, V, 410, 411.

[2] *Ibid.*, IX, 208. *Cf.* also act of 1752, c. 8, *Laws of Md.* (Kilty), I.

[3] In addition to statutes cited *supra, cf.* act of 1682, c. 19, *Grants and Concessions of New Jersey*, pp. 235, 236; act of 1715, c. 47, § 11, *Laws of Md.* (Kilty), I.

has not invested the Baron with an Absolute property and right of Disposal, are presumed [to] be done by that Influence Power and Coercion, which the policy both of the Divine and Human Law afsd has enabled the Baron to Exercise over his feme, and not to be the free and voluntary Act of the person, to whom ye Estate belongs, without which no Disposition can be valid either in Law or Reason.

To remove this Rational Presumption the Com. Law Enjoins in all Conveyances of her real Estate during Coverture, that she be removed from the Person of her Husband, and then Examined as to her free Consent and voluntary re[linquishment of] her right. This in England must be done by a writ of Dedimus issuing out of the Court of Chancery for that Purpose and in this Province before a Justice of the Peace &c. under ye Act of the 1 Geo. 1. And unless one of those are done, or a fine or recovery Suffered in the present Case, the Deed from Peter Loyd and his wife can not Bar her heir from the recovery of his mothers inheritance.[1]

In *Jones v. Porter* [2] a bill in equity was brought in the Virginia Court of Chancery to supply a defect in a conveyance of a husband and wife in which the wife was not privately examined. In behalf of the appellant it was set forth that since equity will require a livery where it is lacking in a feoffment and a surrender where it is omitted from a copyhold transfer, there is no reason why its intervention should be denied in the instant case where there is adequate consideration. The vendor, it is submitted, " has become a kind of Trustee in Equity for the Vendee & so compellable in Equity to make or perfect " the conveyance. In answer to the objection that no precedent could be found for such relief in the Court of Chancery in England, advantage is taken of the fact that no such situation could arise in England, where

[1] MSS. Miscellaneous Papers (Joseph Galloway), NYPL.
[2] *Va. Col. Dec.*, II, 93-100.

the fine or recovery was required to effect a valid transfer. Apparently the court agreed with the respondent's position that equity could not intervene to annul an act of assembly making the legality of the conveyance under such circumstances dependent upon a special bill; for, according to the report, " the bill was dismissed by the opinion of a great majority of the Court."

(4) The instances where the wife alone executed the conveyance are generally those in which she was living separately from her husband and where the court had conferred upon her the complete proprietary capacity of a feme sole. In 1641 the Massachusetts Body of Liberties provided that " any conveyance or alienation of land or other estate what so ever, made by any woman that is married, any childe under age, Ideott or distracted person, shall be good if it be passed and ratified by the consent of a general court." [1] This provision does not appear in the later revisions of the laws. Apparently it was too glaring a departure from English precedent to survive the administrative scrutiny of the subsequent period.[2] Infrequent examples have been found of conveyances by married women living with their husbands. The New Haven Town Records show that in 1668 Anne Andrews, the wife of William Andrews, conveyed seven acres of meadow-land to Mathew Moulthrop, " as by a writeing under ye hand of ye sd Anne Andrewes & allowed by her prsent husband, now appeared." [3]

Throughout the colonies the most radical conveyancing privileges were granted to married women who lived sep-

---

[1] Liberty 14. *Mass. Col. Laws, 1660-1672* (Whitmore ed., 1889), p. 35.

[2] Whitmore, *Bibliographical Sketch of the Laws of Massachusetts,* p. 27.

[3] *New Haven Town Rec.,* II, 214. But *cf.* Mayson *v.* Sexton (1767) 1 H. and McH (Md.) 275, where it was held that a bargain and sale with warranty by a feme covert was no discontinuance of the estate.

arately from their husbands. In addition to the individual property settlements made in the separation agreements previously discussed, the courts, to protect the wife and family from being left unprovided for by the husband, sequestered the wife's property, a procedure anticipatory of the more modern equity proceedings or the "protection order." [1] In all respects she was treated as a feme sole.

As typical of this procedure may be cited the Massachusetts case of 1644, where the Court of Assistants

. . . Ordered that John Richardson should be sequestered from Elizabeth Fryer, to whom he was married, yᵉ 12 of the 8th Month, and neither to meddle with hir Person, nor estate, till thinges bee cleared by advice from England . . . [2]

In 1670 Nicasius de Sille and his wife, who were incompatible, petitioned Governor Lovelace of New York to compose the difference between them in regard to the control of their estates. A commission was appointed, and, as a result of its report, an inventory of all property was taken to satisfy creditors; the remainder was divided equally. It was not considered fair "that the one should draw more from the overplus" than the other. As against such property as the wife brought with her at her marriage and expended on the children of de Sille by his first wife, there was set off the latter's salary as fiscal. [3] In 1674 the General Court of Connecticut empowered Mary Dowe of Hartford, whose husband had gone to sea and had not been heard of for almost two years, to execute a valid conveyance of her house and lot in order to ward off destitution for herself and family. [4]

[1] 20 and 21 Vict., c. 58, § 21: *Statutes at Large*, XCVII, 536.

[2] (1644) *Assistants*, II, 139.

[3] *Executive Council Minutes*, I, 327 *et seq.*; Fernow, *Rec. Amst.*, VI, 227.

[4] *Conn. Pub. Rec.*, II, 239.

In 1718 the legislature of Massachusetts empowered Mary Evans, who had been deserted by her husband, to execute a mortgage on her own realty;[1] and as late as 1763 an act was passed to validate a conveyance of Faith Cookson's real estate which she had inherited from her father. The fact that she was married was disregarded because she had lived separately from her husband and was the sole support of her children.[2]

Virginia, customarily conservative in property law, adopted a progressive stand in this situation as it had in the case of the separation agreement. In 1752 the House of Burgesses and the Council passed a bill to enable Frances Greenhill to sell and dispose of her lands and other estate by deed or will notwithstanding that her husband Joseph Greenhill should happen to be living. From the bill it appears that her husband had deserted her and had not been living with her for over twenty years.[3] On legislative review in England, a committee of the Board of Trade reported unfavorably and the act was disallowed on the committee report of June 16th, 1745 on the ground that

this is the first Instance wherein the Legislature in any of the Colonys Abroad have taken upon them to alter the Law in so Settled and known a point as giving a power to a Feme Covert to sell or dispose of her Real and Personal Estate in the Supposed life time of her Husband and as it may not be adviseable to countenance any attempts of this kind.[4]

The haphazard supervision of colonial statutes by the King in Council was not calculated to produce a consistent legal

---

[1] *Mass. Acts and Resolves*, IV (App. I), p. 103.

[2] *Ib.*, p. 192.

[3] *Journal of the House of Burgesses, 1742-1747* (Richmond, Va., 1919), pp. 21, 24, 27, 34, 60, 61, 70.

[4] *Acts of the Privy Council, Col. Ser.*, IV, 4, 65, 252, 513, 527.

policy in the colonies, for, both before and after this disallowance, such bills were passed by colonial legislatures without interference on the part of the home authorities.

1. *The Married Woman's Interest in her Husband's Realty*

An important proprietary interest of married women
which the colonial courts protected was the dower right.
Generally, in accord with the common law, statutes established the dower portion as a life estate in one-third of the
realty of which the husband had seisin during coverture.[1]
What was in effect the common-law writ of dower with its
grant of damages,[2] was brought repeatedly by widows in
the colonial courts.[3] The eighteenth-century statutes more
clearly recognized the nature of the action, and empowered
the widow after demand to sue out the writ within one or
two months following the death of her husband.[4] Under
these circumstances the legal basis for the dower interest
was generally recognized as the common law.[5]

The consent of the wife was required in a conveyance to
bar her dower and transfer clear title.[6] Where she was not

---

[1] *Lawes Resolutions*, pp. 101, 106; *Charters and General Laws of Mass.*,
pp. 99, 100 (act of 1641); Brigham, *Compact*, pp. 43, 281, 293 (1636,
1671, 1685); *Ply. Col. Rec.*, XI, 188 (1661[4]); Hening, *Statutes at
Large*, II, 212, 303 (1673).

[2] Stat. 10 Hen. III, c. 1; act of 1749, *N. C. Col. Rec.*, XXIII, 317.

[3] *Cf.* e. g., Griffen *v.* Gaynes (1662) *Essex*, II, 368; petition of Clarke
and Buckminster (1671) *Assistants*, III, 208; petition of Mary Savage
(1683) *ibid.*, I, 229; petition of Coomes (1687) *Westchester Court Rec.*,
p. 58; Streeter *v.* Burbage (1655) Hening, *Statutes at Large*, I, 405;
petition of Simpson (1703) *N. C. Col. Rec.*, I, 585.

[4] *Mass. Acts and Resolves*, I, 450, 451 (1701); *ibid.*, VI, 197 (1764);
Conn. Pub. Rec., VIII, 56 (1736).

[5] Common Council, Palace Court (1734) *Ga. Col. Rec.*, II, 64.

[6] Brigham, *Compact*, p. 86 (1646, 1658); bill of sale of Richards and
wife (1668) *New Haven Town Rec.*, II, 213; acknowledgment of Catherine Rumsey (1680) *New Castle Rec.*, p. 344; acknowledgment of

a party to the deed and did not consent to the sale, her dower interest was generally affirmed, although the Deal Court, in 1683, did not apply this general rule with consistency in dealing with a widow's petition.[1]   In 1709 the King in Council disallowed a Pennsylvania statute for acknowledging and recording of deeds, which it held to be " unreasonable and repugnant to the Laws of this Kingdom," as it provided that no woman should recover her dower in lands which had been sold by her husband during her marriage, even though she were not a party to the deed and did not consent.[2]

To protect the best interests of the widow, the colonial courts and legislatures were not circumscribed in their activities by the rigid precedents of the English courts.   In some instances, where fine distinctions between real and personal property were not drawn, the widow was awarded half of her deceased husband's estate.   At a council held at Philadelphia in 1683, the question was put: " All that are of opinion that halfe of an Intestate's Estate shall goe to ye Wife," and was passed in the affirmative on condition " that she shall have no more." [3]   Typical of this assimilation of realty and personalty in actions at law is the case of *Sewall et ux. v. Goffe et ux.*,[4] in which the latter's suit for a "moyety or half part " of her deceased husband's property of which

---

Bartree Rowle (1682) *Deale Court Rec.* (Del.), p. 94; power of attorney of Ann Freak, Westmoreland County, Va., 1664, to acknowledge her consent to her husband's sale of six hundred acres of land, Emmet Papers, No. 13389, NYPL; acknowledgment of Elizabeth Hunt (1703) *N. C. Col.* Rec., I, 584; power of attorney of Mary Evans (1704) *ibid.*, p. 609.

[1] Petition of Ann Newcome, *Some Records of Sussex County, Del.*, p. 114 (hereafter *Deale Court Rec.*). The court "thrue away " the petition.

[2] *Pa. Arch.*, 1st ser., I, 156.

[3] *Pa. Col. Rec.*, I, 48.

[4] MSS. Mass. Sup. Crt. Judic. (1721-1725), fol. 16.

he died seised was sustained on appeal in the Superior Court
of Judicature of Massachusetts in 1721. This case repre-
sents still another analogy to the custom of gavelkind,
whereby the wife's dower portion was one-half; and, according to which, in a writ of dower for the moiety she had to
allege the custom and the fact that she was sole.[1]

Where the husband by will left his wife but " a small,
inconsiderable part of his estate " and it appeared that she
was " a frugall and laborious woman in the procuring of
the said estate," the Plymouth court took steps to right the
wrong.[2] In fact, a New Hampshire statute of 1714 provides that, where the husband's will is proved to be to the
injury of his wife, the widow " shall have such proportion
of her late Husbands Estate Assigned her as if he had dyed
Intestate." [3] She was given the alternative of declining her
legacy under the will and of suing out her writ of dowr.[4]
Among the questions propounded in 1773 to William Smith,
the noted New York lawyer, concerning the estate of Andries Stockholm, were queries whether the widow was entitled to dower in lands purchased by the deceased subsequent
to the making of his will, and whether the widow might
entertain as many persons as she pleased on the property or
merely out of the proportion assigned to her in the will.
To this question, Smith replied that, if the widow chose to
take her legacy under the will, she would forfeit her dower
interest in the testator's real estate,[5] and that she might
" entertain in the Apartments assigned to her whom she

---

[1] *Lawes Resolutions*, p. 108.

[2] Naomi Silvester's case (1663) *Ply. Col. Rec.*, IV, 46.

[3] Act of 1714, *New Hamp. Prov. Laws*, II, 133. *Cf.* Gage *v.* Gage
(1854) 29 N. H. 540.

[4] Bateman's case (1694[5]), *N. C. Col. Rec.*, I, 443.

[5] But *cf. Va. Gen. Court Rec.*, p. 506, where in 1658, it was declared:
" Legacy to widow no bar to dower."

pleases and at her Pleasure dispose of the Grain and Fruits of the Orchard. But I think she can demand no more Firewood than is necessary for one Hearth and but one Bed & no more Household Furniture than is requisite for her own Convenience." [1]   Where the widow chose the legacy rather than the dower portion, she could bring an action on the case against the executors of her deceased husband's estate " for neglecting or refusing to deliuer unto her " such property, and would be entitled to recover damages.[2]

In other cases where the property of the husband was not adequate for the support of the wife and family, the widow was frequently either given control over the entire property, or her portion, either of realty or of personalty, was enlarged; [3] where she was about to remarry, the court was insistent that she give security for the maintenance of her children and the protection of their portion of the estate.[4]   In situations where the dower portion was inadequate and the principal legatee was not in such relation to the widow as would involve legal responsibility for her support, such legatee, according to a Connecticut statute, was to be held liable to contribute in proportion to his share of the decedent's estate under penalty of being prosecuted in the same manner as children might be for the support of their indigent parents.[5] At the request of the wife, the court might grant her permission to sell the lands assigned her as dower in order to

---

[1] MSS. Miscellaneous Papers (William Smith).   NYPL.

[2] *Cf.* Sad *v.* Sad's executors (1695) *Conn. Pub. Rec.*, IV, 152, where the court awarded the widow damages of £20.

[3] Estate of Henry Smith (1679) *Ply. Col. Rec.*, VI, 3; estate of John Smith (1679) *ibid.*, p. 5; act of 1715, *Conn. Pub. Rec.*, V, 438, 439.

[4] Estate of Barnaby (1677) *Ply. Col. Rec.*, V, 247; estate of Lindon (1664) *New Haven Town Rec.*, II, 81.   A somewhat analogous situation is presented in Ward *v.* Weeks (1650) *Md. Arch.*, X, 228.

[5] *Conn. Pub. Rec.*, XIII, 124, 125.

pay her deceased husband's debts, where his estate was insolvent.[1]

Other types of aid for indigent widows and their children were frequently granted by the colonial legislatures.[2] In those jurisdictions where the estate of a felon was forfeited, special allowance was generally made out of his property for the maintenance of his wife and children. In New Netherland, it was provided in one instance that, upon clearing the wife of the suspicion of being accessory to the felony, she was to receive one-half of the estate.[3] Among the laws for Pennsylvania agreed upon in England, 1682, was the provision " that the estates of capital offenders, as traitors, and murderers, shall go one third to the next of kin to the sufferer, and the remainder to the next of kin to the criminal." [4] Subsequent legislation reduced the share of the murderer's family to one-half of his estate.[5] In Maryland, John Dandy's estate was forfeited to the Lord Proprietor because of a conviction for murder, but upon petition of his wife, asking for relief for herself and children, the court allowed her to remain in possession of the estate, both real and personal, provided that court costs and just debts be first satisfied, and that she render an accounting.[6] Dower was exempted in Maryland in the case of the forfeiture of lands for manslaughter, malicious trespass, forgery, attacks on high officials, being accessory to a felony, or receiving stolen

[1] Petition of Smith (1706) *Conn. Pub. Rec.*, IV, 530.

[2] *Cf.* e. g., Britton's case (1743) *Ga. Col. Rec.*, VI, 64; *Mass. Acts and Resolves*, IX, 11 (1708) ; *ibid.*, p. 87 (1709) ; *ibid.*, pp. 94, 95 (1709). *Cf.* also *Grants and Concessions of New Jersey*, p. 235 (1682) : " Whoever shall afflict the widow or fatherless, shall be punished by the judges according to the nature of the transgression."

[3] Case of Catrina Lane (1673) *N. Y. Col. Docts.*, II, 668.

[4] *Duke of York's Book of Laws*, p. 101.

[5] *Ibid.*, pp. 144 (1683), 210 (1693) ; Bioren, *Laws of Pa.*, I, 2 (1700).

[6] (1657) *Md. Arch.*, X, 546, 547.

goods.[1]   A Virginia statute prescribed the forfeiture of a
forger's estate, but directed the governor and council to
" make out of the offender's estate such an allowance as they
shall think necessary for the maintenance of his wife and
children." [2]   The New England statutes generally abolished
forfeiture of estates for felony,[3] and, as a matter of course,
the heirs in those jurisdictions inherited in accord with the
prevailing rules of descent.   The Massachusetts act of 1692
provided attainder for " conjuration, witchcraft and dealing
with evil and wicked spirits." [4]   This act was disallowed by
the King in Council in 1695 on the ground that it was not
in agreement with the " Statute of King James ye First
whereby the Dower is saved to ye widow and ye Inheritance
to ye heir of ye party convicted." [5]   In this instance the English law set the standard for compassionate treatment of the
widow of a felon; for, while at early common law, dower
was barred for every felony,[6] by the period of seventeenth-
century colonial settlement, treason was the sole offence that
worked forfeiture of dower.[7]   In colonial statutes enabling
creditors to attach the realty of the debtor, the wife's dower
interest was reserved.[8]   Where, in the administration of a
decedent's estate, the debts were first paid and then dower
set off, the legislature of Massachusetts, by a private bill,

[1] Act of 1639. *Ibid.*, I, 72.

[2] Act of 1771, Hening, *Statutes at Large*, IX, 303, 304.

[3] Body of Liberties (1641), Liberty 10, *Mass. Col. Laws* (*1660-1672*),
p. 35; *Lawes and Libertyes* (Cambridge, 1648); code of 1660, *Mass.
Col. Laws* (*1660-1672*), p. 168. *Cf.* also act of 1779, *Mass. Acts and
Resolves*, V, 967. Pennsylvania exempted the estate of a suicide from
forfeiture (1701), *Pa. Arch.*, 4th ser., I, 122, 123.

[4] *Charters and General Laws*, pp. 735, 736.

[5] *Mass. Acts and Resolves*, I, 90, 91.

[6] *Lawes Resolutions*, p. 152.

[7] *Ibid.*, p. 152; 2 Bl. Comm. 126 *et seq.*

Act of 1720, *Mass. Acts and Resolves*, II, 150.

ordered the error rectified and one-third of the " whole of
the produce and Premises " set aside for the petitioner during her natural life.[1]

Certain striking variations from the common-law interpretation of the widow's dower interest are occasionally, but
with no great consistency, found in the colonial records. At
common law, the dower interest of the wife was a mere life
estate. In *Grose v. Guardians of Grose*,[2] which came up to
the Court of Assistants of Massachusetts in 1661, it is not
clear whether the wife's interest which was litigated was the
property under the legacy or her dower. In respect to the
court order, granting a third of the estate to the wife, the
jury brought in a special verdict to the effect that

. . . if the meaning of the courts order for a third of the
whole for the wife be onely for her life the jury finde for the
defendant one third and noe more, if the meaning of the aforesaid order be for ever the jury findes reason to revoake the
judgment of the former court and finde for the plaintife the
whole: and for the determination thereof with costs of courts
the jury leave it to the honoured court.

The record goes on to state: " The magists. considering of
this Speciall virdict declare they cannot find by a third for
yᶜ whole is to be vnderstood for life only therefore find for
yᵉ plaintiff Costs of courts." It would appear that the record
of the following case litigated in Connecticut in 1697 presents
a similar enlargement of the widow's dower interest, although
here again it is not entirely clear that such an estate is at
issue :

Anna Wilcockson widdow and relict of Joseph Wilcockson
late of Killenworth deceased being aggrieved with the act of

[1] Petition of Webb (1742) *Mass. Acts and Resolves*, XIII, 162.
[2] *Assistants*, III, 90-93.

the countie Court at Newlondon, June 6, 1683, concerning her interest in the reall estate of the said Joseph, whereby ye said court did order that the said Anna should have onely one third part of the profitts of the reall estate of the said Joseph; which act being an abridgment of her just right according to lawe, this Court doth declare the same to be void, and doe order that the said Anra shall have the one third part of the reall estate of sd Joseph according to lawe to be to her during her natural life, ye said act notwithstanding.[1]

The restrictive common-law interpretation, as stated in the Plymouth Laws of 1671, was in general acceptance: " if any Married man dieth Intestate, his Widow shall have one third part of the Rents and Profits of his Lands during her life." [2]

While the law was clear that a claim to dower could only arise where the husband had been seised of an estate of inheritance during coverture, it appears from the limited facts presented in the Plymouth action of *Man v. Cowin* [3] that the court recognized the dower interest of Cowin's wife in one-third of the lands of which her husband had only possession for a term of five years.

At common law divorce was regarded as terminating dower, whether or not the wife were the innocent party,[4] and " elopement," as the situation where the wife deserted her husband to live in adultery with another man was quaintly called, likewise barred her proprietary interest.[5] This rule was in force in a majority of the colonies. Thus, the Plymouth statute of 1685 provided that a married woman

---

[1] *Conn. Pub. Rec.*, IV, 227.

[2] Brigham, *Compact*, p. 281.

[3] (1670) *Ply. Col. Rec.*, V, 45.

[4] " *Ubi nullum matrimonium, ibi nulla dos.*" 2 Bl. Comm. 130; 4 Kent's Comm. 54.

[5] *Lawes Resolutions*, pp. 144, 145; Godolphin, *Reportorium Canonicum*, pp. 474, 475.

would be entitled to dower except where she had "not de-merited the contrary by her wilful Absence or Departure from her Husband or other notorious fact without reconciliation to him in his lifetime." [1] The Duke of York's laws provided that "if any Woman shall Causelessly absent herself from her Husband of which he shall make Complaint to the Court of Sessions If upon certaine time given her by the Court, shee shall refuse to return, shee shall forfeit her Dowry unless the Husband shall afterwards upon a New agreement Confirm the same." [2] In South Carolina the English Statute of Westminster, 13 Edw. I, c. 34, § 4, barring dower in the case of the wife's elopement, was extended by legislative enactment to that jurisdiction. [3]

It is gratifying to record that a more equitable view of this situation was taken in most of the New England colonies. In Massachusetts and Connecticut, dower was by statute granted the wife, where she was living with her husband, or where her absence was with his consent or "through his mere default, or inevitable providence, or in case of divorce, where she is the innocent party." [4] Prior to the restrictive statute of 1685 in Plymouth, that colony clearly recognized the right of the innocent wife to her dower interest after a divorce had been granted for her husband's misconduct. [5] In Massachusetts, in one notable instance, the court went much further:

James Luxford being prsented for haveing two wifes, his last marriage was declared voyde, or a nullity thereof, & to bee

---

[1] Brigham, *Compact*, p. 293.

[2] *Duke of York's Book of Laws*, p. 24.

[3] Act of 1712, *S. C. Statutes at Large* (Columbia, S. C., 1837), II, 422.

[4] Act of 1641, *Charters and General Laws of Mass.*, p. 99; *Laws of Conn. Colony* (1673), p. 21; Peck, *Law of Husband and Wife in Connecticut*, § 120; act of 1736, *Conn. Pub. Rec.*, VIII, 56.

[5] Burge v. Burge (1661) *Ply. Col. Rec.*, III, 221.

divorced not to come to the sight of her whom hee last tooke,
& hee to bee sent away for England by the first opportunity,
all that he hath is appointed to her whom hee last married, for
her & her children . . . [1]

This privilege of dower for the innocent divorcée has been
granted in modern times by many of the American states,[2]
and the right has even been extended to guilty wives; for
this latter position there is some precedent in colonial Massachusetts.[3]   In conclusion, it may be stated that a frequent
method of barring dower in colonial America as well as in
England was by jointure.[4]

2. *The Husband's Interest in his Wife's Realty: Curtesy*

At common law, where a man married a woman seised of
an estate of inheritance, and had issue by her, born alive and
capable of inheriting her estate, he held her lands upon her
death as tenant for life by the curtesy of England.[5]   In
the colonies, the husband's right of curtesy was respected,[6]
and it is clear that his proprietary interest was confined to
a life estate, and that he could not execute a valid conveyance in fee.[7]   There is no evidence of a reciprocal incapacity
being imposed upon the husband to enjoy his wife's estate

[1] (1639) *Assistants,* II, 89.   Italics mine.

[2] Stillson *v.* Stillson (1878) 46 Conn. 16; Wait *v.* Wait (1850) 4 N. Y.
95; *Mass. General Laws,* c. 190, § 1.

[3] Peck, *Domestic Relations,* pp. 138, 139, and cases cited.

[4] Act of 1641, *Charter and General Laws of Mass.,* p. 99; act of 1705,
Hening, *Statutes at Large,* III, 374.   An excellent example of an early
colonial jointure, 1650, is found in *Md. Arch.,* X, 12, 13.

[5] 2 Bl. Comm. 126 *et seq.*

[6] Smith *v.* Cheeseman (1673) *Va. Gen. Court Rec.,* p. 353; Bowler's
case (1676) *ibid.,* p. 450.

[7] Johnson *v.* Lynde (1723) MSS. Mass. Sup. Court of Judic. (1721-
1725), fol. 128; heirs of Greenough *v.* Greenough (1760) *Conn. Pub.
Rec.,* XI, 394, 395.

by the curtesy in cases where he had abandoned his wife, though this is the rule in some American states today.[1] Nevertheless, in those colonial jurisdictions where the wife was allowed her separate property when deserted by her husband, it may be safely concluded that a like incapacity arose from this practice.

The husband generally brought suit for his wife's dower right by a former marriage,[2] and sued " by the right of his wife," for her inheritance portion.[3]   In one instance in Connecticut, the court actually ordered that the land for which the petitioner was suing in right of his wife " be recorded to him in the records of Wethersfield." [4]   In *Chapman v. Barry,*[5] the court ruled that, where a wife is named as legatee under a will but dies without issue before the time of payment, the husband cannot sue for the legacy after her death.   In other instances the husband and wife were joined in suit for the wife's inheritance portion.[6]   There is like inconsistency in suits brought to recover property held under the wife's claim of inheritance, in some cases suit being brought against the husband alone,[7] and in others, the hus-

---

[1] Henry Wynans Jessup, *Law for Wives and Daughters* (New York, 1927), p. 34.

[2] Lambe's case (1677) *Assistants*, I, 103; Knight's case (1679) *ibid.*, p. 147; Johnson's case (1694) *Chester Co. (Pa.) Rec.*, p. 332.

[3] Case of Robin the Indian (1674) *Ply. Col. Rec.*, V, 140; Halloway *v.* Bobbit, MSS. Mass. Sup. Court Judic. (1715-1721), fol. 32; conveyance of Meekes (1664) *New Haven Town Rec.*, II, 128 (1664); Hubbard *v.* Turner (1687) *Westchester Court Rec.*, p. 40; petition of Shepard (1682) *Deale Court Rec.*, pp. 93, 94.

[4] Shelton's case (1699) *Conn. Pub. Rec.*, IV, 295.

[5] (1681) *Assistants*, I, 205.

[6] Bigg *v.* Harwood *et ux.* (1691) *Assistants*, I, 339, 340; Barnard *et ux. v.* Holding (1722) MSS. Mass. Sup. Court Judic. (1721-1725), fol. 64.

[7] Fiske *v.* Hill (1694) MSS. Mass. Sup. Court Judic. (1692-1695), fols. 92, 93.

band and wife being joined as co-defendants.[1]   Because of
the control exercised by the husband over his wife's realty,
typical statutes exempted married women from liability during their coverture under the statute of limitations,[2] and
from forfeitures of lands and chattels in jurisdictions where
such confiscation was made for certain felonies.[3]

3. *The Husband's Interest in his Wife's Personal Property*

The common law gave the husband unlimited right over
his wife's chattels which he reduced to his possession during
his marriage.[4]   An adequate summary of the proprietary
control vested in the husband is found among the law papers
of John M. Macdonald, a New York attorney of the provincial era.[5]   Under the chapter heading, " Baron and
Femme," it is stated, probably on the authority of the standard abridgments, that

> The Husband by marriage acquires an absolute title to all
> the personal property of the wife wh she had in possession
> at the time of the marriage.
>
> The Husband's liability to ye Creditors of the Wife lasts no
> longer than coverture.
>
> Husband and wife must be joined because if ye suit cd be
> maintained against wife alone she might be imprisoned and
> wd be wholly destitute of the means of extricating herself
> from confinement depending wholly on the good will of
> her husband to pay the debt and release her.
>
> Husband has a right to his wife's personal property in action
> to wh she was entitled at the time of the marriage, as bonds,
> notes, and may sue, collect and dispose of them at pleasure.

[1] Curtis *et ux. v.* Godsoe (1722) MSS. Mass. Sup. Court Judic. (1721-
1725), fol. 54.

[2] *Cf.* e. g., act of 1684, *Conn. Pub. Rec.*, III, 147.

[3] *Cf.* e. g., act of 1639, *Md. Arch.*, I, 40, 41.

[4] Holdsworth, *Hist. Eng. Law*, III, 526.

[5] MSS. John M. Macdonald Papers. NYHS.

To render an assignment of a chose in action valid against
a surviving wife it must be for a valuable consideration.

If an Husband cannot recover the choses of his wife without
the intervention of a Court of Equity, as where the legal
estate is in trustees, such Court will refuse to lend him
any aid, unless he has made a previous decent provision for
his wife, or has agreed to make one out of the property
sued for.

Where the Husband cannot avail himself of the Wife's property without the aid of Chancery, the Court will refuse its
aid unless the husband will make a suitable settlement on
ye wife—Even where the Husband has assigned his title
to a Creditor the Court will not aid that Creditor unless he
makes out of it a reasonable provision for ye wife.

If the Trustees be willing to pay the Choses to ye husband
Chancery never prevents it.

Ch. 1

A Husband who survives his wife is entitled to all her choses
in action whether reduced into his possession in her life
time or not. (John.)

And after his death they go to his personal representatives.

If the Husband without taking out letter of administration
obtain possession of his wife's personal property he may
retain it against his wife's next of kin. (John.)

The Administrator of the wife is Trustee to the Husband and
after his death for his representative. (John.)

In accord with this view, which was the accepted one in
the colonial courts, the husband brought suit for the chattels
belonging to his wife,[1] and for her legacies;[2] her choses in
action he reduced to his possession.[2] A Virginia statute of

[1] Baker *v.* Jacquet (1681) *Newcastle Rec.*, pp. 515, 516; Hall *v.* Peyton
(1658) *Md. Arch.*, XLI, 79; Anon. (1740) *Va. Col. Dec.*, II, 107.

[2] Johnson *v.* Revell (1642) *Md. Arch.*, IV, 185; Eltonhead *v.* Banks
et al. (1649) *ibid.*, p. 527.

1727 provided that, where slaves were conveyed, bequeathed, or passed by descent to a married woman, the absolute property in them vested in her husband, and, in like manner, upon the marriage of a feme sole, her slaves vested absolutely in her spouse.[1] In addition, the husband brought suit for the ante-nuptial debts due to the wife.[2] The policy behind this was not consistently respected, for, in numerous Massachusetts and New York cases of the provincial period, the husband and wife joined in actions for the recovery of the ante-nuptial debts owing to the latter or for her legacy.[3]

The husband's control of his wife's personalty imposed upon him a reciprocal obligation to pay his wife's ante-nuptial debts; he was joined with his wife in such actions,[4] and was sued jointly with her where she acted either in the capacity of executrix or of administratrix.[5] The husband was frequently bound for the good behavior of his wife, after a criminal prosecution of the latter, such action being indicative of the fact that she had no separate chattels.[6]

---

[1] Hening, *Statutes at Large*, IV, 223.

[2] Hall *v.* Knap (1644) *New Haven Col. Rec.*, I, 142; Powllen *v.* Humber (1671) *Essex*, VI, 415.

[3] Jeffries *et ux. v.* Ledget (1693) MSS. Mass. Sup. Court Judic. (1692-1695), fols. 46, 47; King *et ux. v.* Estate of Cutt (1693) *ibid.*, fols. 83, 84; Hutchinson *et ux. v.* French (1695) *ibid.*, fol. 195, where the wife is administrator; Anderson *et ux. v.* Wilson and Crommelin (New York, 1725) James Alexander Papers, I, NYHS.

[4] Lidget and Foxcroft *v.* Colman *et ux.* (1694) MSS. Mass. Sup. Court Judic. (1692-1695), I, fols. 104, 105.

[5] Bradstreet *v.* Sherratt *et ux.* (1669) *Essex*, IV, 118; Bellingham *v.* Hammond and wife (1679) *Assistants*, I, 157; Hoare *v.* Cooke, Executrix, and Cooke (1680) *ibid.*, p. 166. But *cf.* Harwood *v.* Nowell *et al.*, where it appears that, though the wife was the executrix, the husband brought suit alone, and was regarded as an executor, possibly in right of his wife. (1683) *Ibid.*, p. 237, and n.; MSS. County Court Records, Middlesex (1681-1686), fol. 64.

[6] *Cf.* e. g., Carter's case (1641) *Assistants*, II, 107.

From the point of view of the husband, a more objectionable type of procedure was the levying of an attachment on his property for debts which his predecessor in the marital role had contracted, and for which his wife as administratrix had been liable prior to her second marriage.[1] Stephens, in his *Journal* of Georgia events, relates that one John Slack courted a widow energetically and was finally betrothed to her. " But all this at last comes to nothing: Slack got Information, that there were some Debts of her former Husband yet standing out unpaid, and that there had been no Administration, wherefore he would become liable to satisfy such Creditors which he stumbled at, and his Interest outweighing his Love, thought it too great a Price to pay for a wife." [2] Needless to say, the engagement was broken.

In a Virginia case reported by Barradall in 1716,[3] a married woman was made executrix by her husband, who in his will left his realty and personalty to her and her heirs forever unless she failed to make disposition of it at her death. The widow subsequently remarried, and, at her death, disposed of her property to a principal legatee. Sir Edward Northey submitted it as his opinion that, though the will conferred the power to dispose of the realty, it could not empower the wife to do likewise with the personal estate, as her second husband had, upon his marriage, become absolute owner thereof. A query is raised at the end of the opinion: " Whether S'r Edward Northey is not mistaken as to the Psonal Estate Seeing she had it as ExEx and never made any Declaration That she took it as Legatee." From the facts as submitted, it would appear that this last contention was unsound.

[1] Haskett *v.* Searle *et ux.* Writ of attachment (1670) *Essex,* IV, 322.

[2] (1741) *Ga. Col. Rec.,* IV, App., pp. 100, 101.

[3] Estate of Pollock (1716) *Va. Col. Dec.,* II, 4, 5.

The extent to which the husband reduced his wife's chattels to his possession is illustrated in *Hanlon v. Thayer*,[1] a Massachusetts case of the late provincial era. The plaintiff, a married woman, brought trover against a sheriff for attaching her apparel. The case involved the interpretation of the colony law of 1647 and the provincial statute of 1709,[2] which forbade levying execution on necessary household articles, but did not specifically exempt wearing apparel. Gridley, for the defendant, construing the English rule very strictly, confined the statutory exemption to the barest necessities of life. Otis, for the plaintiff, relied chiefly on the evidence that the plaintiff's husband had never purchased any of his wife's clothing, but that she had brought her entire apparel with her at her marriage, and submitted it as universal custom that clothing derived from this source was never seized for the debts of the husband. While Justices Oliver and Cushing both conceded that " the Case was very hard upon the Wife," they nevertheless ruled that " as they are personal Property, they become the Husbands on Marriage," and therefore subject to the levy. The Chief Justice dissented. In his opinion, he cited the customary practice of the Court of Probate during his occupancy of that bench of exempting the wife's clothing from process, and concluded that it would be " safer to verge towards Conveniency than to strain the Word *Necessary*." While the jury in this case brought in a verdict for the defendant, subsequent statutory enactments confirmed the humane and reasonable practice of exempting the widow's wearing apparel from process by creditors of the husband's estate.[3]

[1] (1764) Quincy 99.

[2] *Charters and General Laws*, pp. 155, 390.

[3] Mass. Statutes, 1783, c. 36; 1802, c. 193; 1838, c. 145. *Cf.* note by editor in report of Hanlon *v.* Thayer, Quincy 99. For the English practice, *cf.* Bacon, *Abridgment*, Baron & Feme, C., 3, 1.

In the neighboring colony of Connecticut the situation appears to have been handled differently. In one case the widow was permitted

to receive and injoy to her selfe her owne Apparrell both woollen and linnen and nessisary bedding for her owne person to lye vppon that she shall be allowed her nessisary Charges in gathering vp and presarving of her husbands estate shee giving in an Accot of whatever estate of his She knoweth of in the hands of any other person or persons whatsoever and making oath thearwith that she hath not Concealed any part of the estate of her deceased husband from the Courte or Creditors and if the Relict should desi[re] to bvy any of the movables for her selfe the Court Advises that she should be attended before any other paying to the aforesaid Administrators a valuable Consideration for the same.[1]

4. *The Extent of the Married Woman's Control over her Personalty*

Certain limitations on the husband's control over his wife's personal estate were occasionally imposed by the colonial courts. In a few instances the married woman sued for her personalty virtually as a feme sole.[2] In 1702, Margaret Pastree of Boston, wife of John Pastree, appealed to the Superior Court of Judicature from a sentence passed in the Court of General Sessions, whereby she was required to return to one Sanders a quantity of silk found in her possession. The jury found for the plaintiff, and ordered that the silk be restored to her.[3] In Plymouth there is some evidence

[1] Estate of Cross (1656) "Records of the Particular Court of Conn., 1639-1663," Conn. Hist. Soc., *Publications*, XXII, 166.

[2] White *v.* Duren, Executor (1697) *N. C. Col. Rec.*, I, 479. It is likely that the plaintiff was a feme covert at the time of suit, for, in 1695, she sued her husband on ante-nuptial contract. *Ibid.*, pp. 444, 446, 448.

[3] Pastree *v.* Sanders (1702) MSS. Mass. Sup. Court Judic. (1700-1714), fol. 67.

that the personal property of the wife was considered to be not in the possession, but in the custody of the husband, and subject, at her death, to disposition among her children.[1] In occasional cases the wife was sued alone for her debts, and, in at least one instance, the husband appeared for the defendant and satisfied the judgment.[2]   In an action of debt brought in New York shortly after the English conquest, it was alleged that a payment to a wife was an adequate defense against a suit brought by the husband.[3]

The married woman in colonial America might acquire complete control over her personal estate by making an antenuptial contract by which her husband granted her power of disposition.[4]   Where the wife was living apart from her husband, she could not be sued for his debts in some jurisdictions,[5] and, in others, enabling statutes were passed by the legislatures empowering married women to dispose of their personalty, and exempting such property from attachment for the debts or from the control of husbands who had deserted them.[6]   Similar provision for the disposition of the married woman's private estate and for charging such estate with her personal obligations was made in statutes relating to " feme-sole traders," such as the Pennsylvania enactment of 1718.[7]   According to its provisions, executions could be " awarded against the goods and chattels in the possession of such wives, or in the hands or possession of others in trust for them, and not against the goods and chattels of their

[1] Estate of Phillips (1677) *Ply. Col. Rec.*, V, 239.

[2] Vos *v.* Hendricx (1653) Fernow, *Rec. Amst.*, I, 63.

[3] Wolsencraft *v.* Garland (1667) Fernow, *Rec. Amst.*, VI, 94.

[4] (1661) *Conn. Pub. Rec.*, I, 360.

[5] Berriman *v.* Nayler (1668) Fernow, *Rec. Amst.*, VI, 129; petition of Frances Donell (1667) *Maine Crt. Rec.*, I, 287.

[6] *Cf.* e. g., enabling act for Susannah Cooper (1744) Hening, *Statutes at Large*, V, 294-296.

[7] Carey and Bioren, *Laws of Pa.*, I, 116, 117.

husbands;" unless it appeared to the court where those executions were returnable that such wives had, "out of their separate stock or profit of their trade, paid debts which were contracted by their husbands, or laid out money for the necessary support and maintenance of themselves and children; then, and in such case, executions" were to be levied upon "the estate real and personal of such husbands, to the value paid or laid out, and no more." Other aspects of the separate liability imposed upon married women engaging in mercantile occupations will be treated in the examination of their contractual and tortious capacity in early American law.

The wife's right of succession to her husband's personal property was universally determined by statute. The Parliamentary statute of 1671, providing that a wife should have one-third of her husband's personal property at his death, or one-half if there were no children, was the pattern for colonial enactment.[1] This interest differed from dower in that it was a mere right of inheritance which took effect only in the intestate estate left by the husband after payment of his debts, or by legacies given in his will.

C. THE MARRIED WOMAN'S CONTRACTUAL CAPACITY

At common law marriage destroyed the general contractual capacity of the woman. She could not contract even with the consent or joinder of her husband. Such incapacity developed as a result of the fact that she ceased to possess property which could be bound by her contracts.[2] To the

---

[1] Plymouth Colony Laws of 1685, Brigham, *Compact*, p. 300; act of 1692, c. 8, *Charter and General Laws of Mass.*, pp. 230-232; Duke of York's Laws (1664), *Duke of York's Book of Laws*, p. 5; Penn. act of 1683, *ibid.*, p. 141; act of 1684, *ibid.*, p. 174; Virginia act of 1662, c. 68, *Abridgement of the Laws* (London, 1704), pp. 2, 3.

[2] Isidor Loeb, *The Legal Property Relations of Married Parties* (New York, 1900), pp. 27, 28; Pollock and Maitland, *History of English Law*, II, 432; Ernest Young, "The Anglo-Saxon Family Law," *Essays in Anglo-Saxon Law*, pp. 176 *et seq.*; Holdsworth, *Hist. Eng. Law*, III, 528.

extent that the married woman was relieved of such proprietary incapacity, whether because in certain mercantile communities she was regarded as a feme sole,[1] or because the Court of Chancery had recognized her power to possess her separate estate free from the common-law rights of the husband,[2] such restrictions upon her power to bind her separate estate on her own contracts were removed.   In colonial jurisdictions, where, by analogy to the chancery practice, women were granted varying degrees of control over their own property, and particularly in colonial trading centers, it was only natural that many medieval restrictions against the wife's contractual capacity should have been in a considerable measure removed.   The extent to which this capacity of the married woman was augmented and the consistency with which the courts recognized these new rights varied considerably in the colonies.

The colonial courts frequently allowed married women to bring suit on their own contracts.   The preamble of a Pennsylvania statute of 1718,[3] recites that

Whereas it often happens that mariners and others, whose circumstances as well as vocations oblige them to go to sea, leave their wives in a way of shop-keeping; and such of them as are industrious, and take due care to pay the merchants they gain so much credit with, as to be well supplied with shop-goods from time to time, whereby they get competent maintenance for themselves and children, and have been enabled to discharge considerable debts, left unpaid by their husbands at their going away; but some of those husbands having so far lost sight of their duty to their wives and tender children, that their

[1] *Borough Customs*, Selden Soc., *Publications*, I, 227, 288; II, cxii; Eileen Power, "The Position of Woman" in *The Legacy of the Middle Ages*, edited by C. G. Crump and E. F. Jacob (Oxford, 1926), p. 467.

[2] Loeb, *op. cit.*, pp. 28, 29.

[3] Act of 1718, c. 226.   Carey and Bioren, *Laws of Pa.*, I, 116, 117.

affections are turned to those, who, in all probability, will put them upon measures, what [not] only to waste what they may get abroad, but misapply such effects as they leave in this province . . .

For the prevention of such situations, the statute proceeds to treat wives of absent husbands, who are left in the province to pursue remunerative occupations or conduct mercantile establishments, as " feme-sole traders," with right to sue and be sued in any court in the province without naming their husbands in the action; and to make their separate property liable to satisfy judgments on contracts which they had made, except on such as were for the maintenance of themselves and their children. Goodwife Donell, who had been deserted by her husband, was permitted by the Maine Provincial Court "to demand & Legally to recover all such debts as are due to her made by herself or Contracts by her owne dealings." [1]

Legislative enactments, private in scope, created substantially the same privileges and imposed similar liabilities in particular cases. Thus, a private act of Virginia in 1744, enabling Susannah Cooper to sell and dispose of her personal estate by deed or will, justified the grant of these powers by pointing out that Mistress Cooper, possessed of an estate of personal property in her own right, had been deserted twenty years previously by her husband, an impecunious person, who, prior to his act of abandonment, had dissipated a large portion of her estate and had left a collection of debts behind him. In satisfying his creditors out of her own estate, his wife was reduced to serious straits. Since Cooper's propitious departure, she was able to accumulate some property. New problems then presented themselves. No purchaser would "treat with her on account of her coverture." She could not sue those who trespassed on her lands or bring suit

---

[1] Petition of Donell (1666) *Maine Crt. Rec.*, I, 319, 320.

on contracts which she had made.　The statute, in addition to granting Mrs. Cooper the free disposition of her estate, enabled her to make contracts in her own name and to sue and be sued as though unmarried.[1]

Frequent cases illustrate the practice of married women conducting the business affairs of their husbands in the latter's absence.　In a Newcastle case of 1678,[2] it appears that the plaintiff's wife had sold some spoons to the defendant.　The plaintiff admitted in court that his wife did frequently " as much as himselfe " " make bargains " and bought and sold goods, and that he sanctioned such activities. In the Maryland case of *Trussel v. Pakes,*[3] an action of detinue for an Indian boy was brought.　From the deposition it appears that the defendant's wife had undertaken to cure the lad and return him to the plaintiff, and for her services was to be paid one hundred pounds of tobacco.　When the plaintiff had questioned her authority to make such contracts, " shee made answare that shee had a Lre of Attorney from hir Husband to doe any business whatsoever."

Records of cases in which the wife brought suit alone on contracts are not infrequent.[4]　In Roman-Dutch law the general rule was that the married woman could not bind herself or her husband or the community without the consent or subsequent ratification of her husband.　The married woman's contract was followed by legal consequences in certain cases, such as: (1) where she contracted with her husband's consent or where he subsequently ratified; (2) where she acted

---

[1] Hening, *Statutes at Large*, V, 294-296.

[2] Shackerly *v.* Salter (1678) *Newcastle Rec.*, pp. 209, 210.

[3] (1650) *Md. Arch.*, X, 15, 16.

[4] Waltham *v.* Richards (1641) *Assistants*, II, 102, 103; Martin *v.* Evans (1651) *New Haven Town Rec.*, I, 71, 76; Saull *v.* Cowdall (1658) *R. I. Court Rec.*, I, 49; Bradnox *v.* Estate of Cox (1648) *Md. Arch.*, IV, 446 (suit for services rendered).

as his agent; (3) where she was carrying on a public trade with his consent; (4) where she made contracts for necessaries in her own name; (5) where the contract was unilateral; (6) where the wife received a benefit under the contract; (7) where the husband had deserted his wife and was absent from the jurisdiction; and (8) where, by antenuptial contract, the wife had reserved the free administration of her property for herself.[1] In New Netherland these far-reaching exceptions to the general rule resulted in the extension of the contractual power to married women on a scale more lavish than that which obtained in any other colonial jurisdiction, and typical cases of married women's suits on their contracts for commodities and labor may be cited from the *Records of New Amsterdam*.[2]

In the colonial courts the married woman who had gained contractual privileges was not allowed to shield herself from liability by pleading her common-law incapacity to make binding agreements. To obviate this type of inequitable plea a South Carolina statute of 1712 provides:

Whereas several feme coverts in this Province that are sole traders, do contract debts in this Province with design to defraud the persons to whom they are indebted by sheltering and defending themselves from any suit brought against them by reason of their coverture, whereby several persons are defrauded of their just dues, for the prevention of which, Be it enacted, by the authority aforesaid, that any feme covert being a sole trader in this Province, shall be liable to any suit or action to be brought against her for any debt contracted as a sole trader, and all proceedings thereupon to judgment and

---

[1] Lee, *Roman Dutch Law*, pp. 389 *et seq.*

Jansen *v.* Andriesen's wife (1653) Fernow, *Rec. Amst.*, I, 50; Steenmetz *v.* Verleth (1653) *ibid.*, p. 65; Verleth *v.* Beekman (1655) *ibid.*, pp. 315, 316; Loockerman's wife *v.* Cockril (1666) *ibid.*, VI, 10; Hardenbroecx's wife *v.* Holst (1668) *ibid.*, p. 139.

execution as if such woman was sole and not under coverture, any law or custom to the contrary thereof in any wise notwithstanding.[1]

In other jurisdictions wives were sued on contracts for wages,[2] for goods sold and delivered,[3] for rent,[4] and on a note.[5] These cases are chiefly drawn from the New Netherland court records, where, in accord with Roman-Dutch law, the wife was not allowed to pledge her husband's credit for numerous types of contracts. Most frequent suits occurred where the wife was carrying on a public trade, in unilateral agreements, and where the married woman had taken a benefit under the contract.

Just as the husband under the system of separate property would be discharged of liability from the contracts of his wife except for her necessaries, so, according to the principle of contractual reciprocity, the wife's estate would be no longer chargeable for her husband's obligations. In 1746 one John Fenbey, a porter, inserted in the *Pennsylvania Gazette* a notice that his wife had deserted him; this was done in order to rebut the presumption that she was still acting as his agent in making contracts. The publication of the item inspired an acid surrebuttal:

Whereas John, the Husband of Mary Fenbey, hath advertised her in this Paper as eloped from him &c., tho' 'tis well known they parted by consent, and agreed to divide their Goods in a

---

[1] Act of 1712, c. xii. *S. C. Statutes at Large* (Columbia, S. C., 1837), II, 588.

[2] Jansen *v.* Andriesen (1653) Fernow, *Rec. Amst.*, I, 50.

[3] Vis *v.* Capoens (1654) *ibid.*, p. 148; Nes *v.* Cornelisen (1654) *ibid.*, pp. 170, 171; Mans *v.* Heyman (1654) *ibid.*, p. 268; Van Leyden *v.* Varleth (1655) *ibid.*, p. 385; where the contract apparently was made by the plaintiff's husband.

[4] Backer *v.* van Leeven (1667) *ibid.*, VI, 86.

[5] Sharp *v.* Cooly (1669) *ibid.*, p. 163.

Manner which he has not yet been so just as fully to comply with, but detains Her Bed and Wedding Ring. And as she neither has, nor desires to run him into Debt, believing her own Credit to be fully as good as his; so she desires no one would trust him on her Account, for neither will she pay any Debts of his contracting.

Mary Fenbey.[1]

In the American colonies the contractual capacity of the married woman was not co-extensive with her control over her separate property. The conservative common-law concepts were in fairly wide acceptance. Even in mercantile regions, where the wife's separate control over her property was permitted, the husband frequently brought suit on his wife's contracts without having her join in the action. For example, he frequently sued for the value of his wife's services.[2] In *Hebden v. Hall*,[3] the plaintiff recovered a substantial verdict from the defendant for a surgical operation performed by the former's wife upon the leg of the defendant's servant. Frequently the husband recovered in court for goods sold and delivered by his wife.[4] Ofttimes the wife conducted the prosecution of the suit and engaged the attorney, but actually permitted the action to be brought in

---

[1] *Pennsylvania Gazette*, July 31, August 7, 1746.

[2] Dike *v.* Miller (1721) MSS. Mass. Sup. Court Judic. (1721-1725), fol. 12, for nursing a child; Steenmetz *v.* Verleth (1653) Fernow, *Rec. Amst.*, I, 55, as servant of the defendant; Matysen *v.* van Borsum (1655) *ibid.*, p. 298, for nursing and rearing a child, the contract having been made between the plaintiff's and defendant's wives; Hall *v.* Estate of Wilkes (1648) *New Haven Col. Rec.*, I, 397, on what appears to be the wife's ante-nuptial indenture of services, the plaintiff suing " for a portion for his wife."

[3] (1644) *Md. Arch.*, IV, 268.

[4] Verbraeck *v.* Wessels (1666) Fernow, *Rec. Amst.*, VI, 37; Bedlow *v.* Langestraat (1668) *ibid.*, p. 111, where the contract was between the defendant's wife and the plaintiff's wife.

her husband's name. One eighteenth-century New York lawyer's cost book contains, as a typical item, the following:

> William Chase
> > *vs*
> > Catherine Crow otherwise
> > called Cathl Gavan
>
> Dam[ages]
> £ 19

Decr 29th at the Request of Mrs. Chase I issued a writ and delivered it to her Barkeeper the messenger she sent for it.

In the Evening Mrs Chase told me she had got security and that she and the deft were each to pay half the Costs and That she would see me paid.[1]

From the limited evidence available, it is difficult to distinguish clearly between actions brought on the ante- and post-nuptial contracts of the married woman. Conservative practice was occasionally observed in cases where the husband sued alone on the ante-nuptial contracts of his wife. The irony was doubtless unintentional, but the cases recorded are actions for breach of promise of marriage in which the husband recovered damages from his wife's previous lover.[2] On what grounds such damages were awarded it would be indeed difficult to determine, unless on the theory that the husband had suffered tangible damage because the defendant in his utter selfishness had not married the girl himself and thereby obviated the expense and responsibility which the marriage entailed the plaintiff. There is no record of any women sitting on these juries.

By the same token, the husband was personally liable on the contracts of his wife in some situations where the mar-

---

[1] Anon. " Comon Pleas Reg. A. 331," NYHS.

[2] Sutton *v.* Jacob (1663) *Ply. Col. Rec.*, VII, 108; Cocker's case (1642) *Essex*, I, 144, a prosecution for breach of promise; March *et ux. v.* March (1682) *Assistants*, I, 214, 215, a joint action for breach of promise. The judgment for the husband in the Plymouth case appears to have been awarded in reversal of the original verdict upon appeal.

ried parties were living together and the wife's estate was not sequestered. In *Kitsen v. Philipsen* [1] a married man was successfully sued on the note of his wife's first husband. Here, doubtless due to the complicated legal situation in the colony of New York in 1666, shortly after the English conquest, the individual responsibility of the husband was emphatically recognized in a manner exceeding the rigorous requirements of the common law. In other cases the husband was sued for his wife's post-nuptial contracts. [2] In the Maryland action of *Nevill v. Beach,* [3] evidence was presented of the defendant's ratification of his wife's contract to pay for her transportation, and he was held liable probably on the theory of agency. [4]

At common law, where the husband and wife were living together, the authority of the husband for contracts which the wife made for her necessaries was implied in fact. The colonial courts followed the common law and made the husband's estate chargeable for his wife's contracts for food, clothing and shelter, and, in numerous cases, for medical attention rendered her during illness. [5] Where the wife was abandoned by her husband, such agency was imputed in law. [6] In order to rebut this presumption which appears to have

[1] (1666) Fernow, *Rec. Amst.*, VI, 6, 16.

[2] Walliam *v.* Sinnexe (1681) *Newcastle Rec.*, p. 498, on the wife's acceptance of a note; Vos *v.* Hendrecx (1653) *Rec. Amst.*, I, 63, on a book debt (the defendant in the action being the wife, but the husband being condemned by the court to pay the judgment).

[3] (1644) *Md. Arch.*, IV, 269, 274.

[4] *Cf.* Y. B. 21 Hen. VIII, Mich., pl. 64; Manby *v.* Scott (1659) 1 Sid. 109.

[5] Garnett *v.* Nevill (1642) *Md. Arch.*, IV, 128; Ellyson *v.* Hervey (1644) *ibid.*, p. 294; Smith *v.* Newell (1656) *ibid.*, X, 468; Cording *v.* Bishop (1663) *Essex*, III, 75.

[6] James *v.* Warren (1707) Holt (K. B.) 104, where the wife is called an " agent of necessity."

been raised in the colonies even before the view became crystallized in England, colonial husbands hastened to advertise their refusal to pay future debts of their wives' contracting where the latter had deserted them or had been guilty of acts of extravagance. As early as 1664, William Tubbs, who had tried in vain to separate from his wife, appeared in the Plymouth court to disown " all debts that shee shall make unto any from this time forward, as not intended to pay any of them to any person whatsoeuer." [1]   Such advertisements were not always permitted to go unchallenged. For instance, the *Boston Evening Post* in 1761 contained the following remonstrance:

> Weston, July 1, 1762.
>
> Messrs. Fleet,
>
> I find in your last Monday's Papers that my Husband has informed the Publick That I have eloped—and that I run him into Debt, and has given a Caution not to Trust me on his Account. Although I am very sensible that neither he or I are of much Importance to the Publick, for he has not an Estate to entitle me to any Credit on his account; yet I desire you to be so kind to me, as to let the Publick know That I never run him in Debt in my Life, nor ever eloped, unless it was to Day Labour, to support me and the Children, which I am of necessity Obliged to do; and shall be ever glad to do my Duty to him, and wish he would for the future behave to me in such a Manner that I may do it with more Ease than heretofore.
>
> Her
> Mary X Wellington
> Mark.[2]

Even in cases where married women carried on business enterprises apart from their husbands, and were considered by law to be feme-sole traders and therefore liable with their

---

[1] (1664) *Ply. Col. Rec.*, IV, 66.
[2] Cited by Dexter, *op. cit.*, pp. 186, 187.

own estate for their contracts, they were permitted by statute to charge the property of their absent husbands with debts contracted for the necessary support and maintenance of themselves and their children, and the creditors were enabled to sue out process of attachment against the husband's estate.[1]

In a plurality of cases the common-law rule requiring the joinder of parties in suit for the wife's causes of action arising from her ante-nuptial agreements [2] was followed in the colonial courts.[3] The husband and wife sued jointly on ante-nuptial contracts of labor performed by the wife,[4] and on her ante-nuptial covenants.[5] Occasionally husband and wife joined as parties to a contract where services were required of them both. Thus, Nathaniel Morton and his wife Lydia, of Plymouth, agreed in 1667 with William Harlow to care and provide for his son until he reached the age of twenty-one. In case Nathaniel were to die before Harlow's son was seven years of age, Harlow agreed to pay Morton's wife £10 toward the living expenses of the child. The document, however, was not signed by Lydia Morton.[6]

---

[1] Act of 1718, c. 226, § 4, Carey and Bioren, *Laws of Pa.*, I, 116, 117.

[2] *Lawes Resolutions*, p. 212.

[3] *Cf.* e. g., White *et ux. v.* Wilson (1694) General Court of the County of Albemarle, *N. C. Col. Rec.*, I, 406; same *v.* Terry (1694) *ibid.*, pp. 406, 407; same *v.* Kitching (1695) *ibid.*, p. 444; same *v.* Kitching *et ux.* (1695) *ibid.*, p. 444; same *v.* Steel (1695) *ibid.*, p. 446; same *v.* Lawson (1695) *ibid.*, p. 446; same *v.* Moline (1695) *ibid.*, p. 448.

[4] Brookes *et ux. v.* Mitchell (1653) *Md. Arch.*, X, 268, 269; Easterbrook *et ux. v.* Flint (1724) MSS. Mass. Sup. Court Judic. (1721-1725), fol. 210. The judgment for the plaintiffs for £30 damages and costs was reversed in 1725. *Ibid.*, fol. 249. The plea of John Read in his brief for the appellee that the statute of limitations barred recovery appears to have been effective. MSS. File Sup. Court Judic., No. 18233 (5).

[5] Young *et ux. v.* Wallingford (1723) MSS. Mass. Sup. Court Judic. (1721-1725), fol. 111.

[6] *Ply. Col. Rec.*, V, 10, 11.

At common law the husband and wife were jointly liable for the wife's ante-nuptial debts. Not only did the law require a joinder of parties in personal actions, but failure of either party to make his or her appearance constituted insufficient answer.[1] By cleverly alternating the appearance of the two defendants,—a type of legal chicanery known as *fourching,*—litigation was notoriously delayed.[2] In accord with this practice, on a circuit of Kings County in 1695, a New York court stated in *Howe et ux v. Whitly*[3] their " opinion that the accon cannot ly against the wife unlesse the husband be taken he being alive," and the case was " adjourned (sine) die." In general in the colonies the husband and wife were joined as defendants in suits brought on the latter's ante-nuptial contracts;[4] but here, as in other cases, the common-law rules regarding the married woman's incapacity were not consistently enforced. Both were sued for the wife's breach of an ante-nuptial contract of service,[5] on her promise to the selectmen of the town to support an indigent person,[6] and on her pre-marital contract for the payment óf rent.[7]

---

[1] 44 Ed. III, fol. 1.

[2] *Lawes Resolutions,* pp. 218, 219.

[3] New York Hist. Soc., *Collections,* XXV, 88.

[4] *Cf.* e. g., Hassold *v.* White *et ux.* (1694) General Court of the County of Albermarle, *N. C. Col. Rec.,* I, 412; Young *et ux. v.* Wallingford (1723) MSS. Mass. Sup. Court Judic. (1721-1725), fol. III; Kelly *v.* Fraser *et ux.* (1767-1769) Common Pleas Register of John McKesson, p. 304, NYHS.

[5] Johnson *v.* Tennis *et ux.* (1654) *Md. Arch.,* X, 405.

[6] Herd *et ux.,* appellants *v.* Selectmen of Town of Wells (1701) MSS. Mass. Sup. Court Judic. (1700-1714), fol. 44.

[7] Dolbear *et ux. v.* Brock (1723) MSS. Mass. Sup. Court Judic. (1721-1725), fol. 115.

D. THE MARRIED WOMAN'S CAPACITY IN TORT

The rights which married women gained in the field of liability at early American law were not co-extensive with their newly-won authority in other branches of the law. As in the nineteenth-century advance of woman's civil rights, the rights and liabilities in tort of the colonial woman followed upon her proprietary and contractual rights, and at a much slower pace. The conservative influences of the common law were not easily disregarded. On the other hand, a lack of ready acquaintance with the rules of pleading, which, in the field of common-law liability, placed the woman in a favored position before the court, resulted ofttimes in the failure to confer the full benefit of the special protective devices of the common-law system designed for the feme covert.

At common law the husband and wife sued jointly for both the ante- and post-nuptial torts committed against the wife.[1] As to any tort committed before the marriage, the right of action was a liability cast upon the husband by law; during the marriage such liability existed in a suit brought against him and his wife as co-defendants.[2] The husband and wife were likewise joined at common law for torts committed by the wife during the marriage relationship,[3] except in so far as the law presumed that she acted under his compulsion when in his presence. Fine distinctions between ante- and post-nuptial torts were seldom found in colonial court reports. In order to discover the rationale of the pleadings and of the substantive law in the field of tort in

[1] *Lawes Resolutions*, p. 197; *A Treatise of Trover and Conversion* (London, 1696), pp. 24-26.

[2] Y. B. 4 Ed. II (Selden Soc.), pp. 153, 154; E. Peck, *The Law of Persons or Domestic Relations* (Chicago, 1913), p. 62.

[3] Y. B. 36 Hen. VI, pl. 2; *Treatise of Trover and Conversion*, pp. 35-37.

which married women were involved, it is proposed to treat the specific problems involved in the leading tort remedies.

(1) In the action of trespass for assault and battery, uniformity of pleading is not found. Generally in the seventeenth-century cases, the husband sued alone for such torts to his wife,—in the majority of cases for a trespass committed during coverture,[1]—while in the eighteenth, when the common-law rules were more rigorously prescribed by the courts, the husband and wife joined in bringing suit.[2] Many of the seventeenth-century cases where the husband brought suit for an assault upon the chastity of his wife or to recover damages for rape[3] may be explained by analogy to the husband's action at common law for criminal conversation.[4] It is clear that in the eighteenth century the wife was under a disability to bring suit, without joining her husband, for torts committed against her. Because of this disability, the Council and House of Representatives of Massachusetts in 1767 passed a private act to empower Abigail Conqueret, a married woman, to sue as a feme sole for her post-nuptial torts.[5] It appeared from the petition that Mrs. Conqueret's

[1] Longley v. Newhall (1663) *Essex*, III, 33; Boynton v. Browne (1682) *Essex*, VIII, 277 (the plaintiff included in the damages the loss of his own time in caring for his wife); Carpyn v. Quicq (1667) Fernow, *Rec. Amst.*, VI, 60; Rider v. Garland (1668) *ibid.*, p. 132; Willemsen v. Gerrits (1669) *ibid.*, p. 166; Jansen v. Wessels (1670) *ibid.*, p. 225.

[2] Hart *et ux. v.* Wright (1722) MSS. Mass. Sup. Court Judic. (1721-1725), fol. 41. But *cf.* also Craford *et ux. v.* Ashby (1667) *Essex*, III, 420, 421 (writ for defamation, unjust molestation, and false imprisonment).

[3] Rosse v. Greenland (1663) *Essex*, III, 88, assault; Kirke v. Phepoe (1654) *Md. Arch.*, X, 407, rape (the wife may possibly be regarded here as a party-plaintiff); Ford v. Cooke (1667) *New Haven Town Rec.*, II, 210, 211 (assault and battery with attempt to commit rape); also quoted in MSS. Chalmers Papers, Connecticut, I, fol. 7, NYPL; Worden v. Crowell and Maker, assault (penal action) (1668) *Ply. Col. Rec.*, V, 8.

[4] Peck, *op. cit.*, pp. 36-38.

[5] *Mass. Acts and Resolves*, VI, App. I, 209.

husband had gone to sea and had not been heard from for four years. In his absence his wife had suffered two grievous assaults and batteries from which she had been ill for over six months, and, as a consequence, her damages were material. One of the tortfeasors had agreed with her to submit the case to a group of arbiters who were to render an impartial award. As a result of the arbitration an award was made in favor of Mrs. Conqueret, which the loser refused to satisfy. In her husband's absence Mrs. Conqueret was under a disability to maintain any action in her own name. The statute empowering her in her own name to prosecute to judgment and execution her actions against the two malfeasants was disallowed by the Privy Council in 1768.[1]

When the husband was sued alone for the battery committed by his wife, it was frequently because such tortious act was performed in his presence and by his command, or at least with his consent. At common law the wife's will was supposed to have been subordinated to that of her husband. In this instance, such subordination operated in her favor and to her husband's disadvantage, for a conclusive presumption was raised that she acted under his compulsion; and she was wholly freed from liability, the husband being liable alone. If the wife committed the tort in her husband's presence, though without any evidence that he commanded or consented to it, a rebuttable presumption was raised that such act had been under his domination.[2] For the ordinary run of post-nuptial batteries committed by the wife, the husband and wife were joined as party-defendants.[3]

[1] Upon the reading of the adverse report of Sir Matthew Lamb upon this act, dated Jan. 18, 1768, a draft of a representation was ordered to be prepared proposing its repeal. The draft was prepared and signed, Feb. 18, 1768. *Mass. Acts and Resolves*, IV, 994, note.

[2] Peck, *op. cit.*, p. 62; Bennett *v.* Migillegan (1667) *Essex*, III, 414.

[3] Lane *v.* Higgins *et ux.* (1662) *Westchester Court Rec.*, p. 30; Beale *v.* Downing *et ux.* and Benett (1667) *Essex*, III, 419, 443.

Cases in which the wife was sued personally for the damages resulting from her assaults and batteries are infrequent.[1]

(2) In the colonial courts the appeal of larceny and the action of trespass *de bonis asportatis* were in use side by side with the remedy of trover to recover personal property or damages for such loss. No consistent practice in regard to the participation of married women in these remedies is found. At common law actions of the type of replevin and detinue, which affirmed the property in the husband, could only be brought in his name; but the action of trover, where damages were sought, was brought by the husband and wife jointly in cases where the trover took place before coverture and the conversion afterward.[2] The strict rules of pleading which the common law imposed in such cases were ignored in the colonial courts, where informal actions were frequently brought to recover chattels. Such prosecutions, analogous to the appeal of larceny, were on numerous occasions brought by the husband for the conversion of his wife's chattels.[3] Occasionally in such suits judgment was given with great informality to the wife.[4]

Uniformity is likewise lacking in the appeals which were brought for chattels purloined by a married woman or for conversion. For example, where the husband and wife were joined as defendants, it appeared in one New Haven case that the trover had been committed by the husband and the conversion by the wife. Nevertheless the court ordered the

---

[1] Siampan *v.* Marlin and the " wife of Adrian Vincent " (1668) Fernow, *Rec. Amst.*, VI, 143; Seston *v.* wife of Pietersen (1675) *Minutes of the Court of Albany, Rensselaerswyck and Schenectady*, II, 21, 47.

[2] *Treatise of Trover and Conversion*, pp. 24-26.

[3] Whitehead *v.* Armstrong (1666) *New Haven Town Rec.*, I, 173, 174.

[4] Howell *v.* Oliver (1648) *Md. Arch.*, IV, 424; *cf.* also Andries *v.* Tarkinton (1677) *Newcastle Rec.*, p. 136.

former to pay the damages.¹   In the majority of cases the husband alone was ordered to satisfy the judgment.²   Such personal liability, resting on the husband's control of his wife's chattels, was extended to cover the ante-nuptial acts of conversion of the wife.³   With a degree of inconsistency which we have come to accept as characteristic of legal administration in this period, the courts occasionally allowed the plaintiff to sue the wife alone for her acts of conversion.⁴

(3) In the action of defamation, a favorite tort in the American colonies, if we are to judge from the extensive litigation relating to offences of this character, it is even more difficult to explain the haphazard methods of pleading on any other basis than on that of indifference to or ignorance of the English rules.   Suits for post-nuptial defamation of the wife were at times brought by husband and wife jointly.   Thus, Thomas Moulton and his wife sued William Stidson and his spouse in an action of " trespasse upon the case," for the false report which Stidson's wife had raised. The latter had declared that Moulton's wife had raised an accusation of rape against a creditor for the purpose of forcing him to cease attempts to collect a debt she owed him.⁵ In what constituted by far the greater number of cases the

---

¹ Davenport *v.* Smith *et ux.* (1665) *New Haven Town Rec.*, II, 147.

² Whitheare *v.* Lord's wife (1638) *Essex*, I, 5; case of Felton's wife (1641) *Assistants*, II, 108; Gedny *v.* Archer's wife (1650) *Essex*, I, 185; van de Dilliman *v.* Rogers' wife (1679-1683) *Conn. Pub. Rec.*, III, 41, 140, and n.

³ Turner *v.* Gennings (1643) *New Haven Town Rec.*, I, 105.

⁴ Cockshott *v.* Whitcliff (1654) *Md. Arch.*, IV, 154; van Leyden *v.* Vorwanger's wife (1655) Fernow, *Rec. Amst.*, I, 335. (The defendant's husband appeared for her and the nature of the pleading is by no means clear.)

⁵ Lechford, *Note Book*, pp. 259-261. For other cases, *cf.* Hollis *et ux. v.* Boys (1642) *Md. Arch.*, IV, 149; Andries *et ux. v.* Staalcop *et ux.* (1680) *Newcastle Rec.*, pp. 403, 410.

husband sued alone for damage which his wife suffered as a result of slanderous remarks. Numerous instances where the husband brought action for defamation of his wife during coverture do not comprise sets of facts different from the preceding cases where the husband and wife joined as party-plaintiffs; although in the defamation cases, where the slanderous statements were uttered of both the husband and wife, it is apparent that the wife's cause of action has been merged in that of her husband.[1]

Nor is the nature of the husband's personal damages any clearer in other types of cases which arose. In *van Neck v. Teunissen*,[2] the plaintiff sued for damages resulting from a statement of the defendant that his wife's sister had been executed on the scaffold in Holland for having committed a crime. In a Maryland action, which arose in 1649, the plaintiff sued in behalf of his wife in an action of defamation for a slanderous utterance of the defendant in repeating a report sponsored by his own wife that the plaintiff's wife had said " that the king dyed unjustly." The court gave judgment for the plaintiff for three hundred pounds of tobacco; but in this muddled lawsuit the record states that the plaintiff's wife, " present in Court on behalf of her husband," was willing to remit the penalty because of the defendant's inability to pay, and stood satisfied with the payment of costs.[3]   In the Essex County Quarterly Court of Massachusetts one defendant was sued in 1648 " for raising

---

[1] *Cf.* e. g., James *v.* Pitford (1650) *Essex*, I, 204; James *v.* Gatchill (1651) *ibid.*, p. 229; Osgood *v.* Flanders (1653) *ibid.*, p. 312; Collings *v.* Coldam (1653) *ibid.*, p. 276; Beckley *v.* Hitchcock (1659) *New Haven Town Rec.*, I, 413; James *v.* Pitford (1667) *Essex*, III, 413 n.; Gifford *v.* Hutchins (1668) *Essex*, IV, 30, 31; Urgent *v.* Ashman (1668) Fernow, *Rec. Amst.*, VI, 128.

[2] (1669) Fernow, *Rec. Amst.*, VI, 128.

[3] Banister *v.* Browne (1649) *Md. Arch.*, X, 38.

an evil report " of the plaintiff's deceased wife.[1] In England, the famous maxim of the common law, *actio personalis
moritur cum persona,*[2] precluded recovery in all cases of this
character which arose in trespass, case, trover, deceit, and
defamation.

The recognition of the right of the husband to sue alone
for defamatory remarks regarding his wife's fidelity and
respectability is explainable possibly on the ground of the
husband's interest in the consortium of his wife and by
analogy to the colonial actions which the husband brought
for assault to his wife and to the suits for criminal conversation. Frequent instances of actions for damages, both for
ante-nuptial statements tending to discredit the reputation of
the married woman for chastity,[3] and for slanderous remarks
concerning the illicit sexual activities of the wife during her
marriage,[4] are found in the early American court records of
both the seventeenth and eighteenth centuries, and form the
bulk of the defamation cases in which the husband sues
alone. Because of the personal responsibility which was
imposed upon the husband for his wife's acts of conversion
or larceny, it would follow that he would have a cause of
action alone for statements falsely attributing theft to his
wife. These cases amounted substantially to the action at
common law for malicious prosecution.[5] Where the defendant had made a statement defamatory of the plaintiff's
wife and tending to bring the plaintiff himself into disrepute

[1] Willix *v.* Hethersai (1648) *Essex*, I, 150.

[2] Bracton, f. 101 b.

[3] Martyn *v.* Sargent (1669) *Essex*, IV, 129 and n.

[4] Stanton *v.* Sipperance (1649) *Conn. Pub. Rec.*, I, 193, 194, Goderis
v. d'Wys (1651) Fernow, *Rec. Amst.*, I, 51; Coerton *v.* Mrs. Gerrits
(1653) *ibid.*, p. 96; Cornish *v.* King (1653) *Essex*, I, 280; Cloice *v.*
Putnam (1722) MSS. Mass. Sup. Court Judic. (1721-1725), fols. 55, 56.

[5] Leigh *v.* Sanders (1665) *Essex*, III, 313.

or public ridicule, a cause of action was given him. Thus, Abraham Dickerman of New Haven recovered from Thomas Wheadon for the slanderous statement that Goodwife Dickerman had beaten her husband and thrown him " out of doores crying." [1]   In some early New Netherland cases the married woman sued as a feme sole to recover damages for defamation.[2]   Among criminal prosecutions for slander, a procedure which was practiced throughout the colonies,[3] there is a record of a suit prosecuted by the parents of a married woman against several individuals who had maligned their daughter by spreading a report that she did not cohabit with her husband.[4]

The cases are about equally divided between those in which the husband and wife were joined as defendants for the defamatory statements attributed to the latter,[5] and those in which the wife was sued alone,[6] a procedure contrary to the common law.   Of the latter actions, a considerable number, it should be noted, were brought in the courts of New Netherland, and in early New York before the rules of the common law had been deeply planted.   In the New Haven

---

[1] (1661) *New Haven Town Rec.*, I, 484, 486.

[2] Jorisen *v.* de Haes (1655) Fernow, *Rec. Amst.*, I, 322, 328, 329; Woutersen *v.* Fellewer (1655) *ibid.*, I, 381, 387.

[3] *Cf. supra*, Chap. I.

[4] Case of Keely *et al.* (1659) *New Haven Town Rec.*, I, 389, 390.

[5] Barly *v.* Hall *et ux.* (1649) *Essex*, I, 164; Turner *v.* Lenore *et ux.* (1650) *ibid.*, pp. 198, 199; Nurce *v.* Porter *et ux.* (1654) *ibid.*, p. 363; Sutton *v.* Sutlife *et ux.* (1659) *Ply. Col. Rec.*, III, 179; Clarke *v.* Tompson *et ux.* (1667) *Essex*, III, 438; Selectmen of Lynn *v.* Richards *et ux.* (1670) *Essex*, IV, 295.

[6] Bartoll *et ux. v.* Peach (1644) *Essex*, I, 62, 78, 81 (also criminal); Edmonds *v.* Jennings (1648) *Conn. Pub. Rec.*, I, 171; Moran *v.* Pinion *et al.* (1665) *New Haven Town Rec.*, II, 122; Jansen *v.* Spyser (1653) Fernow, *Rec. Amst.*, I, 61, 62; Haughton *v.* Cooper (1651) *New Haven Town Rec.*, I, 86; Benat *v.* Willems (1666) Fernow, *Rec. Amst.*, VI, 12, 17.

action of *Fuller v. Newman et ux.,*[1] it appeared from the evidence that Mistress Newman had spread the tale that Goodwife Fuller had indiscreetly entertained some young men at her home in her husband's absence. The court took this occasion to point out that Newman had fallen " short of his duty " in not insisting that his wife give due satisfaction for the slander and settle the affair privately, and for adding fuel to the fire by making other defamatory remarks. The judgment which was rendered against him for £5 is evidence of the judicial sanction behind private arbitration.

On the other hand, the legislators apparently did not regard the imposition of the damages upon the husband for the indiscretions of his wife as in the nature of an equitable distribution of responsibility for such tortious actions and as one calculated to curtail this pernicious habit. To equalize the burdens, a Virginia statute of 1662 provided:

Where as oftentimes many brabling women often slander and scandalize their neighbours for which their poore husbands are often brought into chargeable and vexatious suits, and cast in greate damages; Bee it therefore enacted . . . that in actions of slander occasioned by the wife as aforesaid after judgment passed for the damages the women shalbe punished by ducking; and if the slander be soe enormous as to be adjudged at a greater damage than five hundred pounds tobacco then the women to suffer a ducking for each five hundred pounds of tobacco adjudged against the husband if he refuse to pay the tobacco.[2]

The husband was impaled on the horns of a dilemma, for it is doubtful if any solvent married man was brave enough to risk domestic turmoil by refusing to pay the expenses of his

---

[1] (1649) *New Haven Col. Rec.*, I, 473.
[2] Hening, *Statutes at Large*, II, 166.

wife's loquacity. In any event, duckings were fashionable in colonial Virginia. The statute is evidential of the practice of suing the husband alone for the defamatory acts of his wife, a procedure which was occasionally found in the northern and middle colonies as well.[1]

(4) Liability was likewise imposed upon the husband for the illegal acts of his wife which were prosecuted in *qui tam* actions or by purely criminal suits. Such liability was extended to cover the ante-nuptial crimes and misdemeanors of the married woman. In 1647 the General Court of New Haven ordered one recreant husband to pay a fine for his wife's acts of insobriety committed prior to their marriage. The husband stoutly denied that it was his debt, but " it was tould him that his wives debts were his." At a subsequent session of the court, this unfortunate again demanded that the court state the legal basis for imposing the penalty upon him, and again " it was tould hime, by the lawe of his marrying the widdow, wch owed it before he marryed her." [2] No harder case can be imagined than the one in which the bond of £10, which Gabriel Hicke of Rhode Island was forced to post for his wife's appearance to answer a charge of committing adultery, was forfeited for her default.[3] A Maine court sitting at York in 1667, fined two husbands for " tollerating " their wives to sell beer without a license.[4] In general, in seventeenth-century colonial law, the husband was commonly fined for his wife's offences.[5]

---

[1] Clough *v.* Conner (1668) *Essex*, IV, 22; Witt *v.* Croft (1667) *ibid.*, III, 422; Bartlet *v.* Martyn (1669) *ibid.*, IV ,184 (the wife, however, was ordered to make acknowledgment in court) ; Beale *v.* Hollingworth (1670) *ibid.*, p. 280; Higgins *v.* Turner (1662) *Westchester Court Rec.*, p. 30.

[2] Pell's case (1647-1648) *New Haven Col. Rec.*, I, 334, 362, 363.

[3] Hick's case (1661-1662) *R. I. Court Rec.*, I, 76, 77, 79.

[4] Cases of Harris and Grant (1667) *Maine Crt. Rec.*, I, 289.

[5] *Cf.* e. g., cases of Wardall and Hussey (1663) *Essex*, III, 100;

When it came to the imposition of corporal punishment, the married woman did not enjoy any degree of vicarious liability for her offences. Wives were whipped and in other ways corporally chastised,[1] and, in a few jurisdictions, chiefly New England ones, they frequently were held personally accountable for their fines, although doubtless their husbands who controlled their personalty were ultimately responsible for the satisfaction of the penalty.[2] In the case of ante-nuptial crimes and other wrongful acts, liability occasionally rested on the wife alone. The Plymouth court ordered one father to pay three pounds as his daughter's fine for having illicit relations with her husband before marriage and before contract.[3]

(5) At common law the wife was under a disability to sue her husband in tort as well as in contract. All common-law inhibitions were abandoned in a Maryland action on the case brought in 1657 before the Provincial Court by Elizabeth Robins against her husband Robert for assault and battery and defamation. The plaintiff secured a postpone-

---

Trowbridge's case (1660) *New Haven Town Rec.*, I, 460, 461; Smith's case (1663) *R. I. Court Rec.*, II, 28; Cowdall's case (1667) *ibid.*, p. 57; Sheriff *v.* Camdal (1668) Fernow, *Rec. Amst.*, VI, 113; Fiscal *v.* vander Spiegel (1674) *N. Y. Col. Docts.*, II, 689; Fitzrandall's case (1678) *Ply. Col. Rec.*, V, 265.

[1] *Cf.* e. g., Wilson's case (1662) *Essex*, III, 17.

[2] *Cf.* e. g., cases of Kitching's wife *et al.* (1662) *Essex*, III, 19; of Longly's wife (1663) *ibid.*, p. 79; Pinnion's wife (1663) *ibid.*, p. 83; Linsford's wife (1663) *ibid.*, p. 109; Buffum's wife *et al.* (1663) *ibid.*, pp. 116, 223 (1664); Gardner's wife *et al.* (1665) *ibid.*, pp. 292, 293; Buffum's wife *et al.* (1665) *ibid.*, p. 343; Gardner's wife *et al.* (1666) *ibid.*, p. 381; Wilson's wife *et al.* (1667) *ibid.*, p. 434; Oakes' wife (1667) *ibid.*, p. 460; Bishop's wife (1665) *ibid.*, p. 244; Pudeater's and Mason's wives (1671) *ibid.*, IV, 410; Hoskins' and Rickard's wives (1664) *Ply. Col. Rec.*, IV, 50; Pels' wife (1648) *Rensselaerswyck Rec.*, pp. 47, 52 (husband appears).

[3] Adkinson's case (1670) *Ply. Col. Rec.*, V, 51.

ment of the suit on the ground of her ill health, and the further disposition of this interesting case is not found in the record. A different angle of the story is adequately presented in the information subsequently brought by Robert Robins against his wife for being *enceinte* despite his long absence from her.[1]

(6) The greatest degree of relief which certain colonial jurisdictions afforded the woman in the field of liability consisted in conferring upon her the right to sue for damages for the death of her husband as a result of a wrongful act attributable to the defendant in certain situations. This substantial tort remedy may be considered an extension of the archaic appeal of felony,[2] and as such marked a notable advance over the contemporary English practice. The common-law rule that personal actions did not survive the death of the injured party precluded recovery in such cases.[3] A detailed treatment of the colonial cases is given in the following chapter.[4]

To recapitulate briefly the ground gained by colonial women in the field of liability, it may be observed that (1) these rights were not co-extensive with the privileges gained by women in other branches of the law; (2) the common-law responsibility imposed upon the husband continued where his control of his wife's personalty was not substantially reduced; (3) great irregularity in the pleading of tort actions is found, a condition attributable to the anarchical state of the law of remedies which prevailed in the colonial courts in the seventeenth century, and which is discussed at greater

---

[1] (1657) *Md. Arch.*, X, 500, 501, 503, 519, 555.

[2] *Cf.* Glanvil, *Tractatus*, Lib. IV, translated by Beames, chs. I-III; 4 Bl. Comm. 312.

[3] Higgins *v.* Butcher (1606) Yelverton 89.

[4] *Cf. infra*, chap IV, § c.

length elsewhere;[1] (4) considerable evidence is available of
the tendency to impose exclusive liability for certain torts
upon the married woman alone; while extensive generalizations cannot be drawn from *Robins v. Robins,* the case
suggests a growing recognition of the individual status of
the married woman in the law of liability; (5) the woman's
right to recover for damages suffered as a result of the
death of her husband or other relative was the most substantial remedy in tort which was won by her in the colonial
period.

E. THE MARRIED WOMAN'S EVIDENTIAL CAPACITY

At common law husband and wife were incompetent to
testify in behalf of each other. The rationale of this testimonial incapacity is placed by Gilbert on the ground that, if
either testified for the other, credibility could not be attached
to the testimony, " because their Interests are absolutely the
same." Hence, the disqualification was on the identical
grounds upon which rested the incapacity of a party to
testify in his own interest. Because of this incapacity of the
wife, the law did not regard it as equitable to compel her to
testify against her husband, particularly since such testimony, it was thought, would inevitably lead to family divi-
sions.[2] Therefore either married party could exercise the
privilege for anti-marital facts and refuse to testify against
his or her spouse.[3]

There is ample evidence that such a rule of testimonial
incapacity obtained generally in the colonial courts in the
eighteenth century, and even earlier in some of the middle
colonies and in the south. In connection with the act for the

---

[1] *Cf. supra*, chap. I.

[2] Gilbert, *Law of Evidence* (Dublin, 1795), pp. 252 *et seq.*; O'Connor
v. Marjoribanks (1842) 4 Man. & Gr.

[3] Wigmore, *Evidence*, § 1164.

punishment of incest, adultery and fornication, a New Jersey statute of 1682 provided that the husband should not " be taken as a witness against his wife, nor the wife against her husband, for any offence punishable by this act." [1]   A clear-cut holding is found in a Pennsylvania case which arose in 1700.[2]   William Smith had been imprisoned in the county gaol of Philadelphia pending trial for rape.   Application was made to admit him to bail.   The distinguished counsel, David Lloyd, argued for the prisoner that " felonies had often been bailed, tho' felony of death."   The attorney-general countered by asserting " that this was only where yᵉ Presumption of Innocence was Strong, wch here was the contrary."   Yet he conceded that, as the case stood, the prisoner should be admitted to bail, for, through lack of adequate evidence, it appeared impossible to convict him.   It seems that the prisoner had clandestinely married in prison the woman who had been the subject of his attack, and " as they were now one flesh, she could give no Evidence agst her Husband."   On her own testimony it was revealed that the bride had been persuaded to contract the marriage in order to save the defendant's life by setting up this evidential impasse.   The prisoner was thereupon admitted to bail. There is little doubt but that the common-law incapacity in matters of evidence existed in the courts of eighteenth-century New York.   In fact *Gilbert on Evidence* was carefully studied by New York attorneys and the very passage cited above was quoted in full in the law note-book of William Smith, jurist of provincial New York.[3]

[1] *Grants and Concessions of New Jersey*, pp. 244, 245.

[2] Smith's case (1700) *Pa. Col. Rec.*, II, 5.   Accord: Kaul *v.* State (Okla., 1929), 277 Pac. 278.

[3] MSS. William Smith Papers, NYPL.   This close adherence to the English practice is clearly seen in the anonymous treatise on the law of evidence, *c.* 1770, in NYHS, which appears to be a composite of various English texts on the subject.   Thus, compare the sections on general and specific laws with Bathurst's treatment (1767) in Buller, *Trials at Nisi Prius*.

In seventeenth-century colonial jurisdictions where the metaphysical concept of the legal unity of husband and wife did not obtain a firm foothold, the married parties were not excluded from testifying for each other and the privilege for anti-marital facts was, as a general practice, not claimed. Thus, Rebecca Roes, whose husband had been indicted in the Westchester court for stealing a hog, testified that she had concealed the hog under orders from her husband and that she knew of no other *particeps criminis*.[1]

In the jurisdictions of Massachusetts Bay, Plymouth, New Haven and New Netherland, married women frequently testified under oath in behalf of their husbands who were either bringing suits or defending actions of contract or tort. An examination of type cases noted herewith reveals the fact that such testimony on material issues disclosed valuable information otherwise unobtainable, and, in general, was evidential of the close familiarity of colonial women with the business activities of their husbands.[2]

Evidence is not lacking that colonial wives testified against their husbands in civil actions. A typical situation is afforded by the suit of William Bunell of New Haven to have his son and daughter released from their indentures of apprenticeship. The plaintiff claimed that when he went to England his wife and father apprenticed the children without his consent. For the defendant, Goodwife Bunell testified that her husband had left little or nothing for the maintenance

---

[1] (1660) *Westchester Court Rec.*, p. 25.

[2] Shatswell *v.* Quilter (1664) *Essex*, III, 141 n.; Duncan *v.* Elwell (1663) *ibid.*, p. 185 n.; Darbey's case (1674) *Ply. Col. Rec.*, V, 158; Howe *v.* Cooper (1650) *New Haven Town Rec.*, I, 29; Blachly *v.* Larabee (1655) *ibid.*, pp. 262, 263; Ward and Ward *v.* Eaton *et al.* (1647) *New Haven Col. Rec.*, I, 329; Perry *v.* Meggs (1648) *ibid.*, p. 417; Langodyck *v.* van Holsteyn (1655) Fernow, *Rec. Amst.*, I, 289; Terhaer *v.* Jansen (1655) *ibid.*, p. 297; Waterhout *v.* Woutersen (1655) *ibid.*, p. 400; van Brountangie *v.* van Groeteboecken (1654) *ibid.*, pp. 262, 263.

of the children, and when " she asked him what she should doe wth them, hee said they were hers as well as his, and he left them wth her." The boy confirmed this conversation, and the court upheld the indentures.[1]

These frequent testimonial practices, in which little or no deference was shown to restrictions existing under the common-law system, render the additional service of illustrating the extent to which the married woman in the American colonies had achieved emancipation in the law.

[1] Bunell *v.* Whithead (1651) *New Haven Town Rec.,* I, 89.

CHAPTER IV

Responsibility for Tortious Acts in Early American Law

A. THE DOCTRINE OF NO LIABILITY WITHOUT FAULT

Considerably prior to the settlement of the American colonies it appears that liability had at common law become a corollary of fault. Such exceptions to the present standard as were found in actions arising from trespasses by cattle, the use of firearms, and damages resulting from fire have been regarded by eminent authorities as survivals of the general rule of absolute liability.[1] In the colonies there is no evidence that any such general rule imposing absolute liability was ever encouraged or even recognized. In fact, even the special class of cases imposing absolute liability at common law was reduced by the subtraction therefrom of actions for damages by domestic animals. Aside from these few exceptions, liability could flow only from culpable conduct or from assumed duties.

1. " Due Care " and " Inevitable Accident "

This dogma was seldom referred to in any of the colonial cases; but respectable evidence of its acceptance is disclosed in the colonial actions of negligence which lay down standards of due care. At the outset we are confronted with a

---

[1] Ames, *Lectures on Legal History* (Cambridge, 1913), pp. 436, 437; Wigmore, "Responsibility for Tortious Acts, Its History" (1894) *Harvard Law Review*, VII, 315, 383, 441; *Selected Essays on the Law of Torts* (Boston, 1924), pp. 18 *et seq.*; *Select Essays in Anglo-American Legal History*, vol. iii.

type of case where the defendant is held liable even though the damage is stated to have been the result of accidental circumstances. The term " accident " is seldom, if ever, defined in colonial cases; from the attendant circumstances it may, however, be deduced that, in civil cases where the defendant is liable, the court imposed responsibility upon him because of an absence of due care on his part. Thus it would be difficult to believe that Roger Miles, Jeremiah Akenes, and Hendrick Cornelisen, of the Borough Town of Westchester in the colony of New York, were not culpable when the court held them liable to pay damages of thirty shillings and costs to the owner of swine which they had killed. It is likely that the killing is characterized by the court as accidental to distinguish the act from a deliberate and malicious tort.[1]

A study of early English cases has encouraged a similar conjecture. On such grounds has the contention been criticized that " there has never been a time, in English law, since (say) the early 1500s, when the defendant in an action for trespass was not allowed to appeal to some standard of blame or fault in addition to and beyond the mere question of his act having been voluntary." [2]   It may be pertinently queried whether such an appeal could not have been made before the sixteenth century; for an examination of the earlier English reports reveals the presence of the same dubious and misleading terms as are found in tort actions in seventeenth-century America. It has been maintained that such phrases as " acting at peril," " inevitable accident," " utterly without fault," " inevitable necessity," and similar expressions, " are so vague and general that almost anything can be read into them," and that " the few cases and illustrations of responsibility for unintentional hurts which ap-

---

[1] Quinbe *v.* Miles *et al.* (1657) *Westchester Court Rec.*, p. 3.

[2] Wigmore, *Selected Essays on the Law of Torts*, p. 66.

pear, in so far as the facts are given, could as well as not be instances of highly probable, though unintended, hurts." [1]

2. " Due Care " and Assumed Duties

Colonial decisions very rarely give any exposition of the technique of the judge in determining whether the defendant is under a duty to exercise due care. Some light is revealed by an examination of typical cases. In the group wherein a special standard of reasonable care is imposed upon the defendant as a result of his contractual and relational position, the court applied an objective standard for determining negligence.

In the first situation, liability is imposed upon the defendant because he is acting in some supervisory capacity. In a New Netherland action the master of a vessel is sued for the loss of his employee's clothing which was stolen from the boat by the Indians as a result of the master's "carelessness," it is alleged. The case is referred to an arbiter. [2] In addition to being responsible to seamen for losses occasioned by culpable conduct attributed to him, the master was liable to the owner for damages resulting to the vessel and cargo and attributable to faulty navigation. The court imposed upon the individual placed in command higher technical requirements in the field of navigation than upon the ordinary seaman.

In 1647 a suit was brought in the New Haven General Court against John Charles [3] for £100 for " grosse, if not wilfull, negligence & default " in permitting the vessel of

[1] Leon Green, " The Duty Problem in Negligence Cases: II," *Columbia Law Review*, XXIX, 259. *Cf.* also Winfield, " The Myth of Absolute Liability," *Law Quarterly Review*, XLII, 37.

[2] Jansen *v.* van der Donck (1653) Fernow, *Records of New Amsterdam*, I, 71.

[3] Evance *v.* Charles (1647) *New Haven Col. Rec.*, I, 281.

which he was master to be damaged and the cargo to be lost or spoiled. Upon the disagreement of expert arbiters, an umpire had brought in a verdict in which the loss was attributed to the negligence of the defendant, who thereupon refused to accept the decision. In the finding it was set forth that the failure to employ a cable and tackle and to cast anchor had led to the damage. In order to avoid responsibility the defendant maintained that he had not been in charge of the vessel. Upon investigating the customs prevailing in maritime occupations, the court found that an employee shipped in the place of the master and given the power of the latter was liable as a master for the control of the vessel. The witnesses whom the plaintiff produced,— seamen on board the vessel,—corroborated the finding of the umpire. The defendant's own admission, that if he had been master his conduct would have been culpable, was placed on the record. The court found (1) that the circumstances attending the making of the contract with the defendant were evidential of the common understanding that he was to act as master; and (2) that the defendant " had not improved his owne skill, nor exercised the ordynary care of a man takeing chardge, for prservation of ye vessel & goods." Judgment was rendered for the plaintiff for sixty-seven pounds and court costs.

The case imposes a special responsibility upon the master which is founded upon his contractual relationship. The distinction found here between bailees and servants not having control over the goods was clearly raised in the famous action of detinue brought in England in 1601 and known as *Southcote's Case*.[1] *Evance v. Charles* furthermore illustrates the proposition that in an action on the case for negligence, the burden of proof rests with the plaintiff. What this objective standard of due care may be is not clearly

[1] 4 Co. Rep. 83 b; Cro. Eliz. 815.

brought out. " Ordinary care " exercised under such circumstances might well have proved insufficient. Similar ambiguity and confusion has characterized the definition of due care in modern English and American courts.

Another type of supervisory activity involving a standard of due care was the keeping of cattle. To the imprudent conduct of the keeper of the town cattle, who had brought the herd into a barren field and then left them until nightfall, was attributed the loss of several cows which were believed to have been trampled to death by the herd in its rush to enter the more herbaceous salt meadows.[1] Failure on the part of the town-keepers to come to an understanding as to a division of time in their assignment was held as the responsible cause for the loss of a cow.[2] It can be assumed from such evidence that liability rested upon the keeper of the herd for any damage which occurred during the time of his supervision except for such as could be attributed to an act of God. Thus in the New Haven case of *Barnes v. Dighton,*[3] the plaintiff sued the defendant for the loss of a cow which was in the temporary keeping of the latter's son. From the evidence it appeared that the youth had been forced to leave the herd and return to town in order to get aid to rescue a cow from the swamp. By the time the rescue had been effected, it was nightfall, and therefore it was not deemed necessary to rejoin the returning herd as no place of danger was known over the route which the cattle would traverse. Subsequently a cow was found to have perished unknown to the keeper in a perilous section of the terrain. The court held the loss of the cow to have been an act of God and freed the keeper from culpability.

In a second group of cases the colonial law imposed upon

---

[1] Moris *v.* Gibbons and Holt (1656) *New Haven Town Rec.,* I, 288-290.

[2] Morrell *v.* Gibbons and Merrimand (1652) *ibid.,* II, 106, 107.

[3] (1645) *New Haven Col. Rec.,* I, 162.

the bailee responsibility to the bailor for his failure to exercise due care.   While in the action of detinue at common law the theory of the suit was that the bailor was liable as a debtor for the safe-keeping of the chattels, if the bailor brought against his bailee the action of trespass upon the case, it was necessary that the defendant should be shown to be guilty of negligence before he could be held, and all considerations going to rebut the charge of negligence were admissible in his favor.[1]   The supplanting in the seventeenth century of detinue by case as a remedy against the bailee led to the rejection of the ancient principle of absolute liability. The same transition is found in the colonies.   In 1703 a suit was appealed in the Superior Court of Judicature of Massachusetts in which an innkeeper rented a coach and horses to the defendants, who promised to return them " Safe and Sound." [2]   From the brief of the plaintiff's attorney, J. Hearne, it appears that the negligence aspect of the case is not stressed, even though the complaint alleges that the defendants " so unseasonably and unskillfully did drive or Cause to be drove " (that) " one of the s^d Horses was killed."   The brief on appeal states that

it is plaindly proved the Appellts held the Coach & kept it out till two in the morning & then added two horses more to the Coach by which means the Appellees horse was killed, which could not have been had they not been added & the Law implies a promise in any man to returne any horse he hired or else he that hired a horse may be liable to sell him at the same time for a shilling when at the same time he cost ten pounds.

This reasoning illustrates a transition from an earlier era

[1] Beale, " Carrier's Liability: Its History," *Harvard Law Review*, XI, 158.

[2] Valentine and Clough *v.* Simpson (1703) MSS. Mass. Sup. Court of Judic. (1700-1714), fol. 93, 94.

when the mere making of a promise imposed no legal duty whatever, and when the default of the bailee fixed upon him the liability of a tortfeasor. In this period, however, when the contract of bailment had come within the realm of assumpsit, it was difficult to determine whether the action was really in contract or in tort.[1] In the same year as this Massachusetts case occurred the historic English decision in *Coggs v. Bernard*,[2] which determined the liability of a gratuitous bailee for negligence.

The clearest statement of the colonial position on the question of the existence of a duty to exercise due care is found in a Maine prosecution brought against one Nicholas Weekes in 1667.[3] It appears that the wife of Weekes had confessed cutting off the toes of her servant, Nicholas Woodman, a procedure which very likely brought about the servant's death. Although Weekes was freed by the jury after extended litigation, the court sitting at York found him " defective in his duty to his servant, which occasioned the death of the per[ ] as the evidence of the Coroners Inquest Issues it, as alsoe wee find the Townes men of Kittery faulty that when Complaynt to them being made they had not caused his Master to provide for him." Then follows a rare and precious dictum: " *Persons defective in their duty from whom comes dammage or charge must of right pay that dammage that cometh through their defect.*"

In cases in which the individual is engaged in a dangerous occupation or has under his control potentially dangerous things, the basis of culpability is a standard of due care applied to fit the circumstances. The old English notion of absolute liability was clearly disregarded in the action

[1] T. A. Street, *The Foundations of Legal Liability* (Northport, L. I., 1906), II, 267-269.

[2] (1703) 2 Ld. Raym. 909.

[3] *Maine Province and Court Records*, I, 261, 262, 272, 286.

brought against one John Beach of New Haven for damages resulting from the loss of a cow killed by the defendant in felling a tree. The complaint alleged negligence. Two witnesses testified that Beach " had nott done whatt in reason he might, and ought to have done to p^{r}serve the cattell, and that if he had beene as carefull as he might, no hurt need have be[en] done." From the evidence it appears that, though Beach saw the cows advancing toward him when he was about to fell the tree, he did not drive them beyond the danger zone. The court granted the plaintiff his damages of five pounds, stating that the price which he had set upon his cow was exceptionally moderate.[1]

3. *Trespasses by Cattle*

At common law a man was responsible for trespasses by his horses and cattle. " Every man is bound to make recompense for such hurt as his beasts shall do in the corn or grass of his neighbour, though he knew not that they were there," was a contemporary maxim of the law.[2] Various explanations have been resorted to in order to reconcile this rule with the doctrine of no liability without fault. Blackstone resorted to the dogmatic fiction that a man is answerable for the " negligent keeping " of his cattle without requiring of the plaintiff any proof of negligence or without permitting the defendant to show that there was in fact no negligence. According to this line of reasoning, as Dean Pound has shown, " the negligence is established by the liability, not the liability by the negligence." [3]   Furthermore, this rule

---

[1] Smyth *v.* Beach (1643) *New Haven Col. Rec.*, I, 88, 89.

[2] *Doctor and Student*, I, 9 (Muchall's ed. [1518], p. 31); Noy, *Maxims* (1642), c. 44, borrows the same language.

[3] Roscoe Pound, *An Introduction to the Philosophy of Law*, p. 180; *cf.* also Street, *op. cit.*, I, 49.

reflects the characteristic strictness with which the common law treats injuries to real property.[1]

The court, which maintained the doctrine that "a man should so occupy his common that he does no wrong to another man,"[2] would not be expected to impose upon the owner of adjoining land an obligation to fence.[3] Despite this general rule, English grazing communities frequently had local prescriptions requiring the owner of land to fence his close against such cattle as were rightfully on the adjoining property.[4] At common law, however, it is clear that, unless by prescription or through the force of an agreement, no such liability exists. This appears from Williams' notes to Saunders:

It must be observed that the general rule of law is that I am bound to take care that my beasts do not trespass on the land of my neighbour, and he is only bound to take care that his cattle do not wander from his land and trespass on mine; 6 Mod. 314, Tenant *v.* Goldwin. 1 Taunt. 529, Churchill *v.* Evans, 6 B. & C. 329, Boyle *v.* Tamlyn, 9 D. & R. 430, S. C.; and therefore this kind of action (i. e., an action on the case for not repairing a fence) will only lie against a person who can be shown to be bound by prescription or special obligation to repair the fence in question for the benefit of the owner or occupier of the adjoining land. And no man can be bound to repair for the benefit of those who have no right.[5]

Throughout the American colonies the courts and legislatures imposed upon the landowner a universal duty to fence his close against trespassing cattle. Since the majority of

---

1 See especially Ellis *v.* Loftus Iron Co. (1874) L. R. 10 C. P. 10.

2 Y. B. 20 Ed. IV, pl. 10 (1481), cited by Wigmore, *Select Essays in Anglo-American Law*, III, 514, n. 4

Boyle *v.* Tamlyn (1827) 6 B. & C. 337.

Beven, *Negligence in Law* (London, 1908), I, 503.

Note to Pomfret *v.* Ricroft, 1 Wms. Saund, 322 a, n. (c).

liability suits in the early agricultural and grazing communities dealt with trespass to realty by cattle and other animals, this obligation, interpreted broadly, evidenced the refusal of the colonial courts to impose responsibility without accompanying fault. Furthermore, the foundations in America of the defence of contributory negligence can be traced to this rule concerning trespasses by cattle, which has been maintained to the present day.[1]

In New England and in the towns established by the New Englanders on Long Island, in Westchester County, New York, and in northern New Jersey, the method of community settlement and of mixed husbandry prevailed, and therefore the system of common pasturage was adopted.[2] In these regions the imposition upon the commoners of the duty to fence amounted in reality to a diffusion among the community generally of the ever-present risk of damage to property by trespassing cattle. In the middle and southern colonies, where settlements were generally made by individuals without group cooperation, the effect was to throw the burden of liability upon the landowner and to lighten the responsibilities of the cattle-owner. No theory has been propounded which explains the existence of this rule of liability in two agrarian regions settled on opposing principles; but it may be possible to discover the rationale of this prescription, with its accompanying notion of contributory negligence, by examining the colonial statutory enactments and the cases as they arose in the courts.

[1] Buford *v.* Houtz (1890) 133 U. S. 320 at 328; S. D. Thompson, *Commentaries on the Law of Negligence in all Relations* (Indianapolis, 1901), § 904. This rule is by no means universal. New York and Pennsylvania, for example, in their modern decisions and statutes return to the English rule. Wells *v.* Howell (1822) 19 Johns. (N. Y.) 385; Erdman *v.* Gottshall (1899) 9 Pa. Sup. Crt. 295.

[2] Percy W. Bidwell and John I. Falconer, *History of Agriculture in the Northern United States, 1620-1860* (Washington, 1925), p. 21.

In the first typical grazing situation, the landowner sues as plaintiff for damages suffered in his property from trespasses by cattle. He is confronted at the outset in every colony from New Hampshire to Georgia with a statute imposing upon him the duty to fence his property. An early Virginia statute of 1632 provides: "Every man shall enclose his ground with sufficient fences or else to plant, uppon theire owne perill." [1] The same phraseology was employed in a Maryland statute eight years later.[2] Failure of landowners to fence against grazing cattle led in one instance to inter-colonial complications. In 1664 the General Assembly of Connecticut sent a letter to the authorities of East Hampton, Long Island, complaining against the "unneighbourly" shooting of a South Hampton mare by an alleged East Hamptonite and going to the root of the difficulty in their suggestion which follows:

. . . We doe allso desire that you would be pleased this winter season to provide and make a sufficient fence about your improueable lands, that soe you may secure your labour from damage by cattell, (water-fences will not be judged sufficient, where it is passable for cattell wthout swiming, at low water), and in the mean season, that you doe not exact damage, or trouble men by impounding there cattell, until you haue made a sufficient fence about your fields, not els. . . .[3]

Property-owners were held accountable for the risk to which they were subjecting adjacent lands by their neglect to fence their own. Failure on their part to provide adequate fencing justified the erection of a proper fence by the party whose property was thus imperilled and the allocation of the cost to him upon whom the law imposed the obligation.[4] In the

---

1 Act of 1732, Hening, *Statutes at Large*, I, 176, 199.
2 Act of 1640, *Md. Arch.*, I, 96.
  (1664) *Conn. Pub. Rec.*, I, 436, 437.
  Act of 1670, *Conn. Pub. Rec.*, II, 129, 130.

case of meadow-land held by adjacent property-owners the obligation to fence was equally distributed, and the responsibility for damages resulting from the neglect of one of the parties was imposed by law upon the delinquent.[1]

If it were shown that the plaintiff had failed to meet the standards prescribed by the colonial statutes relating to fencing, the courts in an overwhelming number of instances would rule that this deficiency constituted such neglect as would bar recovery.   A typical statute is the New Jersey act passed in the Carteret régime, providing that

. . . if any trespass or damage be done by horses, cattle, sheep or swine of any kind whatsoever, in any man's corn, hay, flax, or any other fruits, when the fence is sufficient, they shall pay all damage whatsoever; but in case there be no fence, or not a sufficient fence, then he that owns the defective fence or fences whatsoever, shall bear the damages and the cattle shall be free.[2]

Colonial legislation and town administrative orders elsewhere are to the same effect.[3]   The burden of proof was on the defendant to show that the plaintiff's lands were not adequately fenced.[4]   The law did not, however, impose a liability to fence against unruly cattle, the owner of which had to bear the historic common-law responsibility.[5]

Elaborate provisions were made by the colonial legislatures to set up a standard of care which would bind property-

[1] Act of 1721, *N. Y. Col. Laws* (Albany, 1894), II, 66; act of 1650, *ibid.*, III, 773.

[2] *N. J. Grants and Concessions*, p. 82.

[3] *Cf.* e. g., act of 1642, Hening, *Statutes at Large*, I, 244, 245; act of 1642, *New Haven Col. Rec.*, I, 82; act of 1652, Brigham, *Plymouth Compact*, p. 96; act of 1666, *Conn. Pub. Rec.*, II, 50; *New Haven Town Rec.*, I, 65, 66 (1651); act of 1662, *Mass. Ancient Charters*, p. 65.

[4] *Cf.* e. g., Vinje *v.* Litchee (1653) Fernow, *Rec. Amst.*, I, 95; Whitman *v.* Guyon (1675) N. Y. State Hist., *Ann. Rep.*, II, 338, 339.

[5] *Cf. infra*, § 4.

owners. Although the term fence at common law comprised
almost any kind of division or inclosure, a hedge, ditch, or
wall being most commonly employed to answer that term,[1]
in the colonies it was generally restricted to a stone or rail
fence. The legal height of the fence varied according to its
durable qualities, the measurements for one of stone being
lower than those for a rail fence. Where a hedge was
recognized, as in Rhode Island, it was provided that it be
three feet in height and above the top of the ditch,[2] or four
feet where there was no ditch.[3] Three feet eight inches was
high enough for a stone fence in New York,[4] but where rail
fences were in use the required height ranged from four to
six feet.[5]

The property-owner, in addition to receiving a definite
legislative standard of fencing in most cases, was in numerous jurisdictions given notice of his deficiency by duly constituted officials. This duty to give notice generally devolved
upon the fence-viewer. A typical order is chosen from
among those issued at the Exeter court in 1643:

It is ordered that Will Cole and Robt. Smith shall oversee

[1] Beven, *Negligence in Law*, I, 503.

[2] Acts of 1666, 1725, 1728, 1753, *Acts and Laws of Rhode Island*
(Newport, 1767).

[3] Acts of 1666, 1725, 1728, 1753. *Loc. cit.*

[4] Act of 1734, *N. Y. Col. Laws* (Albany, 1894), II, 863.

[5] Four feet: act of 1734, *N. Y. Col. Laws*, II, 863; act of 1675,
Brigham, *Compact*, p. 175 ("four foot high or otherwise sufficient by
the judgment of indifferent men"); four feet three inches: act of 1682,
Grants and Concessions of N. J., p. 262; four and one-half feet: act of
1646, Hening, *Statutes at Large*, I, 332; act of 1658, *ibid.*, p. 458; act of
1662, *ibid.*, II, 100, 101; act of 1654, *Md. Arch.*, I, 344; act of 1683,
West Jersey Laws, *Grants and Concessions of N. J.*, p. 459; five feet:
act of 1715, *N. C. Col. Rec.*, XXIII, 61, 62; act of 1682, West Jersey
Laws, *Grants and Concessions of N. J.*, p. 455; five and one-half feet:
act of 1755, *Ga. Col. Rec.*, XVIII, 73, 74; act of 1759, *ibid.*, pp. 354-356;
six feet: act of 1694, *S. C. Stat. at Large* (Columbia, S. C., 1837), II, 81.

the farmes about the town and give warning to them whose fences are defective, and if they be not amended, the owners thereof to pay for any hurt is done through those fences.[1]

A favorable return by the fence-viewers raised a presumption in favor of the plaintiff, which, by subsequent legislation, was rebuttable upon presentation of evidence that the fence was impaired.[2]   Evidence does not appear that the law made notice a condition precedent to establishing contributory negligence, although some such implication may be read into a New Haven order of 1644:

Itt is ordered thatt every quarter shall appoynt comittees for their quarters to view outside fences, and where they finde defects to lett the owners know; *and if they doe not see itt mended upon notice so given,* if cattell breake in, though it canott certainly be found where they gott in, yett they must beare the damage whose fence was found defective and not mended.[3]

In awarding damages, the local courts generally availed themselves of the services of arbiters.   The town of Providence at an early date provided that plaintiff and defendant should each choose an arbiter, but made no provision for the determination of the damages in case of a deadlock.[4]   A Georgia statute of 1755 provided that the damages be adjusted by the free-holders who were further empowered to rule on the "Lawfullness of the Fence."   Each party was to choose one arbiter, and the two so chosen were to select the third.   The appraisal of any damages so determined was to be reported to the Justice of the Peace who was empowered to give execution.[5]

---

[1] *New Hamp. Prov. Laws,* I, 743.   *Cf.* also *Conn. Pub. Rec.,* I, 101.

[2] Act of 1718, *New Hamp. Prov. Laws,* II, 311.

[3] Act of 1644, *New Haven Col. Rec.,* I, 126 (Italics mine).

[4] (1662) *Early Records of the Town of Providence,* III, 15.

[5] Act of 1755, *Ga. Col. Rec.,* XVIII, 73, 74; act of 1759, *ibid.,* pp. 354-356.

The plaintiff who had successfully rebutted the allegations of defective fences and who had established tangible losses would in numerous jurisdictions receive an award of exemplary damages. The Town of Providence made the defendant liable for double damages,[1] but in other jurisdictions, such as Pennsylvania, North and South Carolina, and Virginia, double damages were reserved for the second or repeated trespasses by horses or cattle, undoubtedly on the theory that the defendant was now chargeable with gross negligence.[2]

A minority opinion is expressed in several statutes and decisions of the seventeenth century in which the inequitable consequences of the rule imposing a duty upon the landowner to fence are ameliorated. In one arrangement the damages are divided between the landowner and the cattleowner. Thus a New Haven statute of 1647 provides that

. . . if swine be unyoaked & unrunge & goe into any feild, the fence lyeinge downe, that the dammadge should be borne at halves, & that the fine of 6d a head be still payd to him that finds the swyne & brings them to the pownd.[3]

This rule requiring the landowner of the defective fence to bear half the damage of the trespass was reiterated in a New Haven Town order of 1663, which made the further provision that " if the fence be not defective, then swine & other Cattle to beare all dammage & poundage." [4]

---

[1] (1662) *Early Records of the Town of Providence*, III, 15; act of 1715, *N. C. Col. Rec.*, XXIII, 61, 62.

[2] Act of 1694, *S. C. Stat. at Large* (Columbia, S. C., 1837), II, 81; act of 1700, Carey and Bioren, *Laws of Pa.*, I, 18, 19; act of 1705, Hening, *Statutes at Large*, III, 279, 280; act of 1715, *N. C. Col. Rec.*, XXIII, 61, 62 (treble damages for third offense); act of 1771, c. 6, *ibid.*, pp. 854, 855.

[3] *New Haven Col. Rec.*, I, 277.

[4] *New Haven Town Rec.*, II, 56, 57.

It was clearly seen in Plymouth that the arrangement whereby the landowner had to incur the entire expense of fencing his land because of the inherently destructive character of his neighbor's chattels was inequitable. While no general rule covering all such situations was enacted, in the case of the Indians it was deemed practicable to effect some sort of compromise. Hence, the act of 1667 provides that

. . . . The Townsmen or prticular psons whose horses or any cattle doe treaspas upon the Indians upon theire owne lands out of Townshipes by spoiling their Corn; shall agree with them for the prsevation thereof or to healp them to fence; and in case they shall neglect soe to doe; they shall pay the full damage that shall come by theire Cattle soe trespassing.[1]

The Duke of York's laws went further and provided that, where the Indians' corn had been damaged by cattle as a result of the failure to fence, the town should shoulder the responsibility of compensating them, and should in turn allocate the cost to the delinquent parties.[2]

A typical decision which shows that for reasons of policy the general rule was suspended in such cases may be quoted from the records of the Quarter Court at Hartford in 1659:

A case being ppounded to ye Magestrates by the Townesmen on the Southside Hartford Riuulet about dammadg done by the Heard in Indians Corne Its iudged by the Court that the whole damadge should be Levied vpon the whole heard yt did the damadge and that Retribution should be made to ye Indians by the owners of the Cattle.[3]

The declaration of the General Assembly of Virginia in 1632 to the effect that every man should enclose his ground

[1] Brigham, *Compact*, p. 152.

[2] *Duke of York's Book of Laws*, p. 32.

[3] "Records of the Particular Court of Connecticut, 1639-1663," Conn. Hist. Soc., *Collections*, XXII, 208.

with sufficient fences, and in case of a failure to do so, should suffer the consequences without legal remedy,[1] was not adopted without opposition. The opponents of the measure urged that this act would encourage the owners of swine to dispense with keepers and would result in live-stock committing trespasses unchecked upon private property, and in their being exposed to a great number of casualties.[2] This feeling of discrimination in favor of the large cattle-owners is more pronounced among the Virginia objectors in connection with that colony's treatment of the problem of unruly cattle.[3]

Occasionally this opposing tendency in favor of a rule of absolute liability for harmful agents is given expression, as in the Massachusetts act of 1646. This statute provided that " for *all* harms done by goats, there shall be double damage allowed, and when any goats are taken in corn or gardens, the owner of such corn or garden may keep and use the said goats till full satisfaction be made by the owners." [4]

4. Trespasses by Cattle known to be Unruly

Where the trespassing animals were known to be unruly, an exception of considerable importance was made to the rule requiring the landowner to fence against cattle. In the

---

[1] Hening, *Statutes at Large*, I, 176.

[2] Philip Alexander Bruce, *Economic History of Virginia in the Seventeenth Century* (New York, 1907), I, 313 *et seq.*, citing " Review of the Old Acts of Assembly," *British State Papers, Colonial*, IX, no. 98; Winder Papers, I, 128, Va. State Library.

[3] See *infra*, § 4. Because of objections to this ordinance, the fence law was modified in 1639. Owners of swine were required to confine them securely in pens at night and to provide keepers for them during the day; those persons who failed to observe these directions were to be held responsible for the damages inflicted by the hogs upon the property of their neighbors. Hening, *Statutes at Large*, I, 228. In 1642, the original rule concerning swine was once more revived. Hening, *ibid.*, I, 244.

[4] *Ancient Charters*, p. 64.

absence of specific evidence, the colonies did not generally charge the owner with notice of the unruly disposition of his cattle; actual knowledge of the animal's dangerous propensity was required. The colonial courts were thus enlarging the scope of the English rule that the owner in order to be held liable for trespasses by biting or otherwise wounding committed by his animal must have had knowledge of its vicious propensity.[1] The analogy to the *scienter* rule, as it was called, was applied by the colonial courts to trespasses to land as well as to human or animal life.

And it is interesting to observe to what contrary purport. The common-law rule attempted in dealing with personal injuries to modify the rigorous application of the doctrine of absolute responsibility for damages to realty. In other words, the common-law action of trespass afforded a greater degree of relief to the owner of land than to the owner of chattels which had been injured by trespass. In the colonies the analogy to the *scienter* rule was applied in order to grant relief to landowners from a general rule which discriminated against them and in favor of those who could afford to possess potentially dangerous chattels. This discrimination in favor of wealthy cattle-owners in grazing communities was clearly perceived in Virginia, and a statute " concerning fences," passed in 1670, went to the root of the question:

Whereas the act for fences doth not suffitiently provide for remedy of these many damages done by unruly horses breaking into corne fields, It is by the authority of the grand assembly enacted, that the owner of such horses shall be, and hereby is required and enjoyned to take some effectual course for restrayning them from trespassing their neighbours, from the

---

[1] *Registrum Brevium*, 110; Street, *op. cit.*, I, 52-54; Wigmore, *Select Essays*, III, 512-514, who points out that T. Beven in his article on " The Responsibility at Common Law for the keeping of Animals " [*Harvard Law Review* (1909), XXII, 465] does not distinguish between trespasses by biting or wounding and trespasses *q. c. f.*

twentyeth of July till the last of October in every yeare, *it being much fitter that rich men who have the benefitt of such horses should provide for their restraint, then the poore enjoyned to the impossibility of every* [*sic*] *high fences;* and if any horse or horses shall at any tyme breake into any corne feild, the fence being foure foote and halfe high, then the owner of such horse or horses, upon proofe of the damage, shall pay for the first trespasse single damages and for every trespasse after double dammages to the party greived; And because the question hath been made about the suffitiency of fences according to the former act, of enjoyning them to be close to the bottom, It is hereby declared that being soe close that nothing mentioned in the former act can creep through is only by that act intended.[1]

In a majority of jurisdictions the contributory negligence of the landowner possessing a defective fence would be no defence where the defendant had not fulfilled his duty to restrain unruly horses and cattle. In this connection it should be noted that the action which was brought in England for trespasses by unruly animals was an action on the case for negligence, whereas it would appear from the statutes and the decisions in America that the colonial courts permitted the plaintiff to sue in trespass *quare clausum fregit*.

In the Duke of York's laws there is a section which provides that, for trespasses by " unruly cattle of any sort in which Swine are included which cannot be restrained by ordinary fence," the cattle-owner shall be liable despite the insufficiency of the fence, and a subsequent section imposes upon the owner of such unruly cattle, " after knowledge or notice given," the duty of fencing his own property or of providing shackles, fetters, yokes, or rings.[2] In other juris-

[1] Hening, *Statutes at Large*, II, 279. (Italics mine.)

[2] *Duke of York's Book of Laws*, pp. 16, 17; act of 1676, *Grants and Concessions of N. J.*, p. 114. For an earlier instance, *cf. New Haven Town Records*, I, 216 (1654).

dictions the landowner was relieved of the burden of building such a fence as would be required to keep out unruly
cattle.[1]   Among the laws passed by Governor Andros and
his Council in 1687 was the provision that " all swine unyoaked or unringed shall be lyable to Damage fence or no
fence." [2]   A typical action for damages to realty by unruly
cattle was the case of *Beckley v. Hitchcock* brought in the
New Haven Town Court in 1657.   The report does not state
whether the action was brought in trespass or in case.   The
plaintiff sued for damages " done him in his flax " by the
defendant's oxen, alleging that they were unruly and had
broken his fence and let in swine.   Judgment was awarded
the plaintiff, and the defendant was admonished to " take
care that his oxen doe no further damage to his neighbours." [3]   After the owner had been warned of the unruly
disposition of his cattle by the selectmen of the town, he was
liable, in some of the New England colonies, such as New
Hampshire and Connecticut, to pay twofold damages to the
landowner for a subsequent trespass.[4]

5. *Damages to Cattle or Land where the Person under a Duty to Fence is at Fault*

Where, as a result of the negligence of the " quarter " or
of individuals who were under a duty to fence their land,
cattle trespassed on the land of others, the colonial courts

[1] Act of 1642, *Charters and General Laws of Mass.*, p. 65; act of 1671,
Brigham, *Compact*, p. 292; act of 1676, *Grants and Concessions of N. J.*,
p. 113.   *Cf.* also Weeden, *Economic and Social History of New England*,
I, 66.

[2] *New Hamp. Prov. Laws*, I, 200, 201; *Conn. Pub. Rec.*, III, 420.

[3] (1657) *New Haven Town Records*, I, 296, 297.

[4] Laws of Governor Andros and Council, 1687, *Conn. Pub. Rec.*, III,
420; *New Hamp. Prov. Laws* (1687), I, 200, 201; *ibid.*, II, 311 (1718).
Cf. also New Haven town order (1664) *New Haven Town Records*,
II, 82.

held such defect to be the responsible cause of the tort. Thus, the rule which held defective fencing to be such contributory negligence as would bar recovery in an action of trespass, sought further protection for the owners of livestock by imposing a statutory liability on the landowner for trespasses through his fence. A New Haven town order of 1652 provided that fences be maintained between houselots and that, if damage came to the neighbor as a result of a deficiency in the fence, the fence-owner must pay the damage.[1] Statutes and town orders in other colonies established a similar liability,[2] and innumerable grazing situations which arose in the colonial courts were settled in accordance with this policy.[3]

A New Haven colony statute of 1645 provided that, where a person's corn had been damaged by cattle and he was unable to determine through whose fence the trespass had been made, he might request the fence-viewers appointed for that quarter to examine the fences. The damages were then to be borne by such parties as had defective fences.[4] Here the damages were punitive in character; it was obvious that the

---

[1] *New Haven Town Records*, I, 108.

[2] (1667) *Early Records of the Town of Providence*, III, 92; act of 1698, *Mass. Acts and Resolves*, I, 323; *Charters and General Laws of Mass.*, pp. 310, 311.

[3] *Cf.* e. g., Williams *et al. v.* Allen *et al.* (1639) *Conn. Pub. Rec.*, I, 29; Westcoatt *v.* Plum (1639) *ibid.*, p. 41; Owen *v.* Lamberton *et al.* (1642) *New Haven Col. Rec.*, I, 81; Tompson *v.* Eaton *et al.* (1643) *ibid.*, pp. 121, 122; Nash's case (1644) *ibid.*, pp. 144, 145, 149; Tompson *v.* Gregson (1644) *ibid.*, pp. 152, 153; Malbon *v.* Caffinch (1645) *ibid.*, p. 179 ("the quarter that should have fenced and did not, must beare the damage"); Todd *v.* Wheeler (1650) *New Haven Town Rec.*, I, 46; Langden's case (1650-1651) *ibid.*, pp. 52, 56; Lindon *v.* Camfield (1652) *ibid.*, p. 118 (the cattle-owner is directed to pay the damages, and recover from the owner of the defective fence); Smith *et al. v.* Richardson (1661-1662) *Westchester Court Rec.*, pp. 28-30.

[4] *New Haven Col. Rec.*, I, 55.

cattle did not come through at every defective point in the fences. Liability in such instances was founded upon a statutory standard of due care rather than on actual culpability. The case of *Peck v. Ford et al.*[1] is illustrative of this policy. The plaintiff, a New Haven townsman, sued the defendants in 1658 for damages to his corn resulting from trespasses by swine which were alleged to have come through the defendant's fence. An investigation revealed thirty-three defects in the fence in question. The court conceded that it was " possible and probable that ye swine did not come in at all of y^m, yet because ye Order runns that ye fences y^t are defective, so as damag did or might come by y^m, are lyable to pay," it decreed that each fence-owner pay his proportionate share of the damages.

6. *The Scienter Rule in Injuries by Unruly Animals*

In cases of injuries by biting or otherwise wounding inflicted by trespassing animals, the English rule required that the master have actual knowledge of the animal's vicious tendencies. But by Lord Holt's time *scienter* was not necessary in the case of animals " naturally mischievous in their kind." [2] A parallel to this common-law trend is found in the seventeenth century in the American colonial courts, where the tendency to limit the requirement of knowledge gradually won favor. Thus, in the early part of the century the allegation of the plaintiff that the owner had knowledge of his animal's vicious proclivities seems to have been required in the complaint. Lechford, who drew declarations on the basis of English precedents, at a time when the forms of action were not carefully distinguished in Massachusetts, and who therefore is not representative of the true state of legal knowledge in the Bay Colony, drafted a declaration for

---

1 *New Haven Town Rec.*, I, 352.
2 Mason *v.* Keeling (1700) 12 Mod. 332.

William Sprague of Hingham in 1639 in an action on the case, alleging that the defendant's cow "was wont to push and goare cattle and thereof the defendant had notice and warning." Notwithstanding this, he had failed to keep the animal in check, and the plaintiff's milch cow was gored as a result thereof.[1] In 1647 the magistrates at Salem gave judgment against the owner of a bull which had fatally wounded a mare. Evidence was submitted that the bull had previously attacked others. Upon the advice of the Boston magistrates, it was concluded " y^t ye owner of the Bull (vpon such notice as he had) ought to have taken order to p^{r}uent any future mischiefe."[2] Two years later the colony passed an act which on its face imposes upon the master responsibility regardless of notice. The pertinent section of this statute relating to " Sheep " reads:

. . . if any dog shall kill any sheep, the owner shall either hang such dog, or pay double damages for the sheep, and if any dog hath been seen to Course or bite sheep before, not being set on, and his owner hath had notice thereof, then he shall both Hang his Dog, and pay for such Sheep, as he shall either Bite or Kill, and if in such case he shall refuse to hang his dog, then the Constable of the town, upon notice thereof, shall forthwith cause it to be done.[3]

According to this line of statutes it is seen that, when the owner could not be charged with *scienter,* he could evade liability by paying tribute to the primitive Anglo-Saxon deodand, which, in curious instances, makes its appearance in colonial law.[4] Among the laws passed in the Province of

---

[1] Lechford, *Note Book*, pp. 80, 81.

[2] Taylor *v.* King (1646-1647) *Assistants*, III, 13-15.

[3] *Lawes and Libertyes of Massachusetts* (Cambridge, 1648), p. 47; Whitmore, *Mass. Col. Laws*, p. 191.

[4] *Cf. infra*, § 7.

West Jersey in 1681 was the archaic provision requiring the forfeiture of the destructive animal which had inflicted injury upon a person or which was known to have destructive habits.[1] A New Jersey act of 1682 provided for the surrender of the unruly animal; where the animal's vicious conduct had been habitual and the owner possessed this knowledge, he exposed himself to a penalty in addition to the loss of his animal.[2] A Plymouth statute of 1673, on the other hand, required that the owner have knowledge of the previous trespass of his horse. Trespass subsequent to notice empowered the landowner to kill the horse.[3]

Legislation of the late seventeenth century and of later years did not make responsibility dependent upon such knowledge. Upon negligence rather than upon knowledge rested the liability of the owner of the unruly horse under an order in 1666 of the Casco Court for the western division of the Province of Maine:

It is ordered that all persons liveing within the Western devision of this province who keep unruly Mayres & horses unshackelled, through whose neglect they breake into any mans Corne, gardens, or orchards & do them spoyle, the person to whom the damage is done hath his liberty forthwith to make his Complaynt to the next Justice of pea., who is hereby empowered to summons in seaven of the Neighbours to vew & apprize the Dammage, & whatever it appeareth to bee, Itt shall bee raysed to treble Dammages & forthwith leavied by way of destresse under the said Justice of peace his hand on the person or estate of the Damnifier & payd to the person damnifyed.[4]

The New England courts generally extended their rules of responsibility for tortious acts in order to compensate the

---

[1] *Grants and Concessions of N. J.*, p. 43.

[2] *Ibid.*, pp. 233, 234.

[3] Act of 1673, Brigham, *Ply. Col. Laws*, p. 170.

[4] *Maine Province and Court Records*, I, 268.

Indians for damages done them at the hands of the settlers.
Thus, the Particular Court at Hartford in 1650 ordered two
settlers " to pay Thomas Lord for Curing the Eare of the
Indi(an) Squaw wch theire doggs bitt of, and to pay the
squaw 2 bush: of Indian corne, wch Corne, the next Indian
or Indians that Shall any way by clapping hands or throwing
Stones at any dogg or doggs, prouoake them, Shall pay to
the said Warde againe." [1]

The Rhode Island act of 1698, reenacted in 1729 and
again in 1761, held the owner of a dog liable in an action
on the case for injuries to cattle or sheep. After one such
occurrence the owner was charged with notice of his dog's
mischievous behavior and was liable for double damages.
The statute made the further provision that the dog was to
be put to death. [2] Typical eighteenth-century statutes, such
as the New York act of 1732 [3] and the Massachusetts statute
of 1745, [4] impose upon the master, without requiring notice,
responsibility for the injuries inflicted by his dog on cattle
or sheep. While the English law held that the owner of a
notoriously ferocious animal kept it at his own risk, it did
not render him liable for injuries committed by his dog unless he had notice of the tendency of the animal to do this
specific harm. [5] Thus the colonial statutes broadened the
scope of liability in this instance.

7. Survivals of the Deodand

American colonial law in many instances discarded the
outworn fetishes of the English legal system and pioneered

[1] " Records of the Particular Court of Connecticut, 1639-1663," Conn.
Hist. Soc., *Collections*, XXII, 79.

[2] *Acts and Laws of R. I.* (Newport, 1767), p. 75.

[3] *N. Y. Col. Laws* (Albany, 1894), II, 735.

[4] *Mass. Acts and Resolves*, II, 208.

[5] W. N. Robson, *The Principles of Legal Liability for Trespasses and
Injuries by Animals* (Cambridge, 1915), pp. 71-103.

in the field of law reform. In some instances, however, archaic practices were transplanted and legal progress was impeded. One of the anachronisms of the law which found occasional veneration on this side of the water was the deodand, or the practice of forfeiting the object causing death. Its survival in America accounts to some extent for the failure of the colonists to enlarge the scope of responsibility for the harmful consequences resulting from dangerous possessions. In the more progressive colonial communities the deodand was used chiefly as a protective device and seems to be evidence of a preventive motif in the law. In jurisdictions more emphatically influenced by English precedent, the deodand found a readier acceptance, and encouragement was thus given to the policy of retributive justice. As a curious consequence, the deodand is in more frequent use in the eighteenth century, when English legal conservatism was fast gaining ground, than in the seventeenth.

It has been seen that, where harm had been inflicted by animals, the owner in some instances might evade responsibility by surrendering them.[1] In primitive law the animal was delivered to the injured party for the purpose of his wreaking private vengeance, and, later, it was forfeited to the authorities for public punishment.[2] In like manner, where the harm was associated with an inanimate object, the notion was in widespread acceptance in primitive law that, by a surrender or repudiation of the offending thing, the owner could gain complete exculpation. This principle of *noxae deditio,* incorporated in the Roman law, was rationalized by jurists on the ground that it was unjust that the fault of children or slaves should be a source of loss to their

[1] *Lawes and Libertyes of Mass.* (Cambridge, 1648) ; Whitmore, *Mass. Col. Laws,* p. 191 and *cf. supra,* § 6.

[2] Wigmore, *Select Essays,* III, 492; E. P. Evans, *The Criminal Prosecution and Capital Punishment of Animals* (1907).

parents or owners beyond their own bodies, and Ulpian reasoned that *a fortiori* this was true of things devoid of life.[1] The practice of the deodand was recognized in such typical early codes as the *Lex Visigothorum*[2] and the Laws of Alfred.[3] Finally, the deodand was incorporated in the common-law system.[4]

From England the deodand was introduced into the American colonies. In the king's patent to Gorges, by way of illustration, the proprietor was granted all deodands, together with treasure trove, goods, and chattels of felons, waifs and estrays.[5] The earliest instance of the deodand in America has been found in the proprietary colonies. In January 1637/8 an inquest was taken before the coroner in St. Mary's county, Maryland, to view the body of John Bryant. The finding was returned that Bryant had been killed by the fall of a tree. "And further the Jurors aforesaid upon their oath aforesaid say that the said tree moved to the death of the said John Bryant; and therefore find the said tree forfeited to the Lord Proprietor."[6] Another early example of colonial deference to the deodand is found in "Moses his Judicialls," the code of laws proposed by John Cotton in 1638 for adoption in Massachusetts. The provision referring to personal injuries inflicted by animals reads:

---

[1] O. W. Holmes, *Common Law*, p. 7.

[2] *Lex Visig.* 8, 4, c. 20.

[3] *C.* 24.

[4] *LL.* Henry I, c. 87, 2; Fitzherbert, *Abridgment*, Barre. 290. *Cf.* also Holmes, *op. cit.*, p. 25, and cases cited; Wigmore, *op. cit.*, III, 494, n. 3, and cases cited.

[5] (1639) *Maine Province and Court Records*, I, 16.

[6] *Md. Arch.*, IV, 9, 10. According to the editor, this deodand of the tree is perhaps the solitary instance in the records.

If a mans oxe or other beast goares or bite and kill a man or a woman, whether childe or of riper age, the beast shall be killed and noe benefitt of the dead beast reserved to the owner; but if the oxe or beast were wont to push or bite in times past, and the owner hath been told it, and hath not kept him in, then both the oxe or beast shall be forfeited and killed, and the owner also put to death, or else fined to pay what the judges and persons damnified shall lay upon him. Exo. 21, 28, 29, 30, 31.[1]

The section is almost verbatim from the Mosaic prescription. This very drastic imposition of absolute responsibility was not incorporated in the Body of Liberties, and the only evidence of a deodand survival found therein is among the Capital Laws. The eighth, concerning bestiality, provides the death penalty for the beast as well as the guilty person.[2] Bradford has left us a lurid picture of a series of public executions under this provision of the code.[3] The early trespass rule in East Jersey was founded upon the same text in Exodus as was the provision in Cotton's code. Two modifications are present. The beast is to be forfeited to the nearest relative of the deceased; and where the owner had knowledge of the animal's vicious habits, he is to be fined by the court in addition to the forfeiture.[4] A West Jersey law of the previous year spared the animal from forfeiture except where the fatal injury was " wilfully " done or where the

---

[1] C. VI, § 4.

[2] Whitmore, *Mass. Col. Laws*, p. 55.

[3] "And accordingly he was cast by yᵉ jury, and condemned, and after executed about yᵉ 8. of Septʳ, 1642. A very sade spectakle it was: for first the mare, and then yᵉ cowe, and yᵉ rest of yᵉ lesser catle, were kild before his face, according to yᵉ law, Levit: 20:15. and then he him selfe was executed. The catle were all cast into a great & large pitte that was digged of purpose for them, and no use made of any part of them." William Bradford, *History of Plimoth Plantation* (Boston, 1900), p. 475.

[4] *Grants and Concessions of N. J.* (1682), pp. 233, 234.

animal's past history revealed similar dangerous proclivities.[1]
The Massachusetts statute of 1648, allowing the owner of a
dog which had killed sheep the alternative of having his dog
hanged or of paying double damages,—except where he had
knowledge of his dog's dangerous habits, in which case both
penalties were to be enforced,[2]—is more fairly representative
of a desire to effect adequate protection than to resuscitate
an archaic notion of responsibility.

In jurisdictions under the control of New York in the
latter part of the seventeenth century the deodand was in
accepted usage. The Newcastle records contain a report of
the Baker case which came before the Governor and Council
of New York in 1680.[3] It appears that the daughter-in-law
or granddaughter—the records are not clear—of one Am-
brose Baker of New Castle was killed by a horse, which the
coroner then seized. Baker in his petition presented an affi-
davit to the Council that he did not know that the horse was
" ill Condicioned " and requested that it therefore be restored to him. Because of the failure of the sheriff to give
an account of the proceedings, the Council ordered that he
lose his fees, but that the horse be " knock't in the head."

The eighteenth-century cases on appeal seem to accept the
deodand as routine procedure, although an investigation has
revealed few instances on the records of its usage. In 1721,
Joshua, infant son of William Hilton of Salem, was handling
his father's gun when it discharged and killed another infant,
Thomas Spooner. The court declared the gun deodand and
ordered that the sheriff take the weapon in his custody for
His Majesty's use.[4] A Providence inquest in 1724 found

---

[1] *Grants and Concessions of N. J.* (1682), p. 431.

[2] *Lawes and Libertyes* (Cambridge, 1648), p. 47; Whitmore, *Mass. Col.
Laws*, p. 191.

[3] *Newcastle Rec.*, p. 437; *N. Y. Col. Docts.*, XII, 660.

[4] **Rex** *v.* Hilton (1721) MSS. Mass. Sup. Court Judic. (1721-1725),
fol. 34.

that Joseph Owen had been accidentally run over and killed
by a cart. The jury apprized the cart and wheels at five
pounds.[1]   A Rhode Island statute of 1728 [2] gives the details
of the procedure to be followed. Where fatalities result
from damages inflicted by carts, the kicking of horses, or the
goring of " neat cattles," or " by Means of any other like
Casualty," the coroner by a lawful inquest shall appraise
upon oath the value of the animal or instrument which is to
be forfeited as a deodand for the use of the poor of the town
where the accident happened. In modern law the fossil remains of the deodand are found in the clause of the criminal
indictments stating the value of the instrument with which
a homicide was committed, and in federal statutes forfeiting
goods removed or concealed with intent to defraud the United
States of its taxes.[3]

A comparison with the English practice is favorable to the
colonial. In England the deodand survived until 1846, and
was finally abolished because of the ludicrous consequences
of applying this ancient usage to railroad accidents.[4] Its
survival was an obstacle to the recovery of damages by the
next of kin for fatal accidents which resulted from tortious
conduct. On the other hand, in a number of colonial jurisdictions, despite the occasional application of the rule of the
deodand, recovery for damages resulting from ·death by
wrongful act was permitted.

[1] Rex *v.* Owen (1724) *Early Records of the Town of Providence,* IX,
41, 42.

[2] *Acts and Laws of R. I.* (Newport, 1767), pp. 70, 71.

[3] Grant *v.* U. S. (1920) 254 U. S. 505, at pp. 508-513, where Justice
McKenna delivering the opinion of the court states : " Whether the reason
(for this provision) be artificial or real, it is too firmly fixed in the
punitive and remedial jurisprudence of the country to be now displaced."

[4] *Cf.* Lord Campbell's speech in the House of Lords, April 24, 1846.
Hansard, *Parliamentary Debates,* 3d series, LXXXV, 967.

8. *The Rule of Responsibility as a Special Protection
for the Grazing Interests*

To recapitulate the colonial law concerning trespasses to
land or personal injuries inflicted by cattle and other animals,
it is found that the prescription in grazing communities in
England requiring the landowner to fence against cattle was
universally adopted in the colonies. The prevailing common-
law rule imposing absolute responsibility upon the owner of
cattle for damages was rejected. In general, animals were
differentiated in the colonial law from inanimate dangerous
agents, such as fire, explosives and artificial accumulations
of water. The *scienter* rule was adopted by analogy to grant
landowners relief from a general rule which discriminated
against them and in favor of those who possessed live-stock.

The grazing interests in the community were given special
protection by the colonial courts and the colonial laws threw
around live-stock and animals generally certain humanitarian
safeguards far in advance of provisions in English law. A
Massachusetts act of 1648 reveals this special solicitude.
" Whereas the keeping of Sheep tends much to the benefit
of the Country, & may in short time make good Supply
towards the cloathing of the Inhabitants, if Carefully preserved, and forasmuch as all places are not fit and Convenient for that end," [1] reads the preamble; and the statute
then proceeds to give sheep-owners the liberty to keep sheep
on any common and imposes the death sentence upon dogs
which kill sheep.

Although the deodand and the capital law against bestiality might justifiably be regarded as evidences of a retributive-
justice motif, they do not necessarily convict the colonists
of cruel and inhumane treatment of animals. These acts are
fairly offset by statutes in the colonies for the prevention of cruelty to animals. Liberties 92 and 93 of the

---

[1] *Lawes and Libertyes* (Cambridge, 1648), p. 47; Whitmore, *Mass. Col.
Laws*, p. 191.

Massachusetts code of 1641, referring to the "Bruite Creature," provide:

> 92. No man shall exercise any Tirranny or Crueltie towards any bruite Creature which are usuallie kept for man's use.
> 93. If any man shall have occasion to leade or drive Cattel from place to place that is far of, so that they be weary, or hungry, or fall sick, or lambe. It shall be lawful to rest or refresh them, for a competent time, in any open place that is not Corne, meadow, or inclosed for some peculiar use.[1]

In that jurisdiction cruelty to animals was an indictable offence.[2] Hence, as Reno points out,[3] Macaulay's famous disparagement of the Puritans to the effect that they objected to bear-baiting not because it gave pain to the bear, but because it gave pleasure to the spectator, seems undeserved at least as applied to the Puritans of Massachusetts. The Massachusetts practice is directly opposed to the hard common-law concept of animals as possessed of no rights.[4] At the common law cruelty to animals was not indictable.[5] One critic, writing around 1700, observed that England was "the best country in the world for women, and the worst for horses."[6] The earliest English statute, restricted in scope, for the prevention of cruelty to animals was passed in 1822.[7]

[1] Whitmore, *Mass. Col. Laws*, p. 53.

[2] *Cf.* e. g., Comm. *v.* Leach (1649) *Essex*, I, 174; same *v.* Flint (1649) *ibid.*, p. 174; Woodand's case (1680) *ibid.*, VII, 424.

[3] Reno, *Memoirs of the Judiciary and the Bar of New England* (Boston, 1900), III, 4.

[4] Bishop, *New Criminal Law*, I, § 595.

[5] John H. Ingham, *The Law of Animals*, p. 526.

[6] Hanway's *Journal*, p. 71, cited by Botsford, *English Society in the Eighteenth Century as influenced from Oversea* (New York, 1924), pp. 313, 314.

[7] 3 Geo. IV. c. 71. See also 3 & 4 Will. IV. c. 19 (1833); 5 & 6 Will. IV. c. 59 (1835); 12 & 13 Vict. c. 92 (1849).

In the frequent cases in the American colonies where the obligation to fence rested on the entire quarter or upon a considerable group of landowners, a real diffusion of risk was effected. It does not appear that the policy behind this allocation of risk was inherently equitable. There is no doubt that in a great number of cases the consequences of this policy was to shift the burden of responsibility for such damages from the large cattle-owner, who profited by the possession of dangerous property, to the small landowners. There is no reason to believe that in the latter part of the seventeenth century and in the century following the small proprietor was a substantial livestock owner.

As has been previously suggested, in those colonies in which the agrarian settlements were established on a community basis, the allocation of risk in trespass—at least for the seventeenth century—seems equitable. Under the early town orders in New England it appears that there was a direct relationship between the amount of land owned and the amount of cattle which the landowner could pasture on the commons. Thus, the Plymouth act of 1673 allows the owner of a £20 rateable estate to keep one horse on the commons, the owner of a £40 estate two, and of a £60 estate three.[1] The burden of fencing was often made proportionate to the amount of cattle the landowner possessed. In 1633 the townsmen of Dorchester agreed to run a double rail fence in the proportion of twenty feet to each cow. The largest owners had four cows and each set eighty feet of fence.[2] Ultimately this meant that the wealthier landowners were given greater pasturage rights than the small holders. A rule which was originally imposed on the basis of equality of responsibility could easily be abused. This discrimination was seen clearly in the refusal of the pro-

[1] Brigham, *Ply. Col. Laws*, p. 170.
[2] Weeden, *Economic and Social History of New England*, I, 58, 59.

prietors of New England towns and their descendants to permit newcomers to enjoy the right of commonage, which meant chiefly the right of pasturing on town land.[1]

In theory the reversal of the common-law principle of liability for trespasses by cattle worked for the benefit of the small landowner as it threw open a boundless range for his cattle,[2] whether on the seaboard in the colonial era or on the western frontier of the nineteenth century. In the words of Dean Pound, the rejection of the English rule for a time in America did not imply that it was in conflict with a fundamental principle of no liability without fault; the common-law rule "presupposed a settled community, where it was contrary to the general security to turn cattle out to graze, whereas in pioneer American communities of the past vacant lands which were owned and those which were not owned could not be distinguished and the grazing resources of the community were often its most important resources. The common-law rule, without regard to its basis, was for a time inapplicable to local conditions." [3]

Since the methods of husbandry on this continent were as divergent as were the differences in agrarian conditions obtaining in seventeenth-century America and seventeenth-century England, this explanation does not seem convincing. In the individualistic agrarian system of the South, the large landowner preferred the rule imposing responsibility on the property-owner to a measure requiring him to enclose all the lands in his tract, and thus creating an appreciable financial

---

[1] *Cf.* e. g., act of 1660, *Mass. Col. Rec.*, IV, part i, p. 417; H. B. Adams, "Common Fields in Salem," *Johns Hopkins Univ. Studies in Hist. and Polit. Science*, I, parts ix-x, pp. 67 *et seq.*; Akagi, *The Town Proprietors of the New England Colonies, passim.*

[2] Buford *v.* Houtz (1890) 133 U. S. 320 at 328.

[3] Roscoe Pound, *An Introduction to the Philosophy of Law* (New Haven, 1922), pp. 180, 181.

burden.[1] The framers of the Virginia statute of 1670, " concerning fences," clearly perceived that this was the result of the rule, and therefore declared that it was " much fitter that rich men who have the benifitt of such horses should provide for their restraint, then the poore enjoyed to the impossibility of every (sic) high fences." [2]

B. EXCEPTIONS TO THE DOCTRINE OF NO LIABILITY WITHOUT FAULT

1. Responsibility in early Colonial Law for Harm done by Servants and other Agents

In England in the sixteenth and seventeenth centuries the doctrine was accepted that the master, to be liable, must have commanded the very act in which the wrong consisted, unless the command had been to do a thing in itself unlawful.[3] This rule placed narrow limits on the responsibility of a master for his servants' or agents' actions. It might be expected, therefore, that in the American colonies, where the master was relieved of a great burden of responsibility for trespasses by animals in ordinary circumstances, such a rule would gain ready acceptance. Unfortunately, the early colonial cases are scarce. While no consistent rule can be found, some evidence points to an opposing view.

An act of 1646 in Massachusetts imposed a penalty of treble damages upon persons who robbed orchards, gardens, or yards. "And if they be children or servants," the statute reads, " that shall trespass herein, if their parents or masters will not pay the penalty before exprest, they shall bee openly whipped." [4] Another statute in 1678 provided a penalty for

---

[1] Bruce, *Economic History of Virginia*, I, 313 *et seq.*

[2] Hening, *Statutes at Large*, II, 279, quoted in full, *supra*, pp. 218, 219.

[3] Wigmore, *Select Essays*, III, 525; Waltham *v.* Mulgar (1606) Moo. K. B. 776; Southern *v.* How (1618) 2 Rolle 526.

[4] *Lawes and Libertyes* (Cambridge, 1648), p. 5; Whitmore, *Mass. Col. Laws*, p. 127. The Statute of 1698 provides a greater range of punishments. *Mass. Charters and General Laws*, p. 312.

shooting a gun near any house or highway; the offender was made liable to give full satisfaction to the injured parties.   In cases where the offenders were " servants or youths under their parents or masters " and could not render such satisfaction, their parents or masters were made liable " to make full and due satisfaction in all respects." [1]   A provincial enactment in 1698 imposed a penalty for the making of a pound breach.   Where the animals were conveyed out of the lawful pound by apprentices or persons under age, " not having of their own wherewith to satisfy the law, and their parents or masters refuse to pay the fine and damages which the law in such case does inflict," the court is empowered to impose a prison sentence upon the culprit and the injured party is left " to his remedy at law, to recover his damage of the parent or master of such child or apprentice, which such parent or master respectively shall be liable to have recovered of him upon action to be therefore brought, and execution to be accordingly awarded upon judgment given in that respect." [2]

Evidence of this absolute responsibility resting upon the master for the acts of his servant is occasionally found in the South.   At a court leet and baron of Thomas Gerrard of St. Clement's Manor, Maryland, sitting in 1661, Edward Conray, servant of Richard Foster, was presented because he " did by accident worray or Lugg wth doggs one(e) of the L[d] of the manno[rs] Hoggs and at another tyme Edward Conoray going to shoot at ducks the dog did Run at somebodys Hoggs but we know not whose they were and did Lugg them."   Foster was amerced fifty pounds of tobacco.[3]

With this early colonial policy may be compared the noxal action, which at Roman law could be brought against the

[1] (1678) Whitmore, *Mass. Col. Laws*, p. 349.

[2] *Mass. Charters and Gen. Laws*, p. 310.

[3] Johnson, "Old Maryland Manors," *Johns Hopkins Univ. Studies in Hist. and Polit. Science*, I, no. 7, p. 35.

master for the delicts of the slave. The master had the alternative of either taking the consequences of the delict upon himself by paying a fine and damages or of surrendering the slave to the injured party.[1]

The statutes and cases treated thus far reveal a state of society in which the masters were still looked to for servants' torts, even where not commanded. Dean Wigmore [2] accepts this as an illustration of Brunner's thesis that liability follows and depends on power of control and correction. Such power the master possessed in seventeenth-century colonial law. A typical Massachusetts Bay statute of 1645, in defining the punishment for spreading untrue statements, empowers the parent or master to impose " due correction " upon the culprit in the presence of an officer of the law; [3] the courts desired assurance that the servant would render his master due respect and obedience.[4]

In legal theory no colony permitted the master to exercise his control in an inhumane way. The Body of Liberties, which here again serves as a standard text for colonial humanitarian legislation, protects the servants against abusive treatment,[5] deriving its authority from Deut. 22 : 15. 16. Levit. 25 : 39, 40, 43, Exod. 23 : 12 ; 21 : 2 rather than from the common law. Judicial intervention in cases of exceptional inhumanity is found throughout the colonies.[6]

---

[1] Rudolph Sohm, *The Institutes of Roman Law*, translated by J. C. Ledlie (Oxford, 1892), pp. 191, 331.

[2] *Select Essays*, III, 527 n.

[3] *Mass. Charters and General Laws*, p. 150. *Cf. Duke of York's Book of Laws*, pp. 19, 20.

[4] Perry's case, *Assistants*, II, 18; Wilson's case, *ibid.*, II, 104; Bauldwin's case, *ibid.*, II, 134; *Duke of York's Book of Laws*, pp. 152, 153.

[5] Liberties, 85-88, Whitmore, *Mass. Col. Laws*, p. 51. *Cf.* also *Duke of York's Book of Laws*, p. 38.

[6] *Cf.* e. g., *Assistants*, I, 174, 175; II, 80, 103; III, 24-34; *Mass. Col. Rec.*, I, 311; *Essex*, I, 6, 69, 83; II, 2, 430; VII, 149, 241, 326, 421; *Chester County, Pa. Rec.*, pp. 45, 49; *Md. Arch.*, X, 191, 416, 474.

Typical of this attitude of consideration for the servant is the injunction issued by the Virginia General Court in 1680 in these terse words: " Cruel mistress Pvented from having servants." [1]   Nevertheless the general power of the master to inflict upon an unruly servant moderate chastisement was recognized and the transfer to and authorized exercise of this power by a third party was sanctioned as not running counter to the law of God.[2]   Under this paternalistic system the master brought suit to obtain satisfaction for torts committed upon his servant.[3]   In the slave-holding provinces, where this power of control and correction was measurably greater, the master could recover for damages to his slave in the same manner as for injuries to other property resulting from tortious acts.[4]   By the same token, he was liable for the damages resulting from the criminal acts of his slave. A Georgia statute of 1761 provides that, where the damages done by a slave to a fort, battery, or lookout amount to £5 sterling, the culprit shall be adjudged guilty of felony unless his owner render satisfaction for the loss.[5]

The early part of the eighteenth century marked a period of transition for the law of agency in England which resulted in broadening the scope of the responsibility of the master, who now became liable for the acts of his servant in the execution of his authority or for his benefit and without specific command.[6]   The law raised a presumption that all

[1] *Va. Gen. Court Rec.*, p. 520.

[2] Woodberry's case (1664) *Essex*, III, 224, 225.

[3] Whithead *v.* Thomas (1663) *New Haven Town Rec.*, II, 52, 53; Mascall and Maning *v.* Hill (1666) *Essex*, III, 378, where both servant and master recover.

[4] *Cf.* e. g., act of 1755, *Ga. Col. Rec.*, XVIII, 106; act of 1770, *ibid.*, XIX, part i, p. 214.

[5] *Ga. Col. Rec.*, XVIII, 477.

[6] According to Baty (*Vicarious Liability* [Oxford, 1916], p. 22), the idea of " scope of employment " was historically struck out in Tuberville

acts done in furtherance of the master's affairs were done by his authority. In those colonies where the concept of absolute responsibility had prevailed, the acceptance of the English doctrine meant a limitation of this responsibility to acts undertaken by servants when about their master's business.

In the period of transition, one colonial solution was to divide the responsibility. In the New Haven suit of *Blackman v. Elcock* (1667),[1] an action on the case was brought for damages sustained in the loss of one hogshead of rum. Evidence was shown that the hogshead was lost as a result of a tackle breaking when it was lowered into the vessel. The defendant master asked the owner for a better rope, but the latter was unable to spare any. The damages were assessed between the defendant master and the vessel. With this may be compared the English case of *Boson v. Sandford*[2] in which Lord Holt held that the owners were liable for the freight received by the master and spoiled by his negligence. That both master and servant could be held liable was clearly recognized in English cases in the latter half of the seventeenth century.[3]

The general principle that the master was answerable for the acts of the servant in the former's business was recognized as early as 1650 in a Providence ordinance to the effect " that if any man imploy another, as his workman or servant, & the said servant or workman shall be arrested, for his working there the said master shall pay the damage that shall be required of the said servant, & undertake the suit." [4]

---

v. Stampe (1697) 2 Ld. Raym. 264, as a limitation on the absolute liability of the master to keep in his fire. The extension within the period of a century of Lord Hill's dicta in the Stampe case is seen in Bush *v.* Strinman (1799) 1 B. & P. 404.

[1] *New Haven Town Rec.*, II, 206, 207.

[2] (1691) 2 Salk. 440; 3 Mod. 321.

[3] Michael *v.* Alestree (1677) 2 Lev. 172, 3 Keb. 650.

[4] *Early Records of the Town of Providence*, II, 45.

This doctrine, given recognition in the notable English decision in *Michael v. Alestree*,[1] was not clearly established in the American colonies. In the eighteenth century, when the more conservative English practices prevailed, particularly in the southern provinces, there was a tendency to restrict the scope of responsibility for the acts of a servant in the course of his master's business. In Stephens' "Journal" of Georgia activities there appears the following entry for the year 1738:

My first Care in the Morning was to take a proper Person with me, and view what Damage was done by yesterday's Conflagration, which was found to be very great; however *I very well knew, that little Benefit would accrue by seeking for it at common Law; for the Action must lie against those who kindled the Fire, and they were poor laboring Men (Foreigners) who were in no wise capable of Restitution; whilst he who employed them, little cared what they suffered*: wherefore I summoned them before a Magistrate, and required no more of them than their Labour to make good my Fence again; that would cost them some Days work, which they readily agreed to: And as I was willing to impute it to their want of knowing better, I told them (to show that I forgave them) if they did it honestly and well, that I would give them Something to drink for their Pains: And the Damage I had sustained otherwise, I must make the best of that I could.[2]

This quotation illustrates a popular misunderstanding of the common-law rule. In Sir John Randolph's reports of Virginia cases is found an action antedating the Georgia incident by seven years. In the report of the case, the plaintiff's attorney presents an argument which is a complete negation

---

[1] (1677) 2 Lev. 172, 3 Keb. 650.

[2] *Ga. Col. Rec.*, IV, 138, 139. (Italics mine.) It is clear that at common law the principle of vicarious liability would not have to be invoked in this situation as the landholder was absolutely bound to keep in his fires. Bealieu *v.* Finglam (1401) Y. B. 2 Hen. IV, p. 18; Tuberville *v.* Stampe (1697) 2 Ld. Raym. 264.

of the theory above expressed that the master is not liable for his servant's torts. In this case of *Barret v. Gibson,*[1] the defendant, keeper of a public rolling-house, received from the plaintiff four hogsheads of tobacco for storage. The facts found by the jury in its special verdict were that the rolling-house was maliciously burnt by a negress belonging to the defendant. The negress was convicted. The jury returned the additional finding that a portion of the tobacco might have been saved, but that the defendant took no steps to do so. The question of law was whether the act of assembly imposing upon the owner of a public rolling-house liability for goods damaged when in his custody " for want of due care or by the neglect of the Owner or Keeper of such Rolling-House, his Servant or Servants, to the owner or Owners of such Tob'o &c." applied in the case where the servant's acts had been wilfully or maliciously inspired. The plaintiff contended that, by the terms of this act, the defendant was liable notwithstanding the fact that his servant had been convicted and executed for arson. " There may be a fault in the Master, either in provoking the Servant by ill usage to do him such an Injury or in keeping a Person of so Vicious and wicked Disposition about him." Here, as in the case of trespass by cattle, the plaintiff would have the negligence established by the liability rather than the liability by the negligence. It was further contended for the plaintiff that the law would regard the master as negligent for not keeping an adequate guard in or near the house to prevent the spread of fires. The argument that the warehouse-owner should be the insurer is a cogent and equitable one. Yet, the citations from eighteenth-century English decisions would hardly support the notion that the master is absolutely liable for the torts of his servant or agent when in his employ.[2]

---

[1] (1731) *Va. Col. Dec.,* I, 70-72.

[2] The report cites 2 Rol. Abr. 2 pl. 3. Fitz. Action upon the case 25.

So the court ruled in giving judgment for the defendant, stating as its ground that " the master is not chargeable for the wilful wrong of his servant. Vid. Jones and Nail 2 Salk. 411. Ward and Evans ibid. 442. Something to the purpose." By implication it is perfectly clear that the master is liable for the torts of the servant in the course of his regular employment.

2. *Absolute Responsibility for Fire*

In England down through the seventeenth century the old tradition was adhered to that the individual was responsible " for failing to keep in his fire," and that such responsibility was absolute.[1] The fact that the fire was purely accidental was no defense.[2] In the colonial courts more cases are available of suits for damages resulting from the wilful or negligent spreading of a fire than from non-negligent conduct. Thus, Mehittabell Brabrooke, prosecuted in the Essex County court in 1668 on suspicion of setting a house on fire, was found guilty " of extreme carelessness if not wilfully burning the house," and was ordered to be severely whipped and to pay £40 damages to the injured party. The evidence showed that the defendant had been smoking her pipe and had negligently knocked it upon the thatch on the eaves of the house; due to her fright she had failed to report the fire immediately.[3]   A New Jersey statute provided that " he that carelessly kindleth a fire which shall burn any house,

Brook 30; Waylands Case, 3 Salk 234, 2 Mod. 270. Another question of law raised in the case is whether the defendant, who is an infant, can be held liable. The plaintiff's counsel adroitly points out that in actions founded upon statutory liability both a feme covert and an infant can be made liable. Barret *v.* Gibson may be compared with the English case of Savignac *v.* Roome (1794) 6 T. R. 125.

[1] Wigmore, *Select Essays,* III, 511, 512; Tuberville *v.* Stampe (1698) 1 Salk. 13; Comb. 459; Skinner 681; Carth. 425.

[2] Street, *op. cit.,* I, 49 *et seq.*

[3] Brabrooke's case (1668) *Essex,* IV, 56.

barn, corn, hay or other thing, shall make full restitution to the party wrong'd or damaged." [1]

Other statutes clearly incorporate the notion of absolute responsibility for the spread of a fire originating on the defendant's premises. The Massachusetts act of 1652 provides that

whosoever shall kindle any fires in the woods, or grounds lying in common, or inclosed, so as the same shall run into corn grounds or inclosures . . . shall pay all damages, and half so much for a fine, or if not able to pay, then to be corporally punished, by warrant from one magistrate, or the next county court, as the offence shall deserve, not exceeding twenty stripes for one offence. Provided that any man may kindle fire in his own ground *so as no danger come thereby, either to the country or to any particular person;* and whosoever shall wittingly and willingly burn or destroy any frame, timber, hewed, sawed or riven heaps of wood, charcoal, corn, hay, straw, hemp or flax, he shall pay double damages. [2]

It seems justifiable to deduce from this statute that absolute responsibility devolved upon the maker of a fire whether upon common or inclosed lands or upon his own. It is clear that such an interpretation was placed upon the statute by the framers of the Duke of York's code, who took the Massachusetts law for a model. [3]

In an early Maine action brought in 1640, [4] one plaintiff alleged that the defendant whom he had hired to cut his grass had set it on fire; the other did not set up any contract to hire but merely the allegation that his property had been damaged by the fire. There was no allegation of negligence.

[1] Act of 1682, *Grants and Concessions of N. J.*, pp. 233, 234.

[2] *Mass. Charters and General Laws*, p. 112. (Italics mine.)

[3] *Duke of York's Book of Laws*, p. 28.

[4] Williams and Sanky *v.* Grant (1640) *Maine Province and Court Records*, I, 66.

The defendant answered that the fire was kindled in a manner unknown to him. But the jury returned a verdict of 20 s. damage for the plaintiffs and costs.

3. *Responsibility for Artificial Accumulations of Water*

In the suit brought in *Peabody v. Baker*[1] for damages resulting from the overflowing of the defendant's dam, the theory of the action appears to be trespass rather than negligence, although either negligence or wilful conduct might be attributed to the defendant.[2] In other dangerous occupations objective standards are occasionally laid down by the authorities and the scope of the activity is seriously circumscribed. For example, an early New Hampshire order made by the Court at Exeter in 1643 previous to the union with Massachusetts provides " that whosoever shall dig a saw-pit and shall not fill it or cover it, shall be liable to pay the damages that shall come to man or beast thereby." [3]

4. *Responsibility for the Use of Fire Arms*

Under most circumstances, when damage resulted from the discharge of firearms under immediate control, absolute responsibility was imposed at common law.[3] In a Newcastle action brought in 1676,[4] the plaintiff alleged that the defendants had injured him, apparently by an accidental shooting, as a result of which he had suffered injuries which kept him from his work. He therefore petitioned that the defendant " be ordered to hire a Servant for him untill he bee Restored to health." Although the court found that the

---

[1] (1715) MSS. Mass. Sup. Court Judic. (1715-1721), fol. 76.

[2] The judgment for the plaintiff for £5 5s and costs was reversed on appeal, and the defendant recovered £3 14s.

[3] *New Hamp. Prov. Laws*, I, 739.

[4] Street, *op. cit.*, I, 57.

[5] Powell *v.* Pietersen (1676) *Newcastle Rec.*, pp. 9, 10.

damages were accidental, it held the defendant liable for the payment of the physician's bill, and for the sum of one hundred and fifty gilders to the plaintiff for " his smart and Payne " and costs of suit.

Where the nature of the prosecution was criminal, an accidental and non-negligent shooting would not support an indictment. A typical decision is the Maine prosecution of Charles Frost.[1] According to the evidence, the prisoner had been engaged in hunting geese in the marsh and mistook Heard, who was concealed in the brush, also in readiness to fire, for the game. The grand jury found that the latter's death occurred " by misadventure." In some of the other New England jurisdictions the defendant in such cases was occasionally amerced as compensation to the widow of the deceased for her loss.[2]

In connection with the possession and use of arms the colonies by legislative acts or court orders set up an official standard of care. In violation of such an ordinance, Robert Lee of New Haven, who had come to training with his gun charged with shot, contrary to order, and had carelessly discharged it against Gregson's house, " to the great danger of the lives of divers persons, who were in the chamber when the shott came through the window, was fined 20 s. to the towne, and to repair the window wch was broken by the said shott." [3]

License to hunt wolves was restricted. A violation of this colonial order would subject the offender to legal responsibility for the consequent damages. The town court of New Haven conferred upon two individuals the privilege of shooting wolves. If in the course of their efforts they accidentally killed any swine, the town assumed responsibility, provided

---

[1] (1647) *Maine Province and Court Records*, I, 108, 109.

[2] See *infra*, § c.

[3] Lee's case (1643) *New Haven Col. Rec.*, I, 120.

the privileged parties took up their guns by daybreak. The ordinance further provided " *none else to sett gunns but upon their owne perill,* unless they have order from the Governor to doe it." [1] An earlier New Haven colony order had prescribed a fine of five shillings for every violation of the rule that a call be made whenever a bullet or smaller shot was to be fired within the limits of the town or within a quarter of a mile of the town.[2] The use of firearms by the Indians was naturally a source of great annoyance to the settlers. By a Connecticut statute of 1640,[3] Indians who meddled with the weapons of the settlers were made absolutely liable for all damages which might result, even though accidental, and were to " pay life for life, lymbe for lymbe, wound for wound, and . . . . for the healing such wounds & other damages."

The term " at peril," as eminent authorities have made clear, was not a novel one, nor were these statutes and ordinances embodying this concept. " It is an indigenous one and a classical one in our law." [4] It had been employed in English law to impose an absolute liability for keeping cattle, controlling fires and employing firearms. In the colonial courts the term on occasions acquired this broad significance in the second and third situations; but early American law did not anticipate the broadening of its scope in its enunciation in the nineteenth century by Mr. Justice Blackburn in *Fletcher v. Rylands.*[5] By restricting the scope of this principle, the early American courts were helping to construct the fetish of contributory negligence.

[1] *New Haven Town Rec.,* I, 92 (1651). (Italics mine.) For other restrictions against the use of arms, *cf. e. g.,* Brigham, *Ply. Col. Laws,* p. 176 (1675).

[2] *New Haven Col. Rec.,* I, 48 (1641).

[3] *Conn. Pub. Rec.,* I, 52.

[4] *Cf.* Wigmore, *op. cit.,* p. 519, and cases cited, n. 2.

[5] L. R. 1 Exch. at 282 (1866).

C. LIABILITY FOR DEATH BY WRONGFUL
ACT IN COLONIAL LAW

At common law there was no recovery where death resulted from injury to the person. To employ the phraseology of the leading decision,[1] "in a civil court the death of a human being could not be complained of as an injury." That the most serious of all injuries should go unredressed in the courts of common law as late as the last century is due to a devotion to traditions which were evolved in more primitive society and which had long outlived all vestiges of utility. One ground for this denial of redress was the argument that the right of action had merged in the felony.[2] The wrongdoer had been hanged and his goods confiscated. What remedy could the law then afford? Yet this principle was not carried out with consistency, for civil actions could be brought after criminal prosecutions in such felonies as robbery or larceny.[3]

A more general policy underlying this denial of a much-needed remedy was the rule of the common law that the right of action founded upon torts of any and every description terminated with the life of either participant in such torts, or, as stated in the celebrated opinion of Lord Mansfield in *Hambly v. Trott*,[4] no action survived in which the general issue was not guilty. The non-recognition of an action by the representatives of the deceased for loss of his

[1] Baker *v.* Bolton (1808) 1 Camp. 493. *Cf.* Holdsworth, "Origin of the Rule in Baker *v.* Bolton" (1916) *Law Quarterly Rev.*, XXXII, 431-437; Wigmore, "Death by Wrongful Act—Survival of Liability upon the Tortfeasor's Death" (1910) *Ill. Law Rev.*, IV, 425; Goudy, *Essays in Legal History* (edited by Vinogradoff, 1913), pp. 215-232.

[2] Higgins *v.* Butcher (1606) Yelverton 89.

[3] Dawkes *v.* Coveneigh (1652) Style 346. This distinction between homicides and other felonies is criticized by W. S. Holdsworth, *A History of English Law*, III, 676.

[4] (1776) 1 Cowp. 371.

services does not mean that his survivors had no legal remedy. In the Anglo-Saxon period composition for injuries was treated in a perfectly business-like fashion. Carefully estimated sums of money were established to comprise the *wergeld,* or the composition, which the tort-feasor had to make to the kinsmen of the deceased for the injury inflicted.[1]　When, in the twelfth century, this practice became obsolete, the appeal served as a coercive weapon to force the appellee to make some composition with the relatives of the deceased in order that the appeal might be discharged,[2] and in this manner was established a form of " legalized blackmail." Bargains of this sort were sanctioned by the courts in order to stifle litigation.[3]

There is no evidence that the appeal was employed in the American colonies to recover damages by effecting such a composition.　Parliament, however, was more concerned about abolishing this anachronism in the colonies than at home.　The Parliamentary measure of 1774 " for the improved administration of justice in the Province of Massachusetts Bay " originally contained a clause depriving the New Englanders of the appeal of murder.　The liberal party in the House of Commons was aroused.　Dunning, afterwards Lord Ashburton, one of the leaders of the opposition, defended the ancient custom in the strongest terms.

I rise [said he] to support that great pillar of the constitution, the appeal for murder; I fear there is a wish to establish a precedent for taking it away in England as well as in the colonies. It is called a remnant of barbarism and gothicism. The whole of our constitution, for aught I know, is gothic.

---

[1] Paul Vinogradoff, *Historical Jurisprudence*, I, 309.

[2] Blackstone, *Commentaries on the Laws of England*, IV, 312; Stenton, *The Earliest Lincolnshire Assize Rolls*, pp. xlix and lix.

[3] Pollock and Maitland, *History of English Law* (2d ed., 1898), II, 482-483.

. . . I wish, sir, that gentlemen would be a little more cautious, and consider that the yoke we are framing for the despised colonists may be tied around our own necks.

Even Burke was heard to lift a warning voice against the proposed innovation, and the obnoxious clause had to be struck out before the ministerial majority could pass the bill.[1] The constitution was saved.

In the American colonies in the eighteenth century the misleading maxim of the law, *actio personalis moritur cum persona,*[2] was applied to ordinary delictual actions. The courts denied relief,[3] and the plaintiff was forced as a last resort to have recourse to the legislature where private acts frequently empowered the petitioner to maintain an action.[4]

Notwithstanding these obstacles in the way of relief, the family of the deceased, in numerous jurisdictions, was not left destitute and without recourse to recover for the loss of his services where his death had been due to a wrongful act. There are substantial reasons why, in a number of jurisdictions, the civil action did not merge in the felony. In Massachusetts Bay, for example, the estate of the felon was not forfeited as in England. The tenth Liberty sweeps away in one gesture centuries of accumulated anachronisms:

All our lands and heritages shall be free from all fines and licences upon Alienations, and from all hariotts, wardshipps,

---

[1] Campbell's *Lives of the Chancellors of England*, VI, 112; Henry C. Lea, *Superstition and Force* (Philadelphia, 1866), pp. 172, 173.

[2] *"Actio injuriarum moritur cum persona"* (Bacon's *Maxims* (1639), 52), is probably a more accurate statement of the English law at this time. Goudy, *Essays in Legal History*, p. 227; Winfield, "Death as affecting Liability in Tort," *Columbia Law Rev.*, XXIX, 246.

[3] M'Laughlin *v.* Dorsey (1764) 1 H. & McH. 224.

[4] *Cf.* e. g., petition of Nathaniel East, *et al.* (1712) *Mass. Acts and Resolves*, IX, 222; petition of Rebecca Freeman (1716) *ibid.*, p. 501; petition of Ann Andrews (1719) *ibid.*, p. 664.

Liveries, Primerseisins, yeare day and wast, Escheates, and forfeitures, upon the death of parents or Ancestors, be they naturall, casuall or Juditiall.[1]

Survivals of forfeiture of chattels did remain and were diverted to a useful purpose. A statute of 1652 provided that, in the case of a conviction for arson, the Court of Assistants shall judge the felon " to be putt to death, and to forfeit so much of his lands, goods and chattels, as shall make full satisfaction, to the party or parties damnifyed." [2] A similar forfeiture is exacted by the Duke of York's laws.[3] Another survival is found in the case of robbery and larceny, where, on analogy to the appeal of larceny in early English law, the colonial statutes and judicial decisions provided that the culprit make restitution, double, treble, or fourfold as the case might be.[4] The necessity of a subsequent civil action of trespass *d. b. a.* was in this way dispensed with.

The New England, and in some instances the middle, colonies gave a writ for civil damages resulting from a death by wrongful act in special cases where the act complained of was neither malicious nor wilful. The courts went further, and afforded the relatives of the deceased compensation for their loss in the same judgment as was rendered in the criminal prosecution, although in some cases a separate civil cause of action was recognized.

[1] Whitmore, *Mass. Col. Laws*, p. 35.

[2] Whitmore, *op., cit.*, p. 152. This section supplements the section relating to "Fyre" in *Lawes and Libertyes of Massachusetts* (Cambridge, 1648), p. 22. That chattels were at times forfeited for felonies is seen in the conviction of Leonard Pomery in 1683 for manslaughter. He was sentenced to be burnt in the hand and to forfeit his chattels. *Assistants*, I, 243.

[3] *Duke of York's Book of Laws*, pp. 27, 28.

[4] For a discussion of the colonial technique analogous to the appeal of larceny and trespass *d. b. a., cf. supra*, p. 53.

A Massachusetts statute, attributed to 1648,[1] recognizes this action as a means of imposing stricter accountability upon the community for its public works:

The court considering the great danger that persones, horses, teames, are exposed to by reason of defective bridges, & Country highways in this jurisdiction. Doth Order & declare: That if any person, at any time loose his life, in passing any such bridge or high-way, after due warning given unto of any of the Select men of the towne in which such defect is, in writing under the hand of two witnesses or upon presentment to the shire Court, of such defective wayes or bridges, that then the County or towne which ought to secure such wayes or bridges, shall pay a fine of one hundred pounds, to the parents, husband, wife or children or next of kin, to the partie deceased. And if any person loose a Limb, break a bone or receive any other bruise in any part of his body, through such defect as aforesaid, The County or towne through whose neglect such hurt is done shall pay to the partie so hurt, double damages, the like satisfaction shall be made for any teame, Cart or Cartage, horse, other beast or loadinge, proportionable to the damage sustained as aforesaid.[2]

This statute was substantially reenacted in 1693 and again in 1786,[3] and served as the model for the New Hampshire statute of 1719.[4]

---

[1] It is not found in *Lawes and Libertyes* (Cambridge, 1648).

[2] Whitmore, *Mass. Col. Laws*, pp. 126, 127; *Mass. Charter and General Laws*, p. 55.

[3] *Mass. Charters and General Laws*, p. 269; act of 1786, c. 81. Lord Sumner seems to regard the latter as the earliest Massachusetts provision and as a tentative enactment. *Commissioners for Executing the Office of Lord High Admiral of the United Kingdom and Owners of Steamship Amerika*, House of Lords (1917) App. Cas. 38. A policy which had been in force for over a century and a quarter could scarcely be regarded as tentative.

[4] *Laws of New Hamp.*, II, 332. *Cf.* also Copp *v.* Henniker (1875) 55 N. H. 185.

In other colonies statutes dealt with the problem of death by wilful act. Among the laws agreed upon in England in 1682 for the government of Pennsylvania was the provision that " the estate of capital offenders, as traitors and murderers, shall go one third to the next of kin to the sufferer, and the remainder to the next of kin to the criminal." [1]   An act of 1683, subsequently reaffirmed,[2] reduced the share of property to be spared the next of kin of the criminal to one-half of the total estate in case of murder. In manslaughter the nearest relatives of the deceased were to be compensated from such portion of half of the estate of the deceased as the court in its discretion seized.[3]   The heavy forfeiture which the assembly sought to exact in cases where death was the result of " chance medley " or self-defence brought gubernatorial censure in 1705.[4]

By a notable line of seventeenth-century decisions the courts of Massachusetts and Connecticut, although not specifically authorized by statute, foreshadowed in their decisions the policy embodied in the Pennsylvania legislation. Compensation to the relatives of the deceased was secured in criminal or civil actions. The criminal suits were of two kinds. In the first, the jury returned a verdict of guilty of manslaughter; in the second, of accidental homicide.

In the presentment brought against Samuel Hunting of Massachusetts in 1677 for shooting John Dexter, thé bench considered the evidence and found the prisoner guilty of manslaughter. He was fined the sum of £20 to be paid the widow of the deceased " towards hir losse & damage "

[1] Pa. Col. Rec., I, xxxii; Duke of York's Book of Laws, p. 101; Grants and Concessions of N. J., p. 235, act of 1682, c. xviii.

[2] Duke of York's Book of Laws, pp. 144, 210; Bioren's Laws of Pa., I, 4, 7.

[3] Duke of York's Book of Laws, p. 144; disallowed by the King and Queen in Council in 1693.

[4] Pa. Col. Rec., II, 216.

and £5 " to the Country." [1] In a subsequent action, where the prisoner had been found guilty of manslaughter in shooting an Indian, he was ordered to pay the widow £6 on the following terms : twenty shillings down and twenty shillings for five successive years.[2] Probably the first colonial installment plan is thus revealed. In a prosecution brought in 1691 against Richard Lillie, indicted for shooting and mortally wounding John Robinson, the jury brought in the strange verdict of " Manslaughter by Misadventure," [3] but ordered the prisoner to pay £5 to their Majesties and £20 to the widow.[4]

The earliest case that has been found of recovery for damages resulting from death by a wrongful but unintentional act is the Connecticut conviction of John Ewe, who, in 1643, was found to have been the cause of Thomas Scott's death " by misadventure." He was directed to pay a fine of £5 to the colony and £10 to the widow Scott.[5] A similar division of the fine was provided for in the Massachusetts cases dealing with accidental homicide. John Foster, who had accidentally discharged a gun and fatally shot Samuel Flackes, was ordered in 1675 to pay the father of the deceased £10. Another ten due to the country was remitted on petition.[6] In another case, one who had driven a cart over a child was ordered to give satisfaction to the father.[7]

[1] *Assistants*, I, 114.

[2] Rex *v.* Dyar (1681) *Assistants*, I, 188.

[3] What constituted manslaughter at the common law was never clearly grasped in the colonial cases. The reader is referred to Gard's case (1712) *Conn. Pub. Rec.*, V, 350, 351, and n.; and Brown's case (1738), " Stephen's Journal," *Ga. Col. Rec.*, IV, 188.

[4] (1691) *Assistants*, I, 358, 359.

[5] *Conn. Pub. Rec.*, I, 103; " Records of the Particular Court of Connecticut, 1639-1663," Conn. Hist. Soc., *Collections*, XXII, 25.

[6] (1675) *Assistants*, I, 54.

Ford's case (1676) *Assistants*, I, 60.

Where the prisoner was indicted for murder and the jury returned a verdict of not guilty or of guilty of accidental homicide, this compensation to the widow or the nearest relative was still exacted.[1]

As indicated earlier in this study, such terms as " by misadventure," " chance medley," or " accidental," when used in these early brief reports do not necessarily establish non-culpable conduct. For example, in the prosecution of Thomas Allyn before the Particular Court at Hartford in 1651, it appears that the prisoner had negligently cocked his weapon when just behind a neighbor, and had carelessly discharged it, bringing about the latter's death. The jury found Allyn guilty of " homicide by missadventure." He was fined £20 " for his sinfull neglect and Carless Carriages in the premises " and was placed under bond not to carry arms for twelve months.[2]

An example of a civil cause of action for damages resulting from death by wrongful act is *Button v. Godfrey*, brought in the Essex Quarterly Court in 1669.[3] The declaration charged the defendant with firing his chimney in such a manner as to cause his house and goods to burn and to bring about the death of the plaintiff's wife, and with " running away as soon as he had done." The plaintiff was granted the heavy verdict of £238 2 s.

A distinction must be drawn at this point between damages on the one hand for loss of services and society and expenses incurred from the time of the accident to the time of the death, and, on the other, for these expenses together with the estimated loss of the services of the deceased as

---

[1] Bent's case (1677) *Assistants*, I, 86; Ellacot's case (1684) *ibid.*, p. 251; Dounton's case (1684) *ibid.*, pp. 271, 272.

[2] " Records of the Particular Court of Connecticut," Conn. Hist. Soc., *Collections*, XXII, 106, 107.

[3] *Essex*, IV, 131.

determined by the jury. For the first type of damage relief could be secured at common law, but not for the second.[1]

The Plymouth actions and those of eighteenth-century Massachusetts do not appear to exceed the strict limitations of *Baker v. Bolton*. Thus, Robert Trayes, a negro of Scituate, who was indicted in 1684 of wilfully shooting Daniel Standlake, who died of the wound, was cleared by the jury on the ground of misadventure, and fined as follows:

> Robert Trayes, amerced by the Court to pay towards the charge of the lamnes of Daniel Standlake, unto his father, Richard Standlake, of Scittuate, the sume of . . . .   ££ 03:00:00
>
> And for the negroes wrong that hee hath don in takeing away, or being an instrument in takeing away, Daniel Standlake out of the world, although by misadventure is fined or to suffer corporall punishment by being whipt.[2]   02:00:00

In 1721 Joshua Hilton, an infant of Salem, accidentally shot and killed another boy. The Massachusetts Superior Court of Judicature declared the gun deodand, and ordered Hilton's father to pay the sum of forty shillings to the mother of the deceased " to reimburse her the charge of Doctor Boumes looking after her till he dyed of the wound he received, and other charges." [3]

In other colonial jurisdictions the disability of the common law appears to have continued. In 1675 John Skidmore and his wife, residents of Jamaica, Long Island, petitioned

---

[1] Baker *v.* Bolton (1808) 1 Campb. 493.

[2] (1684) *Ply. Col. Rec.*, VI, 141, 142.

[3] (1721) MSS. Mass. Sup. Court Judic. (1721-1725), fol. 34. With this compare Ford *v.* Monroe (1838) 20 Wend. 210, in which the plaintiff recovered for the loss of service of his child until the age of twenty-one.

Governor Andros for a fair trial for their son who had accidentally shot and killed a neighbor's boy.[1] This petition was shortly followed by one from Samuel Barker, father of the deceased, setting forth that his son was his only means of support, and that at his death he was reduced to poverty. He then cites the ability of the offender's parents and asks " whether or no according to the (Law of God), some restitution ought not to bee made for your peticon'rs future Reliefe." The petition carries the endorsement: " not graunted." [2] The procedure comprises some evidence that a cause of action for death by wrongful act was not recognized in the colony of New York.

Where the remedy was available in the colonies, it was founded either on specific legislative enactments which allowed damages recovered from a criminal prosecution to be assigned to the plaintiff, or from a common practice of assigning damages even where the defendant was freed on the ground of accidental homicide. The relief was afforded in the criminal action; in rare instances a civil suit afforded the nearest relative of the deceased such relief. The modern American jurisdictions, ignoring this desirable remedy available in colonial times, have in the main been influenced by the legal reaction of the eighteenth century and by the English line of cases prior to Lord Campbell's act.[3] This remedial statute provided that whenever the death of a person shall be caused by a wrongful act which would, if death had not ensued, have entitled the party injured to maintain an action to recover damages in respect thereof, the tortfeasor shall be held liable, notwithstanding the death of the person injured shall have been caused under such

---

[1] N. Y. State Hist., *Ann. Rep.*, II, 356, 357. The boy was subsequently cleared by a verdict of chance medley. *Ibid.*, pp. 393, 394.

[2] *Ibid.*, p. 379.

[3] 9 & 10 Vict. c. 93.

circumstances as amount in law to felony. American statutes, such as the Massachusetts statute of 1840, c. 80, granting such relief in transportation accidents, were strictly construed by the courts. This particular statute did not provide
a civil cause of action, but rather, in accord with colonial
precedent, a penalty to be recovered from the carriers by
indictment.[1]

By way of exception, it may be observed that at the end
of the eighteenth century and in the first half of the century
following, Lord Ellenborough's rule denying recovery in a
civil action for death by wrongful act was not universally
recognized in this country. *Cross v. Guthery*,[2] an action
brought in the Connecticut Superior Court in 1794, was a
suit to recover damages against a surgeon for unskillfully
performing an operation on the plaintiff's wife, as the result
of which she died. The defendant moved in arrest of judgment that the declaration was insufficient on the ground that
the offence charged appeared to be a felony, and by the common law, the private injury was merged in the public offence.
The court, however, held the declaration sufficient, pointing
out that the rule urged was applicable in England only to
capital crimes, where from necessity the offender must go un-
punished, or the injured individual go unredressed. Judicial
cognizance was thus taken of the different conditions prevailing in this country. Both *Cross v. Guthery* and a New
York action of *Ford v. Monroe*,[3] so far as they were authorities for the view that an action might be maintained for the
loss of services caused by death, have been overruled;[4] but

---

[1] Carey *et ux. v.* Berkshire R. I. Co.; Skinner *v.* Housatonic R. R.
(1848) 53 Mass. 475. The modern Massachusetts statutes retain these
criminal features. Gustavus Hay, Jr., "Death as a Civil Cause of
Action in Massachusetts," *Harvard Law Review*, VII, 170-176.

[2] (1794) 2 Root 90.   [2] (1822) 2 Wend. 210.

[4] *Cf.* Francis B. Tiffany, *Death by Wrongful Act*, 2d ed. (Kansas
City, Mo., 1913), § 11, and cases cited.

new enabling statutes, starting with New York in 1847 and followed in practically all of the American states, gave substantial relief along the lines of Lord Campbell's Act.[1] Here, as in the many other occasions discussed in these *Studies,* ignorance of the trail which had been blazed by the seventeenth-century pioneers hampered the progress of American law. That recognition of the social importance of this legal remedy should have been found in the colonial courts two centuries before Lord Campbell's act is indicative of the refreshing originality which characterized our legal engineering.

[1] Tiffany, *op. cit.,* § 19; *Columbia Law Review,* XV, 621.

CHAPTER V

BIBLIOGRAPHICAL ESSAY

A. The Secondary Literature

The scholar who has made the literary acquaintance of Maitland, Vinogradoff and Holdsworth, of Brunner, Liebermann and Viollet, has been able to set his course in continental or English legal history with the confidence and accuracy afforded by a gyro-compass. The investigator of early American law is not even furnished with the unreliable magnetic instrument, but has to plot his own course virtually unaided. No general treatise deals at any length with the seventeenth and eighteenth centuries in American law. The absence of abridgments of the reported cases makes the principal source material more inaccessible than the Year Books. The law reports contain material as rich in significance for early American law as are the publications of the Selden Society for English legal history, and sufficient reasons exist for publishing at least important selections from this abundant material on a scale commensurate with the notable work of the society of English scholars.

In the field of secondary literature, the commentaries of Kent and Story called attention in the early part of the last century to the problem of the transplantation of the common law. Story's work particularly shows considerable first-hand acquaintance with colonial legal sources. In at least two collections of papers an attempt has been made to give a general survey of the seventeenth and eighteenth centuries: *Two Centuries' Growth of American Law* (Yale Univ., *Bicentennial Publications,* New York, 1901); and *Select Essays in Anglo-American Legal History,* 3 vols. (Boston, 1907). The latter collection (vol. i, pp. 367-415) contains a paper by Paul Samuel Reinsch, originally published as a doctoral dissertation in the *Bulletin* of the University of Wisconsin (Madison, Wisc., 1899), and entitled: " English Common Law in the Early American Colonies." While certain valuable generalizations have been formulated in this brief study, it reveals little direct contact with the actual sources of the law. The author has included a useful working bibliography of the secondary material (*Select Essays,* II, 164-168).

The tranplantation of the common law and the control of colonial courts and legislatures under the British imperial system have been frequently discussed. Of the more important papers dealing with various phases of this general problem may be mentioned: R. C. Dale, "The Adoption of the Common Law by the American Colonies," *American Law Register* (1882) n. s. XXI; T. M. Dill, "Colonial Development of the Common Law," *Law Quarterly Review* (1924) XL, 227-244, with special reference to the situation in Bermuda; Pope, "English Common Law in the United States," *Harvard Law Review*, XXIV, 6; St. George L. Sioussat, "The Extension of English Statutes to the Plantations," *Select Essays*, I, 416-430; L. P. Kellogg, "American Colonial Charter," Amer. Hist. Assn., *Annual Report*, 1903, I, pp. 175 *et seq.*; C. M. Andrews, "The Royal Disallowance," Amer. Antiq. Soc., *Proceedings*, n. s. XXIV; A. G. Dorland, "The Royal Disallowance in Massachusetts," Queens Univ., *Bulletin* (1917), no. XX; H. D. Hazeltine, "Appeals from Colonial Courts to the King in Council," Amer. Hist. Assn., *Annual Report*, 1894, pp. 299-350; A. M. Schlesinger, "Appeals to the Privy Council," *Political Science Quarterly*, XVIII, 440-449; R. B. Morris, "Massachusetts and the Common Law: the Declaration of 1646," *Amer. Hist. Rev.* (1926), XXXI, 443-453. Two valuable monographs dealing with the British materials and the imperial, rather than the colonial point of view, are the dissertations of E. B. Russell, *The Review of American Colonial Legislation by the King in Council* (New York, 1915) (*Columbia Univ. Studies in Hist., Econ. and Public Law*, no. 155), and of George A. Washburne, *Imperial Control of the Administration of Justice in the Thirteen American Colonies, 1684-1776* (New York, 1923) (*Columbia Univ. Studies in Hist., Econ. and Public Law*, no. 238). Illuminating source material for this particular problem will be found in George Chalmers' compilation, *Opinions of eminent Lawyers on various Points of English Jurisprudence chiefly concerning the Colonies* (London, 1858).

While no comprehensive investigation of the general field of the law has been made, a valuable survey of the legal profession has been contributed by Charles Warren, whose *History of the American Bar* (Boston, 1911) contains useful bibliographical notes arranged regionally. The history of the bar and the organization of the courts have been the chief subjects hitherto investigated in monographs dealing with special localities. For Maine, may be mentioned William Willis, *A History of the Law, the Courts, and the Lawyers of Maine* (Portland, 1863). Massachusetts is plentifully supplied with treatises of this character. Among them may be mentioned: William T. Davis, *History of the Judiciary of Massachusetts* (Boston, 1909); Albert Mason, "Judicial History of Massachusetts," in *The New England States*, edited by W. T. Davis (Boston, 1897), chap. CXXXIV; Emory Washburne, *Judicial History of Massachusetts* (Boston, 1840); and the recent chapter of F. W. Grinnell, "The Bench and Bar in Colony and Province (1630-1776)," in the *Commonwealth History of Massachusetts* (New York, 1928), II, 156-192. Wilkins Updike treats Rhode Island lawyers in his *Memoirs of the Rhode*

Island Bar (Boston, 1842) ; and a compendious survey of New England is furnished in three volumes by Conrad Reno, *Memoirs of the Judiciary and the Bar of New England for the Nineteenth Century* (Boston, 1900), vol. III of which deals with the judiciary. Other colonial judicial systems have been investigated, to mention a few, by Richard S. Field, *Provincial Courts of New Jersey* (New York, 1849) ; and by Ignatius C. Grubb, *Colonial and State Judiciary of Delaware* (Wilmington, 1897). Pennsylvania is the subject of surveys by Lawrence Lewis, " Courts of Pennsylvania in the Seventeenth Century," Pa. Bar. Assn., *Reports*, vol. I, by William H. Loyd, *The Early Courts of Pennsylvania* (Boston, 1910), and by F. M. Eastman, *Courts and Lawyers of Pennsylvania, a History, 1623-1923*, 3 vols. (New York, 1922).

There are a few regional studies dealing specifically with the development of the law. Among them may be mentioned W. C. Fowler, *Local Law in Massachusetts and Connecticut, Historically Considered* (Albany, 1872) ; Charles J. Hilkey, *Legal Development in Colonial Massachusetts, 1630-1686* (New York, 1910) (*Columbia Univ. Studies in Hist., Econ. and Public Law*, vol. XXXVII, no. 2), a convenient compendium of the statutory material ; Zephaniah Swift, *A System of the Laws of the State of Connecticut*, 2 vols. (Windham, 1795) ; Henry Budd, " Colonial Legislation in Pennsylvania, 1700-1712," Col. Soc. of Pa., *Publications, Bulletin*, No. 1 ; St. George L. Sioussat, " English Statutes in Maryland," *Johns Hopkins Studies in History and Political Science*, ser. XXI ; and O. P. Chitwood, " Justice in Colonial Virginia," *ibid.*., ser. XXIII.

Special fields of legal history of interest in these *Studies* have been profitably explored in a number of cases. The evolution of some of the forms of action has been treated in A. G. Sedgwick and F. S. Wait, " The History of the Action of Ejectment in England and the United States," *Select Essays*, III, 611-646 ; and in A. Stearns, *A Summary of the Law and Practice of Real Actions* (2d ed., n. p., 1831). Valuable papers dealing with equitable relief have been contributed by S. D. Wilson, " Courts of Chancery in the American Colonies," *Select Essays*, II, 779-809 ; and by S. G. Fisher, " The Administration of Equity through Common Law Forms in Pennsylvania," *ibid.*, pp. 810 *et seq.* Among numerous treatments of the colonial criminal system may be mentioned W. F. Prince, " The First Criminal Code of Virginia," Amer. Hist. Assn., *Annual Report*, 1899, I, 309 *et seq.* ; A. P. Scott, " The Criminal Law and its Administration in Colonial Virginia," a dissertation abstracted in *Abstracts of Theses* (Univ. of Chicago, *Humanistic Series*, 1922-1923), I, 225-229 ; John Noble, " Notes on the Trial and Punishment of Crimes," Col. Soc. of Mass., *Publications*, III, 51-66 ; A. McF. Davis, *The Law of Adultery and Ignominious Punishments* (Worcester, Mass., 1895), with a supplement in Amer. Antiq. Soc., *Proceedings* (1889) n. s. XIII, 67 *et seq.* ; and Arthur Lyon Cross, " Benefit of Clergy in the American Criminal Law," Mass. Hist. Soc., *Proceedings* (1927-1928), LXI, 154-181. A noteworthy contribution to the history of colonial real property law is presented by Charles McLean Andrews, "The Influence of Colonial Conditions as Illustrated in the Connecticut Intestacy Law," *Select Essays*, I, 431-466.

A contribution of monumental proportions to the law of persons and domestic relations has been made by George E. Howard, vol. II of whose *History of Matrimonial Institutions* (3 vols., Chicago, 1904) treats the colonial period with exemplary thoroughness. This theme is also developed, among others, by A. W. Calhoun, *Social History of the American Family* (Cleveland, 1917); by James Douglas, "The Status of Women in New England and New France," Queens Univ., Depts. of Hist. and Polit. and Eco. Science, *Bulletin,* no. 3, the conclusions of which, at least for New England, should be accepted with the utmost caution, if at all.

No treatment of the secondary authorities would be complete without reference to a group of historical works dealing with the institutional, legal, administrative, social and economic development of the American colonies; noteworthy among these are: Herbert L. Osgood, *American Colonies in the Seventeenth Century,* 3 vols. (New York, 1904-1907); *American Colonies in the Eighteenth Century,* 4 vols. (New York, 1924-1925); Philip A. Bruce, *Economic History of Virginia in the Seventeenth Century,* 2 vols.; *Institutional History of Virginia in the Seventeenth Century,* 2 vols.; *Social History of Virginia in the Seventeenth Century* (New York, 1895-1907); and W. B. Weeden, *Economic and Social History of New England,* 2 vols. (2d ed., Boston, 1896).

B. THE PRIMARY SOURCES

I. MANUSCRIPTS

In the preparation of these *Studies* I have found it expedient to explore beyond the more orthodox boundaries customarily set for legal sources. In addition to consulting official manuscript records of reported cases, I have, wherever possible, consulted the file papers, and pursued my investigation among the correspondence, briefs and cost books of colonial attorneys, among deeds and probate records, and among the private papers of colonial business men.

Massachusetts, Connecticut, New York, and Maryland offer four representative regions for manuscript research in colonial law, as judicial systems in all these jurisdictions were established before the middle of the seventeenth century, and valuable unpublished material is available. In the search for material my attention was directed more especially to depositories in Massachusetts and New York.

In Massachusetts, the most valuable unpublished law reports are in the

Office of the Clerk of the Supreme Judicial Court for the County of Suffolk, Boston. In that office, in addition to miscellaneous minute books of the Court of General Sessions of the Peace, there are thirty-three MS. folio volumes of the Records of the Superior Court of Judicature, Court of Assize and Gaol Delivery in the Province of Massachusetts Bay, 1697-1780. The first volume (1693-1695) has been transcribed. Supplementing the minutes are about nine hundred MS. folio volumes of Early Court Files of Suffolk, 1629-1800, consisting of miscellaneous papers, pleas, depositions, briefs, etc., and additional papers are found in the Greenough Collection (1647-1821), added in 1920, and containing an index. The material is handsomely bound and deposited in dust-proof glass cases in a room devoted entirely to these early archives. An index to the file papers, comprising twenty folio volumes, facilitates the collection by the research worker of the miscellaneous data contained in the scattered volumes, and throws light on the more stereotyped records of cases in the first thirty-three volumes. Of special interest in the field of domestic relations is the collection of court records bound as "Divorce, 1760-1786." These archives constitute the greatest collection of American legal material for the eighteenth century. Scattered correspondence of importance for the legal historian will be found among the Hutchinson Papers in the State House. A calendar is available. (*Cf.* Carroll D. Wright, *Report on the Custody and Condition of the Public Records,* Boston, 1889, pp. 316-332; *Catalogue of Records and Files in the Office of the Clerk of the Supreme Judicial Court,* revised, 1896; Boston, 1897).

A comprehensive survey of the public archives of New York County has been made by Victor Hugo Paltsits, in I. N. Phelps Stokes, *Iconography of Manhattan Island,* VI, 185-223; and a brief survey of the judicial records is found in E. B. Greene and R. B. Morris, *A Guide to the Principal Sources for Early American History* (*1600-1800*) *in the City of New York* (New York, 1929; hereafter *Guide*), pp. 208-212. The records are kept principally in the Hall of Records, the Criminal Courts Building, Center Street, and some of the very earliest are with the City Clerk in the Municipal Building. The colonial records in the Hall of Records fall roughly into three classes: file papers, parchments and libers. The parchments form part of the record of cases not only in the Mayor's Court of New York, but also of the Supreme Court of Judicature, the Court of Oyer and Terminer, and subsequently the Circuit Courts. The file papers relate chiefly to the Mayor's Court of the City of New York and to the Supreme Court of Judicature. The libers are minute books of the Mayor's Court, 1674-1820, with few interruptions; of the Court of Oyer and Terminer, 1716-1717; of the Courts of General Quarter Sessions and General Sessions, 1705-1715, 1722-1742; and of the Supreme Court of Judicature, 1704-1847, with certain gaps. In the

Criminal Courts Building are the minutes of the Court of General Sessions, 1684-1831, 131 libers; and the minutes of Oyer and Terminer and General Sessions, 1784-1895, about 20 libers.

For a survey of the important legal papers at the State House, Hartford, Conn., see L. M. Hubbard and C. J. Hoadley, *Report of the Secretary of State and State Librarian (of Connecticut) on Ancient Court Records* (1889); A. C. Bates, "Report on the Public Archives of Connecticut," Amer. Hist. Assn., *Annual Report*, 1900, II, 26-36. In addition to Mrs. H. D. Richardson's "Report of the Public Records Commission of Maryland," Amer. Hist. Assn., *Annual Report*, 1905, I, 367 *et seq.*, there has recently been published a *Catalogue of Manuscripts and Printed Matter* (Nov., 1926) in the possession of the Maryland Court of Appeals in Annapolis.

Court records, not in public archives, form an important addition to the manuscript material consulted. (See Greene and Morris, *Guide*, pp. 212-218). Among the most important of these are the Calendar of the Proceedings of the Court of Assizes relating to Long Island, 1665-1672, New York Public Library; the Minutes of the Circuit Court of Oyer and Terminer, 1721-1749, and of the Court for Tryall of causes brought to Issue in the Supreme Court, Library of the Association of the Bar of the City of New York; and a valuable collection in the New York Historical Society, comprising: First Book of Minutes of the Parish of Rye, 1710-1795; Minutes of the Mayor's Court, Borough Town of Westchester, 1657-1678, 1696-1706, 1717-1727, 1728-1774, meagre and not continuous; and Minutes of the Court of Sessions, 1687-1688, 1691-1696

Correspondence, briefs, account books, court registers and manuscript law treatises of early American attorneys have been consulted. Important material relating to New England lawyers is contained in the file papers in the Suffolk Court House, Boston. A detailed list of material which the writer has examined is found in Greene and Morris, *Guide*, pp. 219-223. The principal papers include those of John Sherman and John Williams of Connecticut, New York Public Library; and the correspondence of Joseph Reed of New Jersey, 1761-1775, in the New York Historical Society and among the Bancroft Papers in the New York Public Library. Of the New York lawyers, the largest collections of private papers were those of James Alexander (*c.* 1690-1756), over 30 folio volumes in the New York Historical Society; of De Witt Clinton, 1785-1800+, Columbia University; of James Duane (vol. V), New York Historical Society; of Harme Gansevoort (Albany, 1748-1793), Gansevoort Papers, New York Public Library; of John Tabor Kempe, attorney-general of New York (1752-1777);[1] of Rufus King

[1] *Cf.* Greene and Morris, *Guide*, p. 212.

(King Papers, vol. I) ; and of John McKesson (*c.* 1770-1793), in the New York Historical Society.

Among manuscript treatises examined, may be mentioned A Treatise on the Nature and Law of Evidence, *c.* 1770,[1] New York Historical Society; a comprehensive abridgement of Judge Roger Mompesson, and a Form Book of Joseph Murray, 1740-1741, both in the Law Library of Columbia University; and the Common-Place Book of William Smith, Jr., including A Treatise on Evidence (Gilbert's *Evidence*), in the New York Public Library.

The extensive collections of deeds, indentures, patents, surveys, correspondence, and miscellaneous papers relating to real estate in early America and disclosing the relations between landlord and tenant, and other sources relating to the administration of estates, including wills, deeds, inventories, guardianships, and miscellaneous correspondence, which were examined, are detailed in Greene and Morris, *Guide*, pp. 224-246.

2. PRINTED SOURCES

In listing the printed sources for early American law which have been examined in the preparation of these *Studies*, I have not included the numerous imprints of colonial statutes and session laws (only the general collections are cited), or of legislative journals, the printed deeds and probate records, the church and town records and the publications of general and regional historical societies, which have been consulted, as they are listed in Greene and Morris, *Guide*, pp. 10-55, wherein their locations in New York City have been indicated.

(a) *General Collections of Colonial Charters, Statutes and Treaties*

An Abridgement of the Laws in Force and Use in her Majesty's Plantations, London, 1704.

N. Trott, *Laws of the British Plantations in America, relating to the Church and the Clergy, Religion and Learning*, London, 1721.

J. H. Howard, *Laws of the British Colonies in the West Indies and other Parts of America, concerning Real and Personal Property, etc.*, London, 1827.

S. Lucas, *Charters of Old English Colonies in America*, London, 1850.

Pennsylvania Hist. Soc., *Charlemagne Tower Collection of American Colonial Laws*, Philadelphia, 1890.

B. P. Poore, compiler, *The Federal and State Constitutions, Colonial Charters and other Organic Laws of the United States*, Senate *Misc. Docs.*, 44 Cong., 2 sess. (no number, serial numbers 1730, 1731) ; also separately, 2 parts, Washington, 1877. New edition compiled and edited by F. N. Thorpe, *House Docs.*, 59 Cong., 2 Sess. no. 357, 7 vols., Washington, 1909.

[1] *Cf. ibid.*, p. 221.

(b) *Documentary Material grouped by Colonies and States*

CONNECTICUT

Public Records

Public Records of the Colony of Connecticut (1636-1776), compiled by
J. H. Trumbull and C. J. Hoadly. 15 vols. Hartford, 1850-1890.
Two additional volumes of *State Records.* Hartford, 1894-1895.

Records of the Colony and Plantation of New Haven (1638-1649). Compiled by C. J. Hoadley. Hartford, 1857. *Records of the Colony
or Jurisdiction of New Haven (1653-1665).* Hartford, 1858.

Statutes and Court Records

A. C. Bates, *A Bibliographical List of Editions of Connecticut Laws
from the earliest issues to 1836.* Hartford, 1900.

Francis Fane, *Reports on the Laws of Connecticut,* edited by C. M.
Andrews. Hartford, 1915.

" Records of the Particular Court of Connecticut, 1639-1663," Conn. Hist.
Soc., *Collections* (1928), vol. xxii.

DELAWARE

Public Records

Delaware Archives. 5 vols. Wilmington, 1911-1916.

Minutes of the Council of Delaware State, from 1776 to 1792. Dover,
1886.

Statutes and Court Records

Laws, 1700-1805. I-II, New Castle, 1797; III, Wilmington, 1816;
1700-1819. New Castle, 1797-1819.

Laws of the Government of Newcastle, Kent, and Sussex upon Delaware.
2 vols. Philadelphia and Wilmington, 1763.

Records of the Court of Newcastle on Delaware, 1676-1681. Lancaster,
1904. Reprinted from the Geneal. Soc. of Pa., *Collections,* LXVIII,
LXIX.

Some Records of Sussex County, Del., (court records of Deal County,
1681-1695). Compiled by C. H. B. Turner. Philadelphia, 1909.

GEORGIA

Public Records

Colonial Records of the State of Georgia, edited by A. D. Candler, 26
vols. Atlanta, 1905-1916.

Revolutionary Records of the State of Georgia (1769-1784), edited by
A. D. Candler, 3 vols. Atlanta, 1908.

John Perceval (First Earl of Egmont), *Journal of the Transactions of
the Trustees for Establishing the Colony of Georgia in America.*
Wormsloe, 1886.

Statutes

Statutes (*1754-1805*), edited by A. D. Candler. Atlanta, 1910-1911.

C. C. Jones, editor, *Acts passed by the General Assembly of the Colony of Georgia, 1755-1774.* Wormsloe, 1881.

H. Marbury and W. H. Crawford, compilers, *Digest of the Laws of the State of Georgia, from its settlement as a British Province in 1755 to the Session of the General Assembly in 1800, inclusive.* Savannah, 1802.

MAINE

Court Records

Province and Court Records of Maine, I, 1636-1668, edited by C. T. Libby. Portland, 1928.

MARYLAND

Public Records

Archives of Maryland, edited by W. F. Browne, I-XLIV. Baltimore, 1883-. In progress.

Statutes and Court Records

T. Bacon, editor, *Laws of Maryland at Large* (1637-1763). Annapolis, 1765.

W. Kilty, editor, *Laws of Maryland* (1692-1799), 2 vols. Annapolis, 1799-1800.

V. Maxcy, editor, *Laws of Maryland, with the Charter, the Bill of Rights, etc.* (1704-1809), 3 vols. Baltimore, 1811.

C. Dorsey, comp., *General Public Statutory Law and Public Law, 1692-1839*, 3 vols. Baltimore, 1840.

Maryland Reports, 1700-1797, 3 vols. New York, 1809-1813.

Maryland Court of Appeals Reports, 1658-1799, Harris and McHenry.

MASSACHUSETTS

Public Records

Records of the Colony of New Plymouth in New England (1620-1692), edited by N. B. Shurtleff and others, 12 vols. Boston, 1855-1861. Vols. IX, X contain "Acts of the Commissioners of the United Colonies" (1643-1679); XI, "Plymouth Colony Laws" (1623-1682).

Records of the Governor and Company of the Massachusetts Bay in New England (1628-1686), edited by N. B. Shurtleff, 5 vols. Boston, 1863-1854.

"Andros Records," Amer. Antiquarian Soc., *Proceedings*, 1900, XIII, 237-268, 463-499.

Journals of the House of Representatives of Massachusetts, 1715-1731, vols. I-IX. Boston, 1919. In progress.

Statutes

W. C. Ford and A. Mathews, *Bibliography of Massachusetts Laws, 1641-1776*. Boston, 1907.

A. Mathews, *Notes on the 1672 Edition and 1675 Volume of the General Laws*. Cambridge, 1917.

W. H. Whitmore, editor, *Bibliographical Sketch of the Laws of the Massachusetts Colony from 1630 to 1686*. Boston, 1890. (Contains in photographic facsimile the " Body of Liberties.")

W. Brigham, *New Plymouth Colony, the Compact with the Charter and Laws*. Boston, 1836.

The Book of the General Lawes and Libertyes (Cambridge, 1648), reprinted from the copy in the Henry E. Huntington Library. Cambridge, 1929.

Colonial Laws of Massachusetts, reprinted from the edition of 1660, with supplements to 1672, containing also the Body of Liberties of 1641. Boston, 1889.

Colonial Laws of Massachusetts, reprinted from the edition of 1672, with supplement through 1686. Boston, 1887.

Charters and General Laws of the Colony and Province of Massachusetts Bay. Boston, 1814.

Acts and Resolves, Public and Private, of the Province of the Massachusetts Bay, I-XXI. Boston, 1869-1922.

Acts and Laws passed by the Great and General Court or Assembly of the Colony of the Massachusetts-Bay (1775-1780). Boston, 1789.

Perpetual Laws of the Commonwealth of Massachusetts from the Commencement of the Constitution, in 1780 to 1788. Boston, 1789.

Acts and Laws of the Commonwealth of Massachusetts (1780-1797). Boston, 1781-1796. Reprinted, 9 vols., Boston, 1890-1896.

Court Records

Records of the Court of Assistants, I, 1673-1692; II, 1630-1644; III, 1642-1673. Boston, 1901-1928.

Records and Files of Quarterly Courts of Essex County, Mass. (1638-1683), 8 vols. Salem, 1911-1921. Of paramount importance for the study of the county courts.

" Records of the Court of General Sessions of the Peace of Worcester County," (1731-1737) Worcester Soc. of Antiquity, *Collections*, vol. V, edited by F. P. Rice. Worcester, 1882.

Josiah Quincy, Jr., *Reports of Cases argued and adjudged in the Superior Court of Judicature of the Province of Massachusetts Bay, between 1761 and 1772*. Boston, 1865.

NEW HAMPSHIRE

Public Records

Documents and Records relating to the Province [Town and State] of New Hampshire (1623-1800), edited by N. Bouton and others, 33 vols. Concord, 1867-1915.

Statutes and Court Records

Acts and Laws of the Colony of New Hampshire (1776-1780). Exeter, 1780.

Laws of New Hampshire, including Public and Private Acts and Resolves and Royal Commissions and Instructions, edited by A. B. Batchellor, vols. I-X (I-VII, 1679-1801). Manchester, 1904-1922.

NEW JERSEY

Public Records

Archives of the State of New Jersey, edited by W. A. Whitehead and others. 1st series, *Documents relating to the Colonial History* (1631-1800), 27 vols.; 2d series, *Documents relating to the Revolutionary History* (1776-1779), 3 vols. Newark, 1880-1906.

Journal of the Procedure of the Governor and Council of the Province of East Jersey from and after the first day of December, 1682 (-1703). Jersey City, 1872.

Statutes and Court Records

John Hood, *Index of Colonial and State Laws, between 1663 and 1877*. Trenton, 1877.

A. Leaming and J. Spicer, *Grants, Concessions, and Original Constitutions of the Province of New-Jersey* (1664-1682). Philadelphia, 1752. Reprinted, Somerville, 1881.

Acts of the General Assembly, 1702-1761, 2 vols. Philadelphia, 1752-1761.

S. Allinson, compiler, *Acts of the General Assembly of the Province of New Jersey, 1702-1776*. Burlington, N. J., 1776.

W. Paterson, compiler, *Laws of the State of New Jersey* (1703-1798). New Brunswick, 1800.

P. Wilson, compiler, *Acts of the General Assembly of the State of New-Jersey* (1776-1783). Trenton, 1784.

Compiled Statutes of New Jersey, 1709-1910, 5 vols. Newark, 1911.

NEW YORK

Public Records

Documents relative to the Colonial History of the State of New York, edited by E. B. O'Callaghan and B. Fernow, 15 vols. Albany, 1856-1887.

E. B. O'Callaghan, *Documentary History of the State of New York*, 4 vols. Albany, 1849-1851.

Minutes of the Executive Council of the Province of New York (with)
  Collateral and Illustrative Documents, edited by V. H. Paltsits, I-II
  (1668-1673). Albany, 1910.

Statutes

N. Y. P. L., "List of colonial and state laws, journals of assembly,
  senate, etc.," N. Y. P. L., *Bull.*, IV (1900), pp. 165-178.
Laws and Ordinances of New Netherlands, 1636-1674, compiled and
  translated by E. B. O'Callaghan. Albany, 1868.
Colonial Laws of New York from the Year 1664 to the Revolution,
  5 vols. Albany, 1894-1896.
"East Hampton Book of Laws, or Duke's Laws, 1665," N. Y. Hist.
  Soc., *Collections*, I, 305 *et seq.*
Laws of New York, 1691-1762, edited by William Livingston and William
  Smith, 2 vols. New York, 1762.

Court Records

Minutes of the Court of Rensselaerswyck, 1648-1652, translated and
  edited by A. J. F. Van Laer. Albany, 1922.
Minutes of the Court of Fort Orange and Beverwyck, 1652-1660, trans-
  lated and edited by A. J. F. Van Laer, 2 vols. Albany, 1920-1923.
Records of New Amsterdam, 1653-1674, edited by B. Fernow, 7 vols.
  New York, 1897.
Minutes of the Orphanmasters of New Amsterdam, 1655-1663, translated
  and edited by B. Fernow, 2 vols. New York, 1902.
"Minutes of the Court of Sessions (1657-1696), Westchester County,
  N. Y.," edited by D. R. Fox, Westchester County Hist. Soc., *Pub-
  lications*, II. White Plains, N. Y., 1924.
Court Minutes of Albany, Rensselaerswyck, and Schenectady, 1668-1680,
  translated and edited by A. J. F. Van Laer, vols. I, II. Albany, 1926-
  1928.
"Minutes of the Superior Court of Judicature, 1693-1701," N. Y. Hist.
  Soc., *Collections*, 1912, pp. 39-214.
C. M. Hough, *Admiralty Reports in the Court of Vice Admiralty, 1715-
  1788*. New York, 1925.

NORTH CAROLINA

Public Records

Colonial Records of North Carolina (1662-1776), edited by W. I. Saunders, I-X. Raleigh, 1886-1890. From 1776 to 1790 (XI-XXVI,
  Winston, 1895-1906), the series is called *State Records*, and is edited
  by W. Clark.

Statutes

Collection of Private Acts of the General Assembly . . . 1715-1790.
Newbern, 1794.
Public Acts of the General Assembly of North Carolina, 1715-1803.
F.-X. Martin, *Collection of the Statutes of the Parliament of England
in force in the State of North Carolina.* Newbern, 1792.

PENNSYLVANIA

Public Records

[*Colonial Records, 1683-1790,*] 16 vols. Philadelphia, 1852-1853.—Vols.
I-X, *Minutes of the Provincial Council;* Vols. XI-XVI, *Minutes of
the Supreme Executive Council.*—General index, Philadelphia, 1860.
Pennsylvania Archives (1664-), compiled by S. Hazard and others, 91
vols. in 6 series (to 1907). Philadelphia and Harrisburg, 1852-1907.
S. Hazard, *Annals of Pennsylvania, 1609-1682.* Philadelphia, 1850.
——, editor, *Pennsylvania Register,* 16 vols. Philadelphia, 1828-1835.

Statutes

*Duke of York's Book of Laws (1676-1682), and Charter to William Penn
and Laws of the Province of Pennsylvania passed between 1682 and
1700.* Harrisburg, 1879.
Statutes at Large of Pennsylvania from 1682 to 1801, compiled by J. T.
Mitchell and Henry Flanders, II-XIII (1700-1790). Harrisburg,
1896-1908.
A. J. Dallas, compiler, *Laws of the Commonwealth of Pennsylvania
(1700-1790),* 2 vols. Philadelphia, 1793-1797.
M. Carey and J. Bioren, *Laws of the Commonwealth of Pennsylvania
(1700-1802),* 6 vols. Philadelphia, 1803.

Court Records

"Records of the Court at Upland, in Pennsylvania, 1676 to 1681," Pa.
Hist. Soc., *Memoirs,* VII, 9-203. Philadelphia, 1860.
Records of the Courts of Chester County, 1681-1697. Philadelphia, 1910.
S. W. Pennypacker, *Pennsylvania Colonial Cases* (1682-1700). Philadelphia, 1892.
A. J. Dallas, *Reports of Cases in the Courts of Pennsylvania . . .* [1754-
1806], *and in the several Courts of the United States* [1790-1800].
4 vols. Philadelphia, 1790-1807.—Vol. I is entitled *Reports of Cases
ruled and adjudged in the Courts of Pennsylvania, before and since
the Revolution.* 2d edition of Vols. I, IV, Philadelphia, 1806, 1835.

RHODE ISLAND

Public Records

Records of the Colony of Rhode Island and Providence Plantations in New England (1636-1792), compiled by J. R. Bartlett, 10 vols. Providence, 1856-1865.

H. M. Chapin, *Documentary History of Rhode Island*, 2 vols. Providence, 1916-1919.

Proceedings of the First General Assembly of " the Incorporation of Providence Plantations" and the Code of Laws adopted by that Assembly in 1647. Providence, 1847.

Statutes and Court Records

Check List of Rhode Island Laws, containing a complete list of the Public Laws and Acts and Resolves of the State of Rhode Island to date. Providence, 1873-1921.

Acts and Laws, 1663-1745; 1745-1752. Newport, 1745-1752.

Records of the Court of Trials of the Colony of Providence Plantations, 1647-1670, 2 vols. Providence, 1920-1922.

SOUTH CAROLINA

Public Records

B. R. Carroll, compiler, *Historical Collections of South Carolina, with many rare documents,* 2 vols. New York, 1836.

Statutes and Court Records

" Fundamental Constitutions of the Carolinas," John Locke's *Works,* 1823 edition, vol. X.

N. Trott, *Laws of the Province of South Carolina before 1734,* 2 vols. in 1. Charleston, 1736.

J. F. Grimké, compiler, *Public Laws of the State of South Carolina* (*1682-1790*), Philadelphia, 1790.

T. Cooper, editor, *Statutes at Large of South Carolina, 1682-1875,* 15 vols. —Vols. VI-X edited by D. J. McCord. Columbia, 1836-1879.

VERMONT

Public Records

Vermont State Papers; being a Collection of Records and Documents, compiled by William Slade. Middlebury, 1823.

Court Records

" Gloucester County Court Records " (1774-), Vt. Hist. Soc., *Proceedings,* 1923-1925.

VIRGINIA

Public Records

Alexander Brown, *Genesis of the United States*, 2 vols. Boston, 1890.

Records of the Virginia Company of London; the Court Book, from Manuscripts in the Library of Congress, edited by S. M. Kingsbury. Washington, 1906.

Colonial Records of Virginia, 1619-1680, edited by T. S. Wynne and W. S. Gilman. Richmond, 1874 ("Senate Document, Extra").

Calendar of Virginia State Papers and other Manuscripts ... Preserved ... at Richmond (1652-1869), edited by W. P. Palmer and others, 11 vols. Richmond, 1875-1893.

Executive Journals of the Council of Colonial Virginia, 1680-1721, I-III. Richmond, 1926-.

Legislative Journals of the Council of Colonial Virginia, edited by H. R. McIlwaine, 3 vols. Richmond, 1918-1919.

Statutes

W. W. Hening, *The Statutes-at-Large, being a Collection of all the Laws of Virginia* (1619-1792), 13 vols. Philadelphia and New York, 1823.

Court Records

Minutes of the Council and General Court of Colonial Virginia, edited by H. R. McIlwaine. Richmond, 1924.

" Virginia Council and General Court Records, 1640-1641," from " Robinson's Notes," in Va. Hist. Soc. *Collections, Virginia Magazine of History and Biography*, II, 277-284.

R. T. Barton, editor, *Virginia Colonial Decisions: Reports by Sir John Randolph and by Edward Barradall of Decisions of the Supreme Court of Virginia, 1728-1741*. 2 vols. Boston, 1909.

Thomas Jefferson, *Reports of Cases determined in the General Court of Virginia* (1730-1740, 1768-1772). Charlottesville, 1829.

INDEX